The Role of the British Press in the 1976 American Presidential Election

Books by George Coleman Osborn

JOHN SHARP WILLIAMS: PLANTER STATESMAN OF THE DEEP SOUTH

WOODROW WILSON: EARLY YEARS

FIRST BAPTIST CHURCH, GAINESVILLE, FLORIDA, 1870-1970: A HISTORY

JOHN JAMES TIGERT: AMERICAN EDUCATOR

THE ROLE OF THE BRITISH PRESS
IN THE 1976 AMERICAN PRESIDENTIAL ELECTION
(with Ron Martin)

WOODROW WILSON IN BRITISH OPINION AND THOUGHT

JAMES KIMBLE VARDAMAN: SOUTHERN COMMONER

The Role of the British Press in the 1976 American Presidential Election

by

George Coleman Osborn

George Coleman Osborn
with Ron Martin

Exposition Press   *Smithtown, New York*

For five gentlemen who have greatly blessed my life:

Samuel George Osborn—my father (deceased)
Wilbur Truet Osborn—my brother
Paul Burnell Osborn—my brother
Philip Mahony—my brother-in-law (deceased)
Albert C. Polk III—my son-in-law

Contents

Preface

The role of the British press in American Presidential elections, while never decisive, has been of substantial influence. The concern of the British in the 1976 American election was evidenced when the British media sent more than two hundred employees to the United States to cover the campaign.

In 1976, several innovations created fresh interest in Britain. For the first time more than 75,000 expatriate Americans living in the British Isles, as well as 750,000 elsewhere, were allowed to vote in an American election. Both major political parties sought the support of this block of potential voters. Democratic and Republican voters living in the British Isles were organized to work in behalf of their party nominees and to contribute money to their candidates. The Democrats permitted the expatriates to send four delegates to the national convention. For the first time a salaried full-time employee served an American political party in a foreign country during an American Presidential campaign.

The British Broadcasting Corporation (BBC) sent almost sixty employees and tons of equipment to both national conventions to broadcast the proceedings of these meetings live on television and over national radio throughout the British Isles. The British also broadcast live the four debates (three Presidential and one Vice-Presidential) of the pre-election campaign. The British media personnel covered the campaign from the primaries through the election, to quench the thirst of the British for information about the American Presidential election.

No book based on research is done by one person alone. Certainly this was true of this book. In fact, I am indebted to many who aided me. I appreciate the many courtesies shown me by the media during the weeks I worked in the British Press Museum at Colindale. Dr. Gus Harrer, director of the University of Florida libraries, and his co-workers gave me every possible help. Mr. Ron Martin made the manuscript more publishable by his expert editing. I am grateful to Mrs. Carol Giles for typing my manuscript. Most of all I am indebted to my wife, who was cooperative, as she has been for forty-five years, in every phase of the research and the preparation of this book. For any mistakes remaining I am responsible.

GEORGE COLEMAN OSBORN

The Role of the British Press in the
1976 American Presidential Election

1

The
Primaries

The British press paid little attention to the early actions in the 1976 American Presidential primaries. The British reporters as a rule did not use their typewriters or their transatlantic telephones to convey information on the American political scene until late spring. A few exceptions were found, including the London *Spectator,** which saluted Ronald Reagan for his moral victory in the New Hampshire primary and declared that President Gerald Ford, who had not cut an authoritative figure since he succeeded Nixon, "for all his smoothness and charm was a lightweight." Jimmy Carter, who won such an impressive victory in New Hampshire, the conservative journal declared, had "shown himself to be little more than an unscrupulous Southern demagogue."

Henry Fairlie, the *Spectator*'s chief reporter in Washington, reported in March that the "Republican Party was in serious trouble with President Ford certain to be its candidate." The crucial concern, Fairlie wrote, was not so much that Ford had the Nixon albatross hanging about his neck as that Ford was the albatross. Fairlie, however, was only half correct when he predicted that "one of the most remarkable features of this election is going to be the elimination, very early, of the extreme right-wing candidates in the persons of George Wallace and Ronald Reagan." Indeed, with the results in the Illinois primary held in early spring both Reagan and Wallace, Fairlie observed, were effectively out of the race. By the end of March the *Spectator,* retreating from the "unscrupulous Southern demagogue" allegation, recorded that the most remarkable feature of the American election was the mounting strength of Jimmy Carter—who beyond doubt had something about him that was intriguing. This conclusion was supported by the London *Times* and the Manchester *Guardian.*

*The first citing of a source will include the place located and the name; thereafter only the name of the source will be given.

1

From Washington, Fairlie predicted in February that the 1976 American Presidential election was going to be more exciting than any had been for a long time. This English reporter changed his mind before the campaign was over. Moreover, with his final conclusion, a reversal of his earlier statement, there was much more agreement among his fellow British reporters.

By May 1 Carter had acquired more convention delegates in the Democratic primaries than any of his party opponents; he was so far ahead that Democratic rivals began to withdraw from the race. Senator Henry Jackson, declaring that his funds were spent, withdrew when Carter won decisively in Pennsylvania. Hubert Humphrey, the *Times* announced, decided to stay out of the race. The *Guardian* concluded that Humphrey's withdrawal from consideration made Carter's nomination even more assured. President Ford spent four days and nights making speeches and holding conferences among Republicans. After this, the *Guardian* said, the President looked supremely confident and spoke with complete assurance as he concluded his busy four-day stay in Texas.

While President Ford was speaking at Baylor University in Waco, Reagan was proclaiming in Houston. Reagan, the *Times* wrote, was an "accomplished speaker who knows how to touch certain nerve ends of his audience and does it in a precise low-key style. He mixes jokes, that are often off color but not too much so, and gets through to his listeners." While the Lone Star State Republicans were cheering President Ford and applauding Reagan, the Democrats were listening to Carter at Southern Methodist University in Dallas and welcoming their favorite son, Senator Lloyd Bentsen.

The Texas primaries held a day or so later revealed some significant results. Among the Republicans Reagan secured sixty-six percent, while President Ford gained thirty-three percent, which under the unit rule gave the former California Governor all of the delegates to the convention. Among the Democrats there were equally important results, for Carter received forty-eight percent of the votes cast, trouncing Bentsen thoroughly by winning ninety-three of the ninety-eight Democratic delegates. Although Alabama Governor George Wallace's name was on the Texas Democratic ballot, he collected only a relatively small percentage of the votes. Reagan and Carter campaign workers were jubilant, and President Ford despondently blamed his defeat on a crossover of the conservative Democrats who had formerly supported Wallace. All of these specific details the *Times* and the *Guardian* and other members of the British press recorded for their readers.

The provincial *Guardian* editorialized extensively in "Will the Real Gerald Ford Stand Up?" President Ford, who only a few days earlier seemed tranquilly coasting toward nomination, now found his campaign topsy-turvy. With weeping, Humphrey announced he was not running, with Jackson's empty bank account and with Bentsen and Wallace overwhelmed, Carter's nomination ship was sailing on placid waters. President Ford, on the contrary, was bailing water. The *Guardian* concluded that "America was steeling itself for a change" and the "real Gerald Ford would have to stand up for the country soon or he would be counted out."

As early as May 3 Jonathan Steele wrote in the *Guardian* that Carter had captured the black vote. Mayor Coleman Young of Detroit endorsed the former Governor of Georgia, while the Reverend Jesse Jackson of Chicago declared that Carter had delivered the blacks "from the carnage of George Wallace" and displayed a "high profile relationship with the blacks." As the preconvention campaign continued, Carter's political relations with black Americans became more widely discussed. Mark Frankland in the London *Observer* noted that Carter's record on race was impeccable.

With the rapid rise of the Deep South's candidate in the number of delegates to the Democratic convention, two new liberal Democratic leaders from Western states entered the contest for convention delegates. Senator Frank Church of Idaho entered several Democratic primaries with success. The youthful, Jesuit-educated, strongly ambitious Governor Edmund (Jerry) Brown of California began a sudden rise in popularity not only in his native state but as far east as Maryland. The last contender among the Democratic leadership, Brown gained strength as other contenders, except Carter, faded into obscurity.

The Liverpool *Daily Post and Mercury* called Brown California's greatest Governor and probably the greatest in the United States. The *Observer* labeled Brown the "Democrats' secret weapon to stop Carter" and discussed him as a marvelous prophet from the West. Leslie Fines wrote in the *Spectator* that "Brown was the hottest thing in American politics since Bobby Kennedy," and Fred Emery reported in the *Times* that young people seemed wild about the slogan "Brown is beautiful." The *Daily Post and Mercury* quoted Brown as saying, "The race is still open and the process is continuing to expand." Meanwhile Senator Church, with the look of a plump Episcopalian curate, spoke of making "a quantum leap" in his campaign. Eventually, both Brown and Church failed in the last-minute efforts to stop Carter.

Another aspect of British public opinion about the American election that appeared early in May was exemplified by Mark Frankland in the *Observer* when he published an article on "The Man Behind the Smile." For a century, success in Southern politics, Frankland wrote, was an almost automatic disqualification for Presidential success. Even if Jimmy Carter failed to win the nomination, the emergence of a Southerner as a potential national leader set another stage in the slow liberation of the North and the South from their old prejudices against each other,

Frankland observed. Carter, Frankland thought, was a very complex person. Particularly impressive to Frankland was the candidate's ability to show sympathy with and to draw trust from very different groups of people throughout the nation. As a successful Southern farmer, Carter understood, for example, the problems of Southerners, but he never accepted their prejudices, especially on race. As Governor, Carter, said the *Observer,* was conservative on money and liberal in his sympathies toward all forms of human suffering.

By early May the campaign strategies of President Ford and Carter became clear to the makers of British public opinion. As President, Ford lost to Reagan in Texas, in Indiana and several other states; the President, as reported in several English newspapers, accepted the advice of some strategy advisers to remain in Washington, to devote his attention to serving the people as President, and to leave the campaigning to others. Subsequently, poll results revealed that President Ford was losing popularity in Michigan, his adopted state, in California, a significant state because of the large number of delegates, and in other states where neither primaries nor conventions had been held. President Ford abandoned his stay-in-the-White-House strategy for a train whistle-stop tour of Michigan and for vigorous campaigning in several other states.

In short, stated the *Guardian,* Reagan's victories left the once exuberant President Ford and his campaign staff "embarrassed and confused." Moreover, the English, through the media, knew that Ford as President had made some impromptu decisions. He vetoed the Humphrey-Hawkins full-employment bill with the statement that a "government big enough to give you everything you want is big enough to take away everything you have." He embargoed the sale of wheat to Russia, thereby depriving the Western farmers of a lucrative foreign market. He vetoed a $4 billion foreign aid bill and denounced Congress for trying to take over his role as arbiter of American foreign policy. These and other executive decisions made by the President became a significant part of British public opinion on American politics in 1976.

Carter, fortunate to have a brilliant young group of advisers in Atlanta, accepted its strategy of emphasizing his status as an outsider of the Washington establishment and a non-Democratic-party-boss candidate. This stance Carter followed throughout the preconvention race, until mid-June.

Meanwhile, foreign policy made British press headlines, for the first time, when President Ford abruptly postponed the ceremonial signing of a pact with Leonid Brezhnev, the Russian leader, limiting underground nuclear explosives for peaceful purposes. The President stated that the timing was inconvenient for him—but the real reason, said the *Guardian,* was President Ford's unwillingness to be seen making a sensitive agreement with Moscow when the President's campaign was in serious trouble after losing five successive state primaries to Reagan.

While President Ford was postponing the Brezhnev agreement indefinitely, Carter named an advisory task force composed of leading Democrats such as Averell Harriman, Cyrus Vance, Robert McNamara, Theodore Sorensen, Zbigniew Brzezinski, Clark Clifford, and others to advise him on foreign policy. In Chicago, Carter declared that his foreign policy would have four basic principles: (1) To be open, honest, decent and compassionate. (2) To treat the peoples of other countries as individuals with the same dignity and respect as Americans demand for themselves. (3) To aim at building a just and peaceful world order in which every nation could have a constructive role. (4) To have the President assume the responsibility for restoring moral authority in the United States.

Carter said that Dr. Henry Kissinger, the Secretary of State, "simply does not trust the judgment of the American people and constantly conducts our foreign policy, exclusively, personally, and secretly." Carter countered that Moscow had enjoyed the benefits of the Helsinki Agreement without America's requiring Russia to live up to its human rights provisions, which "formed an integral part of the agreement." Additionally Carter declared that Americans should promote a more pluralistic Communistic world. The United States, Carter said, had a significant stake in a nationally independent, secure, and friendly China in which there should be an "open and nondiscriminatory trade."

Fred Emery reported in the *Times* that, as the Republicans continued their divisive and increasingly embittered intraparty fight, the Democrats were overjoyed by the Republicans' squabbles and personal denunciations. In contrast to the bickering Republicans, Carter was holding private personal meetings with Humphrey, Wallace and other Democratic leaders, to discuss party unity.

In May, voters began reacting to the actual campaigning by members of candidate families. Both Betty Ford and Nancy Reagan began to state their views on such issues as abortion, equal pay for women, and premarital sex. Betty Ford, said the *Daily Post and Mercury,* "was loved and admired as a lady with courage and warmth who does not shrink from controversy." Nancy Reagan was, declared this western provincial paper, calculated, relentless, a driving force who always figured in strategy policy decisions, looked after her husband, and supplied the stamina to keep the campaign and the candidate going. Rosalynn Carter, stated the *Daily Post and Mercury,* was a high school beauty contest winner who married her early sweetheart and looked like the "nice wife of a peanut farmer with four kids." Her career had been confined to motherhood and a political partnership with her husband. Bethune Church, continued the *Daily Post and Mercury,* shared her husband's "passion for the economic plight of the elderly and other liberal issues" that came before his United States Senate committee. As the preconvention campaign became more heatedly contested, the wives of the candidates became more involved, with the exception of Brown, who was a bachelor.

When June arrived, Jeremy Campbell reported in the London *Evening Standard* that Carter, conscious of an erosion of his status by Brown and Church, suddenly reversed his strategy and began strenuously to woo the leaders of the Democratic Party establishment, who were "offended at his independent, almost contemptuous style." Carter spoke of his "failure to soothe the ruffled feathers of the party kingmakers as the most serious mistake I have made in my twelve months campaigning for the Presidency. I need them very badly and I am going to correct this problem if I can." Carter succeeded by winning endorsements from Leonard Woodcock, president of the United Automobile Workers of America, and Mayor Richard Daley, boss of Chicago and Cook County. Mayor Daley said, "Carter has got something we need. We should have a little more religion in the community."

The Leeds *Yorkshire Post* informed its readers that Wallace had stated, after Carter won in the Ohio primary, that the people wanted Carter and, therefore, Wallace withdrew from the contest, releasing his 168 delegates with the request that they support Carter. Meanwhile, Congressman Morris Udall, reported the Edinburgh *Scotsman,* had, after coming in second to Carter in seven state primaries, adopted as his official campaign song "Second Hand Rose." However, Patrick Brogan quoted the Arizona Congressman as saying subsequent to his defeat in California, Ohio, and New Jersey, "I am a realist and I can count. I know the difference between a sure winner and a sure loser." Although Carter and Udall pledged their mutual support to the winner of the Democratic National Convention, Udall did not release his 331 delegates to Carter during June.

According to reporter Simon Winchester in the *Guardian,* another problem for Carter was the brunt of a vocal attack by two men. Reg Murphy, who had lived in Georgia most of his life but left six months earlier to become the editor of the San Francisco *Examiner,* said, "I have watched him in great detail and, frankly, I see him for the phony he is. He is misleading the American public and, if he is elected, it will be, frankly, a disaster." Robert Shrum, who gave up a Congressional staff assistantship to write Carter's speeches but left without pay nine days later, declared that Carter was "a highly intellectual and shrewd man, running a brilliantly conceived campaign, but he is totally without political principle; he is largely image and little substance. He gets so angry when things are not going his way. Any real criticism of him and he just blows up. On such an occasion to be around him is frightening."

Jonathan Steele reported in the *Guardian* that more than forty million people would find Carter's crinkle-eyed smile and soft insistent voice, if he were elected President, reaching out inescapably from the TV screen for five minutes on the "Vision of America." The British television viewers would see the two contradictory sides of his image—the gentle, compassionate Southern Baptist and the ruthlessly calculating politician. In this nationally televised brief talk Carter stated, "Our people want a President to be both tough and gentle, both statesman and politician, both dreamer and fighter." Steele was correct in his analysis to the *Guardian.*

Ford's image was dealt a surprise blow, though not a tragic one, in Bowling Green, Ohio, when a university coed's flashbulb exploded with a bang like a gunshot. The Secret Service agents rushed to, surrounded, and covered the President, who, according to the Dublin *Irish Times,* "appeared to have doubled up and nearly fallen to his knees." This story was widely reported in the British press, and several papers accompanied it with a photograph of Ford being covered by the Secret Service agents.

In the meantime, Anthony Delano in the London *Daily Mirror* questioned Jerry Brown's qualifications for the Presidency: "Does a 37-year-old would-be priest and oriental philosopher who has been in real politics only fifteen months," the *Daily Mirror* reporter asked, "honestly think he can be President of the United States?" Brown believed he could be nominated for President or be able to trade off his three hundred convention delegates for the Vice-Presidential nomination. The young Brown was Governor of California. He was popular among Californians, but some were puzzled that he so seldom went out with girls. An exception was Ann Schaffenburger, a young California heiress who met Brown when he ran for Governor. Ann recalled, "We went out, but all that happened was he told me exactly how he planned to become President."

Meanwhile, wrote Delano, it was crisis time for Carter. "That clean-living, God-fearing, seemingly ambitious Presidential hopeful, Jimmy Carter, is now facing the first crisis point of his phenomenal surge to the front." He did not have enough convention delegates to be nominated on the first ballot. This caught up with him most inopportunely just when he and his band of bright young Southerners were physically, emotionally, and financially exhausted after a nonstop four-month struggle for national leadership.

When the final primary results were counted, Carter would have slightly under 1,200 delegate votes of the 1,505 required to win the nomination on the first ballot. It was necessary to secure some four hundred more delegates. Delano stated in the *Daily Mirror* that Carter must "pull on his celebrated ear-to-ear smile to try to convey his way of thinking" to the necessary delegates. If his smile failed, he would have to start haggling with the party's kingmakers, chief among whom was the notorious old Mayor Richard Daley of Chicago. The *Daily Mirror* concluded: "As soon as Carter began to run scared he headed for the churches. In the Redneck Bible belt where Carter comes from . . . they talk to God as though he were a neighbor."

By mid-June the state nominating primaries were over; it remained only for the states that held the old traditional party conventions to choose their national party convention delegates. Carter, the Democratic front-runner, was assured of more than enough convention delegates to be nominated on the first ballot when his challengers withdrew and asked their delegates to support him. Udall now asked his 331 delegates to vote for Carter. Wallace had previously released his 168 delegates to Carter; these, coupled with the 1,118 delegates Carter had won directly, gave him more than the 1,505 delegate votes necessary to be nominated.

In contrast to this favorable situation, President Ford, the Republican leader in delegates to the convention, had 902 delegates pledged to him, and Reagan, his antagonist, could boast of 815, with 128 Republican delegates uncommitted. The Republicans required 1,130 votes for nomination. In Missouri, the first of the state conventions, Reagan shocked Ford by capturing 18 of its 19 convention delegates and cut the President's lead to 79 delegates, thus making Ford's lead more untenable. Moreover, as the London *Daily Telegraph* declared, there were ten states that would select 225 delegates which had not yet acted. Actually, President Ford could well have become the first sitting President since Chester A. Arthur not to receive his party's nomination. That the Reagan forces were determined to win the nomination and were not missing any opportunities to gain delegates is attested by the Ford strategists' appointing nine regional delegate chairmen to keep all delegates pledged to President Ford.

The Glasgow *Herald* editorialized that the American contest for Presidential nomination was exhausting, expensive, and unstable, for it left Carter assured of his nomination and the Ford-Reagan struggle undecided. Carter and President Ford were the winners in the New Hampshire primary, but their progress had been anything but placid and predictable. However, said the *Herald,* some trends in the post-Watergate election were discernible. Not the least among the trends was the longing for new faces unassociated with Washington and big government; thus, the advantages of being the incumbent did not necessarily assure Ford a nomination. After thirty-one state primaries no candidate in either party had the required delegates for nomination on the first ballot. However, as noted, Carter's Democratic contenders began to withdraw and suggest their pledged delegates vote for him.

Edna Robertson expressed the same conclusion in the *Herald* when she wrote that the primaries began in a February blizzard and lasted until the mid-June hot sunshine. The process was too long, too exhausting, too irrational. However, American Presidential candidates did not agree with this British reporter. Carter thought primaries were an absolutely superb system because it was democracy in action, keeping the party bosses at bay and placing the candidates on public parade. But Miss Robertson saw in the American primary system compounded calculated ambiguities, a deliberate emphasis on personality rather than on political issues, and an absence of any political philosophies. She realized that the New South was in the throes of economic changes and population shifts. After the crumbling of the Democratic coalition of the 1930s, the South had appreciably withdrawn from the mainstream of the national Democratic Party. In 1976, as Robertson wrote in this Scottish newspaper, Carter was endeavoring to bring the South back into the mainstream of the Democratic Party, but, she added, what would the South find when it returned?

Fred Emery, for the *Times,* announced the ending of the primaries by declaring that the longest and most confusing side of the American political spring season was finished. While President Ford and the Republicans looked more vulnerable, Carter was over the hump and "approaching his entitlement." Emery thought Carter personified the New South and held out the prospect of recapturing much of Dixie for the Democrats without turning over the disgruntled Wallaceites to the Republicans. Carter's strong leadership over President Ford or Reagan, wrote this reporter, was no surprise when compared with the "Vietnam debacle, Watergate, the convulsions of the American economy, and the persistent government lying. The American voters were demanding change, decency and morality in their government," Emery concluded.

In June the *Times* declared editorially that when the primaries began in February it had appeared that Ford had an easy road to the Republican nomination and, with so many hopefuls among the Democrats contending for the nomination, there would be haggling among the delegates at the Democratic National Convention. Both assumptions proved to be completely erroneous. Other pieces of "American conventional party wisdom" lay scattered in disarray, and critics noted that few registered voters actually participated in the primaries. Many voters defied the conventional party labels; labor unions proved unable to deliver the votes of their rank and file. Stalwarts of the Democratic Party establishment were not able to stop a complete outsider. American blacks voted for a white Southerner. Republicans voted in huge numbers against their own President. In fact, said the independent *Times,* the only thing that emerged clearly was the breakup of the old voting patterns.

Presuming that Carter and President Ford were the nominees of their respective party conventions, the popular *Times* predicted a close race, with the result unknown. Carter was a remarkable political phenomenon, said the *Times* and continued: "He came from nowhere and waged an exceptionally clever campaign. He clearly knows how to respond to the desires of many people for moral leadership, traditional beliefs and a new face uncontaminated by scandals and failures of Washington which have rubbed off on President Ford, partly as a result of his decision to pardon President Nixon." The Georgia candidate was in a strong position to bring logic into the American political system by ending the old split between the Southern conservatives and the Northern liberals in the Democratic Party. Nevertheless, the *Times* said, Carter's cold, penetrating eyes, his lack of humor and difficulty in making personal contact indicated he would have difficulty, if elected, in coping with the stresses and the compromises of the Presidency.

Steele contended, in the *Guardian,* that Carter ended the primary season poised on the verge of leading the Democratic Party into its most united and optimistic electoral campaign since 1964. On the other hand, the *Guardian* continued, President Ford and Reagan were left glaring at each other across a treacherous chasm of more than four hundred un-committed delegates after the primaries, which resulted in division and indecision in the whole Republican Party. The extended series of primaries was the fullest and most volatile in American history, with one surprise following another. The biggest surprise of all, thought Steele, was the emergence of Carter from an originally crowded field without antagoniz-ing any substantial part of the Democratic coalition, whereas the Repub-lican camp was possessed of bitterness and enshrouded in divisiveness.

Editorially, the *Guardian* spoke of the primaries as a long, long trail winding and grinding through more than thirty states throughout America. "Any outsider considering the primaries rationally would think the system misbegotten and madcap," the *Guardian* said. "It drains and humiliates good men. It has forced an incumbent President, or leader, to leave cares of the world on his desk to trek barrenly from plate supper to plate barbecue denouncing an ex-cowboy actor." After discuss-ing the frailties of Carter and of President Ford, this widely read provincial paper concluded that "in essence the choice for America this autumn is not a bad one." Ford, the *Guardian* stated, though uninspiring and uncharismatic, kept stumbling on, while the November outcome would depend on Carter's stamina and stature.

Simon Winchester, a writer for the *Guardian,* reported that President Ford, if nominated, was the man least likely to be elected. The White House workers for the President were undeniably crestfallen. Steele, with great sympathy for Carter and his campaign, labeled the Southerner "God's own candidate for the White House." He discussed at length Carter's campaign and his political perceptions. If Vietnam divided the American electorate, Watergate united it, Steele said. In Steele's view, Carter had concluded that the successful candidate in 1976 should stress personality rather than issues. He saw that the white constituency was leaderless. He realized that one could appeal to blacks in a way that would not alienate others. Carter's strategy, wrote Steele, would have amounted to nothing without his skill as a speaker; he dealt in specifics but he was "soft-nosed and avoids confrontation."

As noted earlier, several candidates' wives became active in their husbands' campaigns. Betty Ford, said the *Guardian,* stepped into the political arena and, as a campaigner, improved daily. She was given a schedule of political engagements to fill and, according to the President, was a better campaigner than he. In the *Daily Mirror,* Jill Evans, who accompanied Mrs. Ford on her campaigning, described America's First Lady as the most popular woman to grace the White House since Eleanor Roosevelt. Betty's smile was relentless in ninety-degree heat or otherwise as she trooped from state to state, winning friends for President Ford. Mrs. Ford insisted that she enjoyed it, but in moments off-guard she looked frail and exhausted. Her popularity with the people was attested when signs reading "Vote for Betty's Husband" appeared where she went.

Mrs. Ford's courage was demonstrated in the Hilton Hotel in New York City when Dr. Maurice Sage, while introducing her for a speech before a large gathering at a Jewish dinner, slumped to the floor as he clutched at his heart. The audience was stunned into silence and watched horrified as Betty Ford approached the microphone, asked the audience to stand, and requested that each person pray in his own way. "It is up to God what will happen," she said. The *Guardian* concluded: "This was one of the moving incidents of the political campaign."

If the President's wife was a successful campaigner, so was Carter's wife. The London *Sun* identified Carter's wife, Rosalynn, as his secret weapon. Although called "The Georgia Peach," Rosalynn looked very much as though she were on the way to becoming the world's most powerful wife. She was a strong-willed, independent-thinking person. Leslie Hinton wrote in the *Sun* that, after thirty years of happily married life, she still handed out the weekly pocket money to the man who aspired to the most powerful office on earth. When Carter was at odds with his aides, someone called Rosalynn to settle the dispute. She, said the *Sun,* was campaigning tirelessly for her husband. "No one has ever told me what to say in the campaign," Mrs. Carter told the *Sun.*

The Dublin *Irish Times* discussed a long, 937-page, document prepared by Carter's aides, which was circulated among a subcommittee to draft the Democratic platform for its nominee. "What is at stake in 1976," read the book, "is whether we are going to begin the process of restoring the precious things we have lost in this country." Recommendations of the Carter headquarters, as revealed in the circulated document, prescribed taking no position on issues that had previously divided the party in the writing of the platform. For instance, an attempt to make abortion more difficult was easily defeated, and the opposition of some of the platform committee to school busing was comfortably sidetracked. Upon learning of his camp's success in forming the Democratic platform (there was no minority report), Carter, acting as if he were already nominated for and elected President, exclaimed, "There is no doubt in my mind that before I go out of office the budget will be balanced and . . . that government organization will be proper; that we will have a government sunshine law and finally that harmony between the White House and Congress will be restored."

Carter's control of the Democratic Party was in contrast to President Ford's position of leadership in the Republican Party. As the primaries gave way to state conventions, Reagan fared better than Ford and lessened the President's lead in convention delegates. As total delegates for each Republican contender for the nomination approached equality, emotions became embittered while enthusiasm intensified.

The *Daily Post and Mercury* discussed the tenseness and precariousness that enshrouded the Ford and the Reagan camps and reports of highly ungentlemanly attempts by both sides to incite rebellion among the delegates pledged to the opponent. These conditions pointed to a heated showdown on the floor of the convention when it met in Kansas City, and would place the Republican Party in a disadvantageous position in the November election.

Early in the summer Ford called for a Western economic summit to meet in Puerto Rico shortly before the Republican National Convention. Invited were Britain, Canada, France, Italy, Japan, the United States, and West Germany. The President hoped to advance his nomination drive in at least two ways through the conference. First, he benefited politically by his appearance on television in Western European countries and established himself as a world leader just before the Republican National Convention assembled. Second, in his speech before the conference, President Ford warned British Prime Minister James Callaghan and the Italian government of overspending on social welfare programs. Overly ambitious social programs, said the President advisedly, were responsible for the inflation that brought on a deep recession in 1974-1975. In his stern lecture President Ford gave his reason for vetoing social legislation in this country.

The *Irish Times* had mixed reactions about the summit, especially questioning whether the meeting was another example of political expediency on the part of President Ford. Nevertheless, the *Scotsman* accepted President Ford's proposal that the industrial nations must cooperate to prevent problems from arising and thus avoid the need for any of them to take emergency action. The London *Daily Express* was interested in the President's assurance that Britain would be able to overcome its problems in 1977 and, more particularly, in his proposal that more extended loans be made by the International Monetary Fund. The

Times treated the San Juan Conference in more detail than did other British public opinion sources, and quoted President Ford as saying, "The complexity of our nation's economy, individually and collectively, requires that we concert our effort to prevent problems from arising— to shape the future rather than reacting to it!"

While President Ford was creating an image of a world leader in San Juan, Carter was denouncing Henry Kissinger, whom he named "The Lone Ranger," for what Carter termed secret, selfish, and sordid diplomacy, adding that the United States must preserve a foreign policy keyed to morality, openness, and cooperation with other democracies. It ought not to interfere in the internal affairs of other nations. In recent years, he declared, "our European allies are deeply concerned, and justly so, by our unilateral dealing with the Soviet Union." According to the *Irish Times,* Carter called for a reduction of ground forces in South Korea on a phase-out basis after consultation with South Korea and Japan; a review of the North Atlantic Treaty Organization (NATO) forces, and a balanced reduction of forces by both sides in Europe. The *Times* reported that in a New York City speech Carter again attacked the "Lone Ranger" secret foreign policy. "A foreign policy based on secrecy," Carter said, "inherently has had to be closely guarded and amoral, and we have had to forgo opinion consultation and a constant adherence to fundamental principles and high moral standards."

As the prenomination, preconvention campaign ended, both leading candidates were busy discussing foreign policy. President Ford was endeavoring to improve his image as leader of the free world. Carter was repeatedly denouncing the diplomacy conducted by Kissinger. Next: the two national nominating conventions.

2

The
Democratic
National Convention

On the eve of the national convention, the London *Times* announced that the Democratic Party was "filled with wonder." It was completely united under the born-again Christian Carter, who had reached his position without alienating any of the other party leaders in any sections of the country. Apparently, Carter in his campaign never refused an opportunity to emphasize religion. Before a convention of the Disciples of Christ in Washington, the *Times* reported, Carter urged a deeper involvement of "men of faith" in the American government. The separation of church and state, Carter believed, did not dictate separation in public and private morality. "It doesn't mean," he said, "we ought to have different standards of ethics. There is no reason why we should be less honest on Monday than we were on Sunday." In Lafayette, Indiana, the *Times* reported, Carter declared that "a true demonstration of Christian strength would show concern, compassion, devotion, humility, love, sensitivity. If we can demonstrate this kind of personal awareness of our own faith, we can provide that core of strength and commitment and underlying character our nation searches for."

The *Guardian,* while acknowledging Carter's dedicated religious faith, noted contrasts between the Democrats and the Republicans on some issues. For example, the Democrats, under Carter's leadership, omitted any discussion of school busing, while President Ford urged Congress to redefine busing and to limit the federal courts, which in several cases had gone too far in their decisions dealing with this issue. The President wanted legislation to compel judges to have proof that legal discrimination had occurred before a court could order busing, and then only for a maximum of five years. He wanted federal judges to be able to order busing only as a "tool to be used with the highest selectivity and utmost

14

precision." Reagan, who remained silent on this emotional issue, was not recorded in the British press.

As reported in the *Daily Telegraph,* President Ford, in a speech tinged with candor—almost with sadness—warned that a fierce struggle with Reagan could drag the Republican Party down to defeat in November. "We must all work together," urged the President, "on the national, state and local levels. It makes no sense for us to scramble down to the wire and have our party fall apart. I want a unified party and a program that will be successful in November. It is important not only for the party, but for the people." Other Republican leaders knew the accuracy of the President's warning and sought to remedy the situation by an agreement from the two contenders for the nomination on a Ford-Reagan ticket to be given to the convention. When presented with the idea, Reagan flatly rejected it—even though the plea came from the Republican National Committee. Reagan declared emphatically, "No way I will accept number two on any ticket." There would be no alliance and no compromise of their contrasting philosophies, or of their vaulting ambitions.

George Gallup reported that if the Presidential election were held in June the Democrats' majority in both houses of Congress would be the largest since the 1930s under Franklin D. Roosevelt. That Gallup poll was supported by a similar poll from the New York *Times* and the Columbia Broadcasting System (CBS). Jeremy Campbell gave the statistics of these polls in the *Evening Standard:* "Carter 50 percent, Ford 29 percent; Carter 55 percent, Reagan 24 percent," and concluded that "Carter was heading for a landslide election" in November. However, Campbell warned Carter and the Democrats of being overconfident.

The London *Observer* informed its readers what a strange sight it was for the British to witness the President of the United States leaving the White House to beat the political bushes for a few delegates to the forthcoming convention. President Ford, continued the *Observer,* had an advantage over Reagan in that he could offer delegates political favors that Reagan could not—appointments to well-paying jobs in the federal bureaucracy, United States district judgeships and so on. The President was an "indifferent, a boring campaigner, [who was] doing little really well except shaking other people's hands or wringing his own." Indeed, concluded the *Observer,* "Ford too often looks like what he is, an accidental President."

Mark Frankland reported in the *Observer* that the writers of President Ford's speeches were not famous for their originality. When they found a nice-sounding phrase they usually repeated it frequently. The term "the spendthrift Congress" appeared over and over in Ford's speeches. As Nixon and his appointed successor struggled with Democratic

Congresses the national debt increased by more than thirty-six percent. In fact, two deficit budgets reached record proportions. Because of these unprecedented deficits, Congress, through its two budget committees chaired by Senator Edmund Muskie and Congressman Brock Adams, induced Congress to adopt a proper fiscal policy.

This policy, as reported by Frankland in the *Observer,* provided for the following steps: (1) Congress must produce in May of every year a budget resolution for the following fiscal year that would begin on October 1. (2) The budget resolution would outline all targets for spending, broken down into broad categories for the guidance of Congressional committees. (3) In September Congress must pass a second resolution confirming or modifying the first proposal. (4) From the time of the second resolution the budget figures would be binding on the Congress for all appropriations.

Some of the credit for this badly needed reform, the *Observer* reported, should go to the men working in the Congressional Budget Office, because, for the first time in American history, Congress had its own fiscal experts to match those of the President. The *Observer* stated that particular credit, however, should be given to Chairmen Muskie and Adams for persuading Congress's traditionally powerful committees, with their often elderly and self-important chairmen, to submit to the discipline of the new process. The new policy promised to produce a budget that would "cut the growth" of government spending to eleven percent, compared with seventeen percent the last three preceding years, and to lop almost $20 billion off the deficit. The taxpayers asked why Congress had taken so long to put itself in order.

Members of the British press called the attention of their readers to President Ford's popularity with American bankers—who hoped for his election. The bankers were proud of his vetoes of social programs legislation but did not appreciate Congress's refusal to appropriate money for some of the President's proposals for excessive military weapons. Definitely, the logical British conclusion was that Wall Street was predominantly Republican. However, a few members of Wall Street accepted Carter because of his own fiscal conservatism. But, warned the *Observer,* Carter-supported labor legislation could bring double-digit inflation before his first term was half over.

If the Democrats won in November, wrote Frankland, Carter as President and head of his party would have had no experience of any sort in government at the national level. To the English this was an astonishing way for a powerful country to pick its leader. In their system the Prime Minister, who was the head of his party, was required to have years of prior experience in national government. "Carter's success," the *Observer* stated, "would have been unthinkable if the South still thought itself a world apart. His luck is that America is willing to accept some of the surviving Southern political attitudes and ways." A suspicion of government and a belief in individual freedom, both of which were prominent in the post-Watergate era, have long been Southern inclinations. Furthermore, Frankland continued, the South had a tradition of leadership, and compassionate leadership at that. For decades this was distorted by the obsession with race. "But in Carter and in other present-day Southern politicians this compassionate leadership idea has been revived." Carter brought the South into the mainstream of American political leadership and secured the success of his campaign. He would never have succeeded had "it not long been prepared in Southern history."

As June ended in the preconvention campaign, several significant incidents occurred. The British press discovered Hamilton Jordan's seventy-page memo, which he had prepared four years earlier, outlining the whole Presidential strategy. It had been followed, explained the London *Sun,* to the letter. "The real difference between this and a British election campaign is that everybody knows a President can make a difference." He can make things happen, concluded Jon Akass in the *Sun.* A second incident occurred at a fish fry in Plains, Georgia, when Carter said of President Ford, "I think he is a very good, very kind, and, I think, honest person [but] who has not done a good job in leading this country." This comment appeared in several English newspapers, including the *Times* and the *Daily Telegraph.*

Carter, having been assured of nomination on the first ballot, spoke kindly of his political antagonist and visited Congress. Democratic Congressional leaders, confided the *Times,* gave their guest a rousing ovation when he stated, "I know we can carry all fifty states. I'll be an aggressive and determined President and will seek cooperation with Congress to the maximum degree possible." He, said the *Daily Telegraph,* "impressed Congress as self-confident, well briefed, and tough-minded." Speaker of the House Carl Albert, an Oklahoma Rhodes Scholar, added, "I have always felt good about him." Senate Majority Leader Mike Mansfield lauded Carter for his repudiation of Kissinger's "Lone Ranger" diplomacy, adding, "I would say that he intends to be his own Secretary of State." Carter's staff informed the *Daily Telegraph*'s reporter that Carter had visited Capitol Hill to make himself better known and planned to undertake a great deal of campaigning for the key members of the House and Senate.

The *Daily Telegraph* devoted its lead editorial to "Jimmy Carter's World." It expressed enormous interest in Carter's statement on America's foreign policy, in which Carter promised to work for closer cooperation among the democracies and for a just and stable world order. "Western Europe," he said, "was worried by the United States' unilateral dealings with Russia. To the maximum extent possible our dealings with Communistic powers should reflect the combined views of the democracies and, thereby, avoid the suspicions by our allies that we may be disregarding their interests. NATO forces must be equipped with more modern weapons to face the Warsaw Pact, but the costs must be shared more equitably by European allies and not borne solely by America. Increased cooperation between the superpowers is desirable but we will never seek accommodation at the expense of our own national interests or the interests of our allies."

This statement, said the *Daily Telegraph,* applied particularly to the American allies, "dependent as we are for our own survival on American strength and loyalty—and also on American skill, realism and imagination in wielding its vast power in a bewilderingly complex outside world." For England the main concern about Carter's statement was his "firmness on such matters as undiminished commitment to NATO and the need for necessary military strength and political will to resist Russia's pressures." Certainly, concluded the *Daily Telegraph,* "Carter's speech hid an element of imperative and imagination necessary in an American president. His heart seems to be in the right place but he has a lot to learn about the outside world."

Ross Mark declared in the London *Daily Express* that Carter was opposite, in many ways, to what he seemed to be. He divided himself on issues deliberately. He used every facet of his personality to his advantage. Mark admitted upon reflection that Britain and sometimes France and the West Germans were utterly dependent for their national survival on American men over whose selection they had almost no influence.

In British eyes, as in France and elsewhere in Western Europe, an important innovation in the American election of 1976 was the Congressional Voting Law, which gave expatriate Americans the right to vote. Although some members of the Justice Department thought the law unconstitutional because the recipients of the law were living outside of the United States, Democratic and Republican headquarters accepted the law and endeavored to locate Americans in Britain. The Democrats Abroad met, selected, and sent a delegation of four to the national convention in New York City. The law required that these Americans abroad vote in the last state where they had voted before going abroad.

Both parties soon had well-organized groups in the British Isles. Anthony Hyde, a gangling, graying management consultant, was chosen chairman of the Democrats. Richard Beeman, a youthful, bouncy, dynamic banker with a pudgy face, was selected to lead the Republicans. The 75,000 Americans in Britain were unique in two ways: first, they had special problems in living abroad that were germane to the American election, and, second, they were in a position to see how an alternative economic system worked. The *Times* and other newspapers spoke approvingly of the new law. Beeman and Hyde held regular meetings of their groups and through interesting programs introduced considerable enthusiasm into the campaign among the members of their respective parties.

The Leeds *Yorkshire Post* reported the Carter people naming Steven P. Cohen, a Boston lawyer in London, as the official Democratic organizer and vote-getter among the expatriate Americans living in the British Isles. He was the first full-time salaried campaign worker appointed to work abroad in American political party history, the *Yorkshire Post* said. These expatriate Americans increased their enthusiasm for their respective party nominees until the end of the election campaign in November.

Back in Washington, Senator Barry Goldwater, the Republican Presidential candidate of 1964, announced his support of President Ford. The Senator said this "was a most difficult decision for me to make," because of the President's meager talents and his lack of leadership qualities. The Ford aides were divided over the result. Some thought the Senator's endorsement would be a "political bonus"; others feared it would be a "kiss of death."

Both President Ford and Reagan, stated the *Guardian,* were dealing and wheeling in classic styles as the Democratic delegates packed their bags in preparation to leave for the national convention, which would soon meet in New York City.

Several British reporters, on the eve of the Democratic National Convention in Madison Square Garden, wrote biographical articles about Carter; Jonathan Steele in the *Guardian,* Terrence Lancaster in the *Daily Mirror,* and Jeremy Campbell in the *Evening Standard* were three of them. Steele saw the Democratic leader as the most secretive, the stiffest, and the least attractive of all the candidates. Carter chatted with the reporters on the plane or on the bus, but he never engaged in frivolous banter, no chitchat, never any exposure of personal feelings. He remained one of the least known and most private of politicians. He was close to being a millionaire, wrote Campbell, "achieved by hard work, long hours and shrewd investments."

Steele described the Georgian's early life on the farm and admired Carter for his record at the Naval Academy, where he graduated in 1947, ranking fifty-ninth in a class of 820. He was in the Navy for seven years, most of the time working under the supervision of Admiral Hyman Rickover in the development of the nuclear submarine, an experience that, Steele contended, would become an asset for a President. Steele quoted the candidate as saying that, next to his father, Earl Carter, Admiral Rickover had had the most influence on his life. When his father died in 1953, Carter, against the heated argument of Rosalynn, resigned from the Navy and returned to Plains to manage the farm.

Steele enlightened the *Guardian*'s readers by relating Carter's life's history. Carter in 1954 was invited by the local police chief and the pastor of the local Baptist church to join the "White Citizens Council." Carter refused, whereupon the police chief offered Carter the membership fee if he would become a member. Carter, with obvious disgust, replied, "I have five dollars, but I'd flush it down the toilet before I'd give it to you for that purpose." Subsequently, Carter and his family cast the only votes to admit blacks to the membership of the Plains Baptist Church. As a result of these incidents, Carter's peanut warehouse was boycotted by the community. The British were particularly interested in Carter's reaction to the race problem, because of increasing racial tensions throughout the British Isles.

Carter entered politics via membership in the local school board, and was then elected to the State Senate. He was defeated in his first try for the Georgia governorship by Lester Maddox, "an obvious oaf who [ultimately] became victimized by his own ignorance and his racial prejudices." Cushioned by his increasing wealth, Carter, according to the *Guardian,* spent the next four years making 1,800 speeches throughout Georgia. Elected Governor, he was more liberal than many Georgians had thought he would be. Would he do the same as President? Steele wrote that many hoped so; some doubted.

Steele characterized Carter as "clearly intelligent, quick-witted, intellectually curious, has a rapid grasp of a complicated brief, is strong-willed and supremely self-confident." As President, this British reporter thought, Carter may "be more brain, less muscle, cool and calculating, rather than rash and vulnerable, especially in foreign affairs."

Lancaster began his biographical sketch of Carter in the *Daily Mirror* somewhat constitutionally: "I hold this truth to be self-evident—that anybody investing a little money now on Jimmy Carter becoming the next President of the United States, will not be out of pocket when votes are counted next November." Indeed, at that moment Carter was so far ahead of the field, Lancaster commented, that Mayor Daley might even have an honest election in Chicago's Cook County. This weekend America was celebrating all things that had shaped it during the last two hundred years—"enormous idealism, wonderful generosity of spirit, loyalty to its flag, plus Coca-Cola and whiskey and apple pie. . . ." "I would add one great tradition of American politics," wrote Lancaster, "robbery at the election polls." Although there were examples of dishonest elections in American history, these were the exception, not the rule, as the *Daily Mirror* concluded.

As other reporters for British agencies stationed in the United States were doing, Lancaster saw in Carter a mass of contradictions. He was a simple Christian who was a millionaire peanut farmer; a Southerner who was liberal on race; a man who had never run for office outside his home state of Georgia, but who now was posed to become the most important man in the Western world. Lancaster contended that behind Carter's built-in grin and apparent country boy naiveté were great political skill, amazing stamina, and towering ambition. Carter, on the British

Broadcasting Corporation's *Panorama* program, said, in an appeal to the expatriate Americans in the British Isles, "I hope that when I go out of office at the end of one or two terms, the American people will say, 'Well, Jimmy Carter made a lot of mistakes, but he never told us a lie.'" Anything, concluded Lancaster, "would be better than the last American elected President, Richard Nixon, who made mistakes and told lies to everybody."

On July 12 the Democrats, bubbling over with the intoxicating prospect of winning, after eight years of losing, started their convention on a "wave of conviviality." Some ten thousand Democrats, stated Lancaster, poured into a party at Pier 88 in New York's Dockland, listening to Dixieland jazz and drinking beer out of big plastic cups. On a street in lower Manhattan the philosophical descendants of Jefferson and Jackson flocked to an open-air jamboree that offered spare ribs, French pastries, fried chicken, clams, acres of pizza, and cups of coffee laced with anisette *(Bartender's Guide)*. For entertainment they were shown excerpts from six Broadway shows, two fashion displays, and an organ grinder with a monkey. Amid the red plush carpets and exotic chandeliers of the Metropolitan Opera, hundreds of women Democrats gathered to demonstrate. These marches took on the flavor of a party. Lancaster wrote that, when hundreds of gay activists bore down on them along Eighth Avenue, "they were heckled by anti-gays, carrying enormous banners bearing scriptural messages (Romans 1:26-27) which blew them along the street like a ship under full sail on windswept waters."

Carter, said Campbell, in the *Evening Standard,* moved like a monarch through the festivities, soothing the militant Democratic women, performing well on a television interview, meeting the press, and generating real excitement as he went about the city. At the mammoth party on Pier 88 late in the evening, Campbell noted, some women were so starstruck that they passed through the receiving line twice. One excited Democratic female threw herself into the candidate's arms, saying, "Do you mind if I hug you?" The British were amused by the information about the American quadrennial convention, which was in great contrast to their party meetings.

The *Guardian* revealed that not all sights around the convention hall in Madison Square Garden were pleasing to the senses. Huge garbage drifts were unsightly to the eye and obnoxious to the nose. Derelicts, completely unaware of the Democratic quest, lay barefoot full-length on the pavement. Prostitutes beckoned solicitously from nearby doorways for customers walking along the sidewalks. As night encompassed the area a few double-XX movie shops advertised their shows with flashing neon signs. Delegates were made aware of stealing when a Wallace delegate was robbed of his wallet containing $500 and by excessively high prices—coffee sold for $1 per cup. All of this, the *Guardian* stated, constituted the metropolitan atmosphere in which the Democrats "converged to crown their prince."

The opening session of the convention, as reported by Jane Rosen in the *Guardian,* was tame as some four thousand delegates and visitors, among whom were some expatriates from England, were smiling and munching peanuts as they sat or moved about the huge auditorium. No one apparently paid any attention to the early speakers, whose speeches were dull and drab—particularly Senator John Glenn's. As the bands played the Democratic theme song—"Happy Days Are Here Again"—Barbara Jordan, a late speaker, made her way to the speaker's podium. A black congresswoman from Texas, Miss Jordan was conscious of being the first black and the first woman ever to deliver a keynote address to a major party convention in America. Possessed of a deep, rolling, Shakespearean voice, her eloquence held her massive audience in delightful attention.

"There is something different and special about this night," she began. "That a Barbara Jordan has been asked to come before you. My presence here proves that the American dream need not forever be deferred." The delegates waved and applauded their approval. In her gifted stentorian cadences, she set forth a single challenge, which no doubt delighted many Britons: "If we promise, we must deliver. If we propose, we must produce. If we ask for sacrifice, we must be first to give. If we make mistakes, we must be first to admit them. We must provide people with a vision of the future that is attainable. We must strike a balance between the idea that government can do everything and the belief that government should do nothing." Throughout her eloquent and elegant oration her audience sat enthralled and gave her a three-minute standing ovation when she concluded.

Carter, comfortably seated in a $750-per-day suite high up in the Americana Hotel, spent his time working on his acceptance speech, watching the convention proceedings on the television screen, and reflecting on his unpopularity with some important political groups. Many Democratic officials, said Rosen in the *Guardian,* had not forgiven him for his rapid rise to the top, a rise that he owed to himself and his aides. The intelligentsia and the political commentators, taken by surprise, repetitiously criticized this born-again Baptist Southerner who claimed to be waging his campaign according to the Lord's will. The *Guardian* pointed out that the urbanites and suburbanites were a hurdle to his popularity because he was a farmer, brought up the hard way, who appealed with emotions and lucidity, to the American dream. All of these political problems Carter knew upon reflection.

The platform was briefly introduced in sections by a series of ten-minute speeches from party leaders—a device conceived to show how the Democrats of great diversity had been brought together in unity. The platform, reported Steele in the *Guardian,* was down from 25,000 words in 1972 to 15,000 words in 1976. Modesty of length was matched by sobriety of tone. The platform called for the reduction of unemployment from 7.5 percent then, to 3 percent by 1980. It committed the party to national planning, a national health insurance program, and a new system of income maintenance for the poor. These planks in the Democratic platform were especially pleasing to the British, because the latter had national planning and a national health program they considered second to none.

All party disputes about the platform were firmly swept under the carpet of political harmony by the Carter managers. The Carter team prevented any disturbance of calm party harmony. Having united the various factions in the Democratic Party, the Georgia candidate was not permitting any schism of the party again. New York City had welcomed the thousands of Democrats with brotherly love.

The platform preamble stated: "We acknowledge that no political party, nor any President and Vice-President, possesses answers to all problems that face us as a nation." The broad, all-inclusive platform proposed programs that no Administration could possibly effect in four or eight years. That fact, wrote Louis Heren in the *Times,* could create a dilemma that could be embarrassing to Carter, if elected. The platform stated specifically that governmental decision making behind closed doors is the natural enemy of the people. The Democratic Party was committed to openness throughout all government. The platform, concluded the *Times,* "certainly proves that Carter dominates the party. It also suggests that, behind those flashing teeth, is a new kind of Democrat."

The *Scotsman* reported that the Democratic Party was well, alive, and in wonderful spirit. For the first time in American history, federal funds were available for Presidential campaigns. This convention, more than any previous major party national convention, was pluralistic in delegates. There were 35 percent women, 11 percent black, 4 percent Latinos. The leadership of the party rarely had been better. The new, energetic men, declared the *Times,* were talented, including Tom Hayden, founder of Students for a Democratic Society. The young leaders were better educated, more intelligent and knowledgeable than many of the old leaders. The Democrats deserved to win in November, stated the *Scotsman,* because once again the party was fulfilling its historical role of assimilation of immigrants, of all religions, and now, finally, of the blacks.

With the platform adopted, with the convention rules agreed upon, with the introductory speeches made, the convention was ready for the Presidential nominating speeches. Although several others were placed in nomination, the final result for Carter and his delegates was never in doubt.

All British sources of public opinion carried excerpts from Carter's acceptance speech, which he made to the convention directly—a practice begun by Franklin Roosevelt in 1932.

Having been notified of his official nomination, Carter kept a promise he had made earlier. Upon arriving in New York for the convention, he told a crowd that had gathered to welcome him, "I would like to announce my personal choice for Vice-President." There was an immediate hush as the members of the crowd eagerly awaited the eventful announcement. After a long pause, Carter added, "As soon as I'm sure who the choice of the Presidential candidate is going to be." The crowd, as George Gale wrote in the *Daily Express,* "roared."

For weeks Carter had invited a number of Vice-Presidential hopefuls to Plains for all-day conferences and visits. He had interviewed several in Washington and some after they arrived in New York City. Then he stated he had limited his list to seven, subsequently to three, and finally to two Senators—Edmund Muskie or Walter Mondale. In presenting Fritz Mondale to the press on the morning after his nomination, Carter said, "This was the most difficult decision I have had to make. There is a compatibility between Senator Mondale and myself on the great issues facing the nation. I have absolutely no doubt that I have made the right decision." In accepting Carter's selection, Mondale said, "Carter is terribly gifted, skilled, and committed. My wife and I are committed to give all that we have and to assist in what I know will be one of the great Presidencies." Mondale, declared the *Yorkshire Post,* "fits the geographical requirements. He is the son of a Methodist minister. Politically, he has been at the right place at the right time." One American wag suggested Congressman Wayne Hays of Ohio to balance the Carter ticket.

While Carter was busy determining his choice for running mate, Winchester was one among several English reporters to write about the Vice-Presidency. Six of the fourteen American Vice-Presidents in the twentieth century have become President. One distinguished American politician, wrote Winchester in the *Guardian,* spoke of the Vice-Presidency as not worth a "bucketful of warm spit." Not all Vice-Presidents were chosen by the Presidential nominee on the basis of qualities needed for the Presidency. Spiro Agnew illustrated the point, though he was not mentioned by the *Guardian,* no doubt because of his disgrace to the office with which the people had entrusted him.

When Mondale's selection was announced, several British reporters, well versed in American Presidential politics, wrote advisedly to the Democrats to clarify for their British readers American Presidential campaign history. Louis Heren stated that Republicans did not win American national elections; Democrats only lost them. Americans, wrote Heren in the *Times,* were ready for a God-fearing President, as long as he does not believe that he has a mandate from Heaven to rule over them. It was not true to say that Carter was fuzzy on the issues, the *Times* stated; "he wisely refused to assume hard and fast positions on most of the issues and, thereby, united the divisive factions of his party as Harold Wilson had united the Labour Party by avoiding identification with any of the divisive factions." Carter, a Southern moderate conservative, had, said Richard Rose in the Glasgow *Herald,* selected his running mate wisely. The *Times* noted Carter's advantage in having a natural affinity with blacks. They sensed that he understood them because he was a Southerner. This was a significant factor in the slums of cities throughout the country and should make the Democrats unbeatable and able to forge a new FDR coalition that could ensure their supremacy for the foreseeable future.

Fred Emery announced in the *Scotsman* that Carter had picked a winner and that his final choice was the result of the influence of Hubert Humphrey, who had conferred with Carter several times in behalf of his intimate friend and fellow Minnesotan. Humphrey considered Mondale a liberal of wide experience, a man of many talents, and a widely recognized wit. Emery said Mondale "is articulate and outspoken and at forty-eight is the youngest liberal leader in the Senate." The *Yorkshire Post* stated that Mondale had spent much of his time working for legislation to help the old and the poor people. He was recognized as an expert on tax reform. In a quiet, effective way, the *Yorkshire Post* stated, the Minnesota Senator had led the fight to weaken the Senate's rules permitting unlimited debate—filibuster—frequently used to prevent the enactment of liberal legislation.

Coleman McCarthy in the *Guardian* reviewed briefly Mondale's recent book, *The Accountability of Power,* and quoted him as saying, "I love to ponder ideas, to reflect on them and discuss them with experts and friends." Mondale, said the *Guardian,* in acquainting the British people with the Democratic choice for the vice-presidency, quietly endeavored to generate a national sense of compassion toward those on the bottom, but he had kept free from rhapsodizing himself with a sense of mission. In 1974, Mondale stated, "We have performed miracles for the American people in Washington. If you don't believe it, consider this—who else would have given you two Presidents and three Vice-Presidents in two years without even having an election?"

In his acceptance speech, which preceded Carter's, Mondale stated, "We have just lived through the worst political scandal in American history and we are now led by a President who pardoned the person who did it." The *Evening Standard* stated that the huge auditorium of delegates rose as a thunderous sound of applause reverberated across the hall. The *Irish Times* described Mondale as being "rare among American politicians in that he renounced a Presidential campaign, rare in his outspoken, articulate, sincerity, rare in his dedication to social reforms and rare in his small financial estate in the Senate millionaire membership." Such a political character as Mondale was of particular interest to British Labourites and socialists because he represented ideologically their aims more nearly than other, more conservative, American politicians.

In accepting the Presidential nomination, Carter delighted many British when he said, "We have been a nation adrift too long. We have been without leadership too long. We have had divided, deadlocked government too long. We have been governed by veto too long. We have suffered enough at the hands of a tired [and] worn-out Administration. . . . I want you to help me evolve an efficient, economical, purposeful and manageable government for our nation. Now I recognize the difficulty but if I'm elected it is going to be done and you can depend on it." In regard to Watergate, he declared, "I see no reason why the big-shot crooks should go free while the poor ones go to jail." To American allies he said, "What united us and commands us is our dedication to democracy; this is much more important than that which occasionally divides us." To the group of Third World powers seeking to help themselves, he stated, "America shares your inspirations and extends its hands to you." To those countries competing with the United States, he declared, "We neither fear competition nor see it as an obstacle to wider cooperation."

The Cardiff *Western Mail* defined the remarkable metamorphosis Carter had made from an outsider to unassailable contender for the Presidency of his country. The *Western Mail* found a contributing factor in the unusual success of Carter, hitherto not intimated in British public opinion. The claims to independence from the Washington establishment profited by the showing of the film *All the President's Men* in every major city in the United States. "Vietnam and the official lying that was revealed in the Pentagon Papers, Watergate and Nixon's sordid reign and exit from the White House," noted the Welsh paper, "have combined with recession and the expense and comparative failure of the big welfare programs to bring Washington into a comprehensive dissipation that even the honest Gerald Ford has failed to dent significantly." While admitting that it was always difficult for the British to evaluate American politics, because the Democratic and Republican Parties were massive and amorphous, embracing far wider points of view than British parties, the *Western Mail* concluded that opinion polls showed the Democrat Tweedledum capable of beating whichever Republican Tweedledee was chosen. The lead that the Democrats held was certain to narrow as the election approached.

Rosalynn Carter, in an interview reported in the Ipswich *East Anglia Daily Times,* stated how thankful she was to have one month free in which to find out what her husband thought of "the campaign issues" before she went canvassing for him again. She mentioned she had already spent nearly one and a half years canvassing for him, apparently without knowing what his ideas were. "What an astonishing achievement!" announced the *East Anglia Daily Times*. If Carter is elected in November it will probably be his character rather than his policies that will be tested thoroughly. The basic reasons for this conclusion, declared the *East Anglia Daily Times,* were first that Carter was a completely unknown quantity and second that Congress, instead of passively accepting Presidential legislative leadership, was assisting its own political leaders in putting their ideas into legislation to be placed before the President.

The *Scotsman* and the *Guardian* endeavored to rival each other in their leading editorials about the convention. The *Scotsman*'s "Great Expectations" was not a replica of the *Guardian*'s "All Aboard for the White House." The *Scotsman* contended that Carter's acceptance speech was inspirational to party workers and to millions of voters, including the expatriates watching television in the British Isles. The *Guardian* predicted that future historians looking for "the final healing of the Civil War wounds would point to Carter's nomination as the final restoration of the healthy Union." Too long had Northern Democratic liberals written of Southern whites as "rednecks"; too long had ancient lingering regional prejudices been permitted to act adversely against Southern political leaders. Now an almost unknown man, continued the *Guardian,* from the Deep South had come to the heart of New York to accept the nomination for President from the oldest political party in America.

The *Guardian* was well aware of Carter's driving ambition to be President, but some Americans, as well as some British, worried about his lack of vision. None doubted his sincere Christianity, but more than born-again Christian faith was needed to be a successful leader of the Western world, including the United States. "The American election in November is to elect our President too," emphasized the *Guardian*. In characterizing the Democratic Presidential nominee the *Guardian* discussed Carter's self-confidence, his determination, his restless energy, his good judgment, and, in his own business affairs, his administrative flair.

The *Scotsman* tried to describe the complexity of Carter's personality. His keen intellect "diagnosed the American psyche more keenly and accurately than his opponents and has, with apparent sincerity, told the patient the most palatable cure." His acceptance speech showed great understanding of the state of America today. The *Scotsman* continued: Carter understood the ugliness of the Vietnam War; he knew how Watergate's criminal politicians had scandalized the people, as had the revelations about the Central Intelligence Agency (CIA)'s illegal activities; "the people of America are thirsty for an inspirational leader untainted by Washington politics, free from conventional ideas and ideals which have ruled the nation for so long." In this Bicentennial year, the *Scotsman* believed that Carter reiterated the hopes of the Founding Fathers and American traditions of living by high, strongly held morals and philosophical principles. The acceptance address was punctuated with such words as "grace," "decent," "love," "sound." This simple style, the *Scotsman* concluded, had been the key to Carter's meteoric success.

On the morning after the convention officially adjourned, Carter held a breakfast for the campaign strategists before shaking hands in farewell as they departed for their respective homes and, in some instances, local welcoming parties. The *Guardian* described pledges of euphoria pouring into the streets over the "Grits and Fritz" ticket, with "Georgia peaches and Minnesota cream" blending with the mental powers of the executive branch particularly. These powers, contended the *Guardian*, were intermingled with the native skepticism that Americans have about politicians and bureaucracy.

The *Irish Times* gave its readers a summary of the preconvention campaign as it centered around Carter. When he began his struggle for the Democratic nomination two years earlier, the *Irish Times* said, he "correctly perceived the national mood." He realized that Americans were not so much interested in the future as they had been in coming to terms with the horrid, painful past. He realized how "the moral ugliness of Vietnam, the corruption and hypocrisy of Watergate, the cynical realpolitik of the CIA and of the Federal Bureau of Investigation (FBI) and other agencies ostensibly created to defend American values and, finally, the unresolved stresses of the civil rights of the blacks—and the counter-culture revolution of the young" had caused millions of Americans to lose faith in the nation's political leaders. The Democratic nominee offered "absolution rather than a program," concluded the *Scotsman*. What America needed, Carter stated repeatedly, "was a government as full of decency and compassion and kindness and love as the American people are."

Carter's strategy to run in virtually every primary and caucus proved a successful gamble. He concluded that he would do well in enough states to prove that a Southerner could win in the North and do well in enough states to absorb an occasional defeat and still win. Both of Carter's calculations proved correct.

The *Daily Mail*'s leading editorial thought Carter's nomination was the nation fully accepting the South as an equal part of the Union. "Dixie, once despised and hated, was in many ways becoming the most forward and dynamic part of the country, while remaining the most stable in its sense of duty and tradition." Carter's success, said the *Daily Mail*, was an interesting lesson for British politicians, even though their system did not permit the overnight rise of a Jimmy Carter.

The *Observer* bade farewell to the convention by discussing Carter's step toward a real alliance with the liberals, his naming of Mondale as his running mate, and his efforts to re-create the coalition of Franklin Roosevelt of forty years ago—namely, the Northern liberals, the blacks, the Southern conservatives, and the elderly. Like Roosevelt, Carter spoke off the cuff much of the time. Although Carter was a poor reader of speeches, the *Observer* informed its readers that Carter had acquired the difficult task of memorizing his speeches so that he could retain the appearance of spontaneity. The *Observer* noted that Carter was relatively small and had a light and high voice. Charles Kirbo, an Atlanta lawyer and adviser to Carter, stated for the *Observer,* "Power sits on his shoulders as easily as a good saddle does on a horse."

The *Daily Express* described the results of the Democratic convention as an American Revolution as bloodless as the English one of 1689. In this revolutionary change, Carter was "part agent, part catalyst, part servant, and chief beneficiary." Wheeling and dealing were casualties of the Carter revolution. There were no conspiratorial meetings in smoke-filled, whiskey-scented hotel rooms at this convention, wrote Brian Vine, adding that the great bosses of the Democratic Party were casualties also and the greatest casualty could be the Republican Party. The *Daily Express* maintained that Carter's crowning moment came when he brushed aside all token opposition at the recent convention to clinch the nomination amid wild, enthusiastic scenes.

"Two quite different worlds existed between Plains where Carter lives and in Washington where he will live in January," wrote Michael Davies in the *Observer,* "and each is extremely suspicious of the other." Indeed, Washington was as nervous as Georgia was confident. Why all of this nervousness as the "Grits and Fritz" ticket began the Presidential election campaign? There were two complex and massive problems that would confront the next Presidential Administration, concluded Davies. There were the ever-increasing bureaucracy of the federal government and the lucrative link between the politicians in Congress and the big-money vested interests outside.

According to the *Observer* reporter, in the last 15 years, 236 new federal agencies were created and only 21 were terminated. In fact, some of these agencies were captives of the very people they were created to regulate. More than 52 percent of the senior staff members of the Nuclear Regulatory Agency were alumni of Babcock and Wilcox, General Electric, and other giant nuclear producing companies, as the American people would learn tragically in 1979. The real problem, declared the *Observer,* was the intimate financial connections between the politicians in Congress and the big-money vested interests. If that link could be broken, wrote Davies, it would be a revolution highly beneficial for America. Can any politician resist the lobbyists of the American Petroleum Institute with its multimillion-dollar lobbying budget, some of which always finds its way into campaign funds? An unbreakable system, legislators, special interests, and bureaucrats joined together with hoops of steel. "Jimmy Carter has his work cut out for him," concluded the

Observer, "to break this selfish corrupting system—even if he means to try."

Stephen Barker declared in the *Daily Telegraph* that Carter's strategy was astonishingly simple—"hard work, a passionately devoted and youthful staff and meticulous cultivation, well ahead of times, of grass roots support far and wide." He was a successful businessman with a razor-sharp mind. Assuredly, said the *Daily Telegraph,* he is no "red-neck hillbilly," but a "go-getter, in every inch the polished managerial executive type. He dresses impeccably, has his hair expensively cut, his hands well manicured. A voracious reader, his mind is like a computerized file bank." Washington officials and the elite's Eastern Establishment were awed by his command of detail.

Dermot Purgavies reported Carter's goodbye to the convention in the *Daily Mail* by addressing himself to the 20,000 who attended, the 14 miles of telephone cable in Madison Square Garden, with the 700 journalists and reporters—the British Broadcasting Corporation alone sent 57 employees to the convention—the 3,000 delegates and the 2,000 visitors. Purgavies thought it interesting that the combined population of Plains, Georgia, and Ceylan, Minnesota, the birthplaces of Carter and Mondale, respectively, was a total of 1,170. Small-town America had certainly triumphed over metropolitan centers.

William Lowther, in the *Times,* was impressed with Carter's having crisscrossed the nation with a fixed ceramic smile on his face, preaching with the religious fervor of a Baptist missionary for a new morality in government. The secret of his success was remarkable only in its simplicity. He realized that all of the nation's ills could be blamed on Washington and cunningly cashed in on his greatest weakness—lack of any federal experience. The establishment, wrote Lowther, frightened and suspicious, tried time and again to stop him, but Carter's story of love and compassion, delivered in a Southern drawl, worked a political miracle. Never, concluded this astute British commentator, "has a candidate reached the top owing so little to so few."

One obvious exception to Carter's freedom from obligations was Dr. Peter Bourne, British-born, who was head of Carter's Washington office. He was a great asset to Carter because of his great talents, his incredible self-discipline, his ability to put his mind to something and to pursue it to the exclusion of everything else.

Alan Brew reported in the *Daily Post and Mercury* that Carter, "the clockwork politician," arose earlier, went to bed later, traveled farther, gave more grins, shook more hands, and believed in himself more serenely than anybody in the present scramble for the White House. He ended the Democratic primaries assured of the nomination—a most remarkable achievement. Only six months earlier he was virtually unheard of. He astonished the party elders, "who dubbed him 'Jimmy Who?'" They were still bemusedly wondering who the nominee was. Carter's success was the hallmark of the primary season; there were no issues, only personalities. Carter, continued Brew, had been the most salable commodity. He was surrounding himself with a formidable brain trust of advisers who would assist him to "allay the strong doubts about his fuzziness on the issues." The national demand for change, decency, and morality in government, Brew thought, ran deep. Carter was skillfully working that vein.

The *Daily Post and Mercury* recorded an early campaign incident of nominee Carter's. In talking to a group of children in a Florida school, he, "with crinkly smiles," asked, "How many of you have mothers and fathers and grandmothers and grandfathers and neighbors and friends? Well, if you ask all those people to vote for me, I could get elected, and if I got elected you can come and see me at the White House." His blue eyes fell coolly on each child in turn. "Because," he promised them all, "I'll remember you personally." It was remarkable but, concluded Brew, "come January he will have to start remembering."

The thoughtful sportsmanship of President Ford was evidenced in the telegram he sent to the Democratic nominee. The *Daily Post and Mercury* quoted the message: "Congratulations, Jimmy. I look forward to a good contest."

In considering British coverage of the Presidential campaign, all sources used so far have been conservative or liberal—none socialist. But one socialist newspaper, the London *Socialist Standard,* called the election "the American Presidential circus." The American President was able to use H-bombs and other nuclear weapons to annihilate countless millions of people. American militarism, the *Socialist Standard* said, showed how a string of glib excuses was ready to explain why poverty, unemployment, and crime continued to blight the lives of most Americans. During primaries and up to election, erosion and cynicism were essential to survival. "Candidates must strike the proper balance between being patriotic, religious and anti-communist." Candidates, said this organ of the British socialists, "must be strongly associated with capitalism, be enterprising, successful, wealthy, rugged, ultra-American."

In America, this leftist source of British opinion continued, the President was regarded as a kind of "national father figure." "The circus and the sickening ballyhoo were indispensable to the final outcome." The entire campaign and election were stage-managed and party boss-controlled so that "only personalities were seen, the issues were glided over or covered up entirely." In 1964 Johnson was for peace and Goldwater for war. Johnson was elected overwhelmingly, but the people got war anyway. It was not long before Americans were chanting, "Hey, hey, LBJ, how many kids have you killed today?" It was not, concluded this socialist voice, that "American workers were more ignorant than their fellows elsewhere; it was just that the circus campaign lasted longer.

The real issues were never treated seriously in American elections," concluded the *Socialist Standard.*

The magazines were not as prolific in discussing the Presidential election as were the newspapers. The Democratic convention, exclaimed the *Spectator,* "was not a convention but a coronation." The Democrats were hopefully shoving all Republicans into that scandal-ridden Nixon kitchen. The convention was extremely dull until Miss Jordan spoke. She was forty and plain, "but, by God, she possesses the gift of tongue." She was superb, concluded the *Spectator.*

After the convention, this conservative journal described Carter's preparations for the campaign and election. Four years ago, it stated, "Carter sat down and prepared the most meticulous, cold-blooded assault on the Presidency that has ever been mounted. He wrote out a plan for projecting himself year by year, first as a successful Governor, then as a good party man, then as a profound thinker, and finally as potential President. He understood the mood of America when no one else did. He sensed the distrust of Washington, of party machines, and of the professional politicians." He acted advantageously for himself toward all of these conditions.

The excessive energy that habitually characterized Democratic conventions, stated the *Economist,* pulsated on the periphery in the lobbies, coffee shops, downtown streets, and in the hotel corridors. But on the rostrum in the convention hall, proceedings were sedate to the point of being perfunctory.

The United Kingdom's public opinion on the American political scene during July was devoted almost entirely to the Democrats: their activities previous to the national convention, comments about the convention, and characterizations of the Democratic nominees. The British press in August naturally shifted its attention to the Republicans, the activities of the two chief contenders for the Presidential nomination, their convention, and their nominees. Next: the Republican activities.

3

The
Republican
National Convention

Governor Reagan arrived from California to a reception of twenty gorgeous girls in short blue skirts and tight white blouses who waved red straw banners in the air as they sang rah-rah songs, including "Rock Around the Clock." About three thousand colored balloons, reported Jeremy Campbell in the *Evening Standard,* took flight from the courtyard and balconies of the Alameda Plaza Hotel, "where waterfalls played and Cadillacs were parked nose to tail with Lincoln Continentals." An avenue of welcome was formed for Reagan and Nancy by forty-three American flags.

Two days before the convention opened, President Ford arrived at the airport. He was met by a group of boys and girls dressed as cowboys and wearing large white hats and high white boots, and a considerable crowd waving small American flags.

John Pilger stated in the *Daily Mirror* that the Republicans were meeting in the "home of the American pig industry" in the hopes of picking the man who could bring home the bacon in the Presidential election in November. Here, continued the *Daily Mirror,* "where the smell of the world's largest pig pens enveloped the huge auditorium, the Grand Old Party met to adopt a party platform and to nominate two candidates for the nation's highest offices.

A fortnight before the assembling of the Republicans in Kansas City the United States held its Bicentennial Celebration. As President, Gerald Ford made several appearances before large audiences on July 4, 1976, usually accompanied with a speech. On this conspicuous occasion the President and Mrs. Ford entertained the British Queen as the nation's guest at the White House, with wining, dining, and dancing. The President was an official host at the public occasions. For ages the

33

British have had a social custom that requires a person in the presence of royalty to back off for a required distance from royalty before turning to leave. When the President, on a public occasion, violated this long-held English tradition, the British press made much ado about the violation of majestic courtesy. However, the Americans thought none the less of their President for the incident.

Ford was extremely busy in his preconvention campaign against Reagan, who, on July 6, spoke for thirty minutes on a national television broadcast. As reported in the *Evening Standard* and several other English newspapers, Reagan attacked both Ford and Carter as authors of "soothing rhetoric, pleasant smiles and reorganization gimmicks." Reagan said he was not a professional politician but, as a citizen running for President, he must state his own beliefs and values.

The *Guardian* noted that President Ford, in a White House lawn press conference, put on a cool, confident front when he stated that the Carter-Mondale ticket was beatable and that he would be selected as the one to beat it. He said he would wage an affirmative campaign and would win. The President promised that he would meet each undecided delegate personally before the convention convened. The *Daily Telegraph* announced that Ford had nearly the magic total of 1,130 delegates pledged to him, and that it was the end of the trail for Ronald Reagan. The *Daily Post and Mercury* quoted Ford as saying that he would let Carter develop the issues and that Ford would stand on his record as President. When Carter stated that he never would have pardoned Nixon, and Mondale added that the pardon violated the sacred principle of equality under the law, Ford replied, "I have no regrets for the pardon."

The *Irish Times* announced Reagan's bombshell in the naming of Senator Richard Schweiker of Pennsylvania as his running mate if he won the nomination. "This unites the Republican Party for November," stated Reagan, "by bringing together the conservative and the moderate wings of our party." The Dublin newspaper said this selection was one of the best-kept secrets in recent United States political history.

The *Economist* branded Reagan's naming of his Vice-Presidential running mate as the "boldest political move since Richard III decided to meet Henry Tudor at Bosworth Field." Reagan's hopes that the announcement would sway the uncommitted delegates to him were blasted when the *Daily Post and Mercury* announced that Clarke Reed, Mississippi's state chairman, declared that he expected all of that state's thirty delegates to support Ford because of Reagan's choice of Schweiker as his running mate. A south Mississippi congressman, Trent Lott, who had voted against all charges against Nixon even after the White House tapes revealed Nixon's attempt to cover up Watergate, told Ford, according to the *Evening Standard,* that, if he chose Elliott Richardson or Senator Edward Brooke or any other liberal, he was finished. With this information, President

Ford left the Oval Office to meet the Mississippi Republican delegation in Jackson. The *Daily Telegraph* reported that the conference was successful. Meanwhile, the *Guardian* declared that Reagan's "candor in naming his running mate three weeks before the convention is a bold and refreshing departure from the old politics."

Besides the switch in the Mississippi delegation from uncommitted to possibly pro-Ford, John Connally, a Texas wheeler and dealer, flew from Texas to confer with the President. Upon emerging from the White House conference, Connally told reporters he would support President Ford and work in Texas for his election. The *Times* quoted Connally as saying, "with inimitable presumptuousness," that "the best interests of the country will be served by my stating my unequivocal position that I do support President Ford . . . will support his election with every resource I have and all of the ability I have." After the Connally conference, President Ford entertained the entire Pennsylvania delegation of 103 members with a banquet at the White House. On this occasion the President carefully kept his lips sealed as to his choice for his running mate, reported the *Yorkshire Post*.

With the Democratic convention concluded and with the Republican convention coming up, the Republicans captured British headlines. Among the interesting headlines was the one in the *Sun,* which declared that Reagan's dream of capturing the Presidency was shattered by his naming his running mate before the convention delegates assembled.

The *Economist* called President Ford a good President, noting that on the political stump he came across exactly as he was—"a good, limited, average conservative man." The President's chief claim to the nomination, the *Economist* said, was that he had managed the country for two years and done no harm. Indeed, the United States, said the popular journal, was in vastly better condition than it was at the dark moment when he became President. He made the White House once again the civil, honest center for the expression of the results of the many primaries.

Several British newspapers and the *Scotsman* reported that President Ford mailed letters to 4,518 delegates and their alternates, Republican governors, Republican mayors, and some influential non-office-holding Republicans, asking each person to vote for five persons for Vice-President in order of preference. "I can assure you that your response will be held in complete confidence." Apparently, no one ever saw the result of this poll except the President, if he ever did. Another poll showed John Connally to be the Republican favorite for the Vice-Presidency. The *Irish Times* pointed out that, two years earlier, Connally had been indicted in federal court for perjury and bribery—tried on the latter charge and acquitted some months later. Thus, uncertainty prevailed among the Republican hierarchy over President Ford's selection. Many of the delegates hoped Reagan would change his mind and go on the ticket with the President. With the convention approaching, the *Irish Times* stated that if President Ford was denied the nomination he would be left the lamest duck in Presidential history.

As pressures mounted on the President to name his choice for the Vice-Presidential nomination, he announced that he would not name his running mate until after he was officially nominated by the convention. Nor would he make any confidential statements to anyone on the subject. He kept his opinion secret, despite efforts to force him to name his Vice-Presidential candidate by the Reagan forces on the floor of the convention.

According to the *Daily Telegraph,* Carter told reporters at Plains that Nixon's pardon was like having an illegitimate child in the family. The *Irish Times* was surprised to find how deep and damaging still was the resentment at President Ford's pardoning of his criminal predecessor, particularly in Middle America, where Nixon once had his principal support. Carter also discussed his problem of convincing the people that as President he would be able to lead in the solution of the problems confronting the country. Americans were acquainted with the President's leadership, but Carter's was an unknown factor. Once the Republicans made their nominations, the Democratic nominee predicted that he would be the object of "unprecedented vicious personal attacks" and so would Senator Mondale. Davies, a reporter, wrote in the *Observer* that Carter was a super politician and enormously intelligent. No one had brought religion and politics so close together since Woodrow Wilson. Yet, added Davies, Carter was not at all like Wilson.

Campbell reported in the *Daily Post and Mercury* that Carter and Mondale were a new breed of liberals. These new liberals ardently believed that America was the only country strong enough to have its presence for freedom recognized throughout the world. The liberals were, Campbell thought, too modest to believe that there were no limitations to their accomplishments. Carter's hallmarks of the new liberalism were seen in his strong, firm roots in the rural South. This was the reason for the loyal support of so many blacks.

Indeed, the ardent appeal to the black voters was one of the most interesting and important aspects of his campaign. For more than a century the South was regarded by Northern urban Americans as a "hotbed of primitive racial antagonisms overlaid with Biblical pieties." The *Daily Post and Mercury* contained quotations from several black leaders, including Congressman Andrew Young: "Blacks have always known that their best allies are those whites in the South who dared to live by their religious principles and had to suffer for them."

Campbell echoed Young's statement, arguing that one of Carter's strongest assets was the way he reached out to people who have been excluded from the political process. He was a liberal who, by promising to run a competent government free of extravagances and waste, stole the conservatives' show. Anchored firmly in traditional values, rooted in a part of the country that had escaped the radical gyrations of the 1960s, Carter offered Americans a chance to be reconciled with their past. Although these and other articles about Carter were found in the British press at this time, the Republican leaders and their party received most attention.

The *Observer* lamented President Ford's lack of control of his party, a condition that enabled Senator Jesse Helms to push the Republican Party toward conservatism and, concluded Mark Frankland, to certain defeat. The *Evening Standard* announced that the Ford aides were ready for a bruising fight at the convention. As the Republican delegates arrived at Kansas City, Senator James Buckley of New York said that his name would be presented at the convention to block any nomination on the first ballot, and to free the convention delegates to make their choice. John Sears, Reagan's chief strategist, stated that Buckley's entrance as a candidate "would hurt Ford more than it will us." When Buckley learned that President Ford had enough delegates to win the nomination on the first ballot, he withdrew from consideration before his name was presented.

Shortly before leaving for the convention, the President entertained all Republican state leaders at a banquet in the White House, where, stated the *Times,* he pleaded with each of them to have all of their delegates on the floor during all sessions and to have them vote for him.

As thousands of delegates, friends, candidates, managers, strategists, and others were arriving in Kansas City, Edna Robertson discussed party national conventions in the *Herald.* They were as American as pumpkin pie but differed from British Conservative and Labour Party conferences "both in atmosphere and intention." Traditionally, American party conventions were colorful—rowdy occasions, much oratory, many slogans, campaign songs, parades, and demonstrations—all under television coverage. This coverage, thought Robertson, made conventions less amenable to party bosses; the era of plotting in smoke-filled rooms had passed. The Democrats selected their delegates from more ethnic and minority groups and their committees were less dominated by the white middle-class males; the abolition of the two-thirds rule for majority rule in 1936 prevented minority control.

Winchester wrote, in the *Guardian,* that on arriving at the Kansas City Airport he saw a pandemonium of conventioneering. A pleasant girl, with a large chest encased in bright red velvet and with a badge saying, "Hi, I'm Linda Comfort," came right up and said, "How are you convention people? How can I help you all?" There were maps, pins, buttons, free glasses of colored drinks, and small telephone directories—

all thrust into the hands of the alighting passengers by dozens of pleasant young volunteers. Dressed in the patriotic colors of red, white and blue, most of the volunteers told Winchester, upon learning that he represented the *Guardian,* "We are simply dying to go to little old London." Without request, they gave their telephone numbers to reporters, saying, "Just in case you get tired."

On the sidewalk approaching the Alameda Plaza Hotel, where the Reagans were staying, and in the hotel lobby, country music groups competed with high school jazz bands. Among the crowd of loyal Reagan supporters, women brandished a placard: "Grandmothers for Reagan."

Senator Schweiker, who had recently returned with Reagan from a hurried trip to Mississippi in the hopes of retaining the thirty delegates who had threatened to go to Ford, handed a note to Reagan in the hotel lobby. The note promised Reagan a great surprise among the Pennsylvania delegates. This information, stated the *Evening Standard,* made Reagan enthusiastic. However, when only three of the 103 Pennsylvania delegates switched from Ford to Reagan the information was obviously anticlimactic.

Disappointed and frustrated by failing to receive the Vice-Presidential selection from President Ford, John Connally appeared suddenly with a group of hired aides who visited the numerous meetings of state delegations and reporters to tell delegates and reporters what a fine fellow Connally was and what a magnificent public record he had made. When asked why he had brought a caravan of aides and professionals to Kansas City if his interviews at the convention were, as he stated, purely social, Campbell reported that "Connally's face took on an expression of cherubic sincerity as he told the assembled press—'Frankly, gentlemen, it is to accommodate your own needs.' "

Although President Ford, upon arriving at the Kansas City airport, made no speech, he walked along the ropes shaking hands with the crowd before entering the Presidential car. Along the route to the Crown Center Hotel at the Alameda Plaza, he waved at people standing on either side. A large number of well-wishers were at the hotel to welcome the President, Betty Ford, and his strategists. The *Irish Times* and the *Scotsman* described a rally of Ford's forces on Sunday where enthusiastic speeches by members of the President's caravan fell largely on empty seats, because Kansas City residents stayed at home and the arriving state delegations failed to show up before the convention officially opened. It was a flat social and political event. The reason, Pilger thought in the *Daily Mirror,* was that "good old Jerry" who was not very bright. "Blundering, headbanging Jerry is the Gadfly of American politics." As quoted by Pilger, the President, when asked what he thought about harnessing the energy of the sun, replied, "It can't happen overnight, you know." President Ford was "dumb but lovable," and Reagan was "smart but lethal," concluded the *Daily Mirror.*

Pilger contended that, as a congressman, Ford voted to emasculate every piece of civil rights legislation. As President he had given more military weapons orders to the munitions manufacturers than any President in American history.

Pilger argued that regardless of whether Carter or Ford or Reagan was elected in November nothing would change in American politics. The outlook for the Republicans was exceptionally bleak, said Stephen Barber in the *Daily Telegraph*. The President's efforts to be a dynamic leader were thwarted by his resorting to fifty-five vetoes of bills, with Congress overriding his veto nine times.

President Ford certainly broke all tradition when, as President, he personally went from state delegation to state delegation seeking delegate votes for his nomination. Moreover, he endeavored to chat briefly with the hundred and more delegates who were uncommitted. The *Daily Express* said that Ford, as President, already was humbled and discredited. For the President to come to a national party convention without its results being a conclusion foregone in his favor was a modern scandal. This, the *Daily Express* said, was the measure of the depth and breadth of a silent revolution that was occurring.

The preliminary speeches at the convention were made by Vice-President Nelson Rockefeller and Senator Howard Baker. Rockefeller, like Reagan, refused the Vice-Presidential nomination on any ticket. Rockefeller's speech, wrote Emery with accurate prophecy, sounded like his last farewell to the party. Rockefeller stated candidly, "I never wanted to be a bridesmaid—that's just not me. I always wanted to be the groom. But somehow I could never get to the church on time." Of the President, the *Scotsman* recorded that Rockefeller stated, "Ford, in taking over after Watergate, kept this nation from being torn apart at the seams." Of Carter, Rockefeller said, "Here's a fellow that one time called himself a 'Georgia Redneck' and just last week in Washington, he tried to pass himself off as a 'Nader-day Saint.' "

Senator Baker, ambitious to be named on the ticket with President Ford, had in his original speech a severe condemnation of Watergate. Learning of the severe criticism, the President, after reading the speech, persuaded the Senator to delete most of the references to Watergate. However, as reported in the *Guardian,* Baker stated, "We did not shy from our duty in that difficult time, even though we knew that Watergate would be embarrassing, humiliating, and even potentially devastating."

The *Daily Express* declared the Republicans were going forward to destruction. The victor at the convention this week would be the victim in November. Reagan would be knocked out politically, and President Ford would be bloodied in the face, groggy, and in no condition to meet the Democratic challenger.

The Reagan forces, through John Sears, challenged the President early in the convention by introducing a resolution that would have compelled all candidates for President to name their running mates twelve hours before nomination of the Presidential candidates began. The convention defeated the tactical measure by a vote of 1,180 against and 1,069 for—a majority of only 111. The Florida delegates split on the resolution, voting 38 against and 28 for. The Mississippi delegation cast 30 no votes. The *Evening Standard* described the scene of the vote as a "deafening racket of whistles, cowbells and a roaring blend of ecstasy and black bereavements." The *Times* thought that by delaying the showdown test until the last possible minute the Reagan forces betrayed a weakness they would not admit. Harry Dent, a White House strategist with a grasp of the trends in the Southern states, said the Reagan resolution effort illustrated that "the fire has gone out of the belly." Meanwhile, Campbell saw in the convention a "yearning for those vanished simplicities, for that exact coincidence of the new and the moment, that perfect matching of desire and promise which went to make the fantastic Nixon landslide victory."

The *Daily Telegraph*'s leading editorial, labeled "The Kansas City Dogfight," analyzed the fierce struggle in the Republican Party, outlining the reasons for it: (1) Ford was not elected as Vice-President or President. (2) Ford was linked with Richard Nixon. (3) Though a conservative, Ford was a moderate man.

Within hours of the proposal on the rules amendment, two Illinois delegates for President Ford stated publicly that they had been offered $1,500 or more to change their votes to Reagan. The *Daily Post and Mercury* described the incident as a new dimension of melodrama hitting the convention. Appalled, the Reagan supporters found themselves facing the specter of a criminal investigation as the whole controversy was turned over to the Federal Bureau of Investigation. There was violent frustration on the convention floor. The British press carried stories of the incidents. The FBI found no evidence of bribery, only rumors. Reagan declared the charges fake and added that the "whole thing stinks!"

The *Times* declared that Reagan had no chance of being nominated unless some demagogic miracle occurred like the mass enthusiasm that seized the Republican convention of 1940 to nominate Wendell Willkie. The *Sun* concentrated on party maneuvering more than the personalities involved. The convention was a mournful occasion for the party, the *Sun* said: "Disgraced by Nixon, embarrassed by Ford, outguessed by Carter, torn by internal strife the Grand Old Party isn't good any more although it remains old." The convention delegates, reported Jon Akass in the *Sun,* were not typical Americans in the way that the Democratic delegates in New York were. The Republicans resembled more a secret society, an exclusive club. The belief was popular among those attending the convention that the Republican Party had outlived its time, the *Sun* concluded.

The efforts of the Reagan people to stall and to create confusion in the convention failed as the nominations and voting went off as scheduled—though with some delay. With Buckley withdrawn, Ford was nominated on the first ballot over Reagan by a vote of 1,187 to 1,070—a majority of 117—the narrowest margin of any Republican candidate in twenty-four years. As soon as the result was known, Betty Ford jumped from her seat in the VIP section and did a dance. President Ford left his suite in the Crown Center Hotel and had his chauffeur drive him twenty-five blocks to the Alameda Hotel for a half-hour meeting with Ronald Reagan. Again, the President offered the Vice-Presidential nomination to Reagan and again the Californian refused. They emerged all smiles from the Reagan suite, but, when asked if his earlier rejection of the running-mate position still stood, Reagan stated, "That is absolutely final." President Ford announced that he and Reagan were in philosophical agreement, that the two had agreed at the beginning of their campaigns that they would still be friends afterwards, and that he had accepted Reagan's offer to aid in the campaign.

The *Evening Standard* described wild scenes back in the convention hall. The delegates used horns and noisemakers for more than an hour, reported Campbell; it sounded like a rush-hour traffic jam in Oxford Street, London. Leaders sitting on the stage sought vainly to bring the noise to a conclusion. Many of the Reagan delegates broke down and wept unashamedly in their seats, unreconciled to the bitter end. Before silence enshrouded the strongly pro-Reagan Texas delegates, Ford managers had packed the high galleries in the auditorium with youthful enthusiasts who, upon the announcement of the Ford victory, "flung down hundreds of squeaker red, white and blue balloons and a blizzard of confetti." In a moment of desperation, Senator Helms grabbed a microphone to complain: "My fellow Americans, we are missing prime time on the television." A band officially neutral, stated the *Evening News,* mistakenly played Reagan's campaign song: "California, Here I Come, Right Back Where I Started From."

Meanwhile, President Ford selected Senator Robert Dole for his running mate. In presenting him, the President stated, "It's a very great occasion for me. I'm really thrilled with the opportunity of having Bob Dole as my running mate." Dole spoke briefly: "I'm realistic. I know there's a lot of work to be done between now and November. I'm not sure what I can add to the ticket but I'll work hard. I did not expect to receive a phone call this morning but I'm very glad we were in. I've known President Ford from the time I could call him Jerry." The *Yorkshire Post* declared that Dole, a tough political gut fighter and a tough campaigner, was just what the President needed in his uphill fight against Democrat Carter.

Reagan immediately endorsed Dole: "I couldn't be more delighted," he stated. Both President Ford and Dole were Midwestern right-wing conservatives. The Republican moderates, especially in the Northeast, were left out in the cold. Their reactions, as reported in the *Times,* were glum, their feelings crushed. Dole, a native of Russell, Kansas, educated at the University of Arizona and Washburn University, spent more than five years in the Army, was wounded twice, decorated twice, left with a shattered right arm, entered politics and rose rapidly to the top. Dole was best known nationally as the Republican National Chairman in 1972 whom Nixon unceremoniously fired immediately after the election was over.

In the *Times,* Barry Goldwater praised Dole: "Thank God, we finally have someone who will grab the other side [the Democrats] by the hair and drag them down the hill." Dole's ex-wife, Phyllis, declared that her former husband was a "workaholic. He was off, day and night, seven days a week." In the last year of their marriage, she added, "she, Dole and their daughter ate supper together only four times." Patrick Brogan declared, in the *Scotsman,* that Dole did not balance the ticket in any way. He came from the Middle West, like President Ford. He was an archconservative, like the President; although he undoubtedly was a better orator than President Ford and also a far more vicious political campaigner than the President, he was not likely to make any particularly memorable contribution to the 1976 Presidential campaign. In discussing the Republican ticket the *Daily Express* stated, "The only thing that Carter has to fear is Carter himself."

The next morning Reagan, said the *Times,* with Nancy standing beside him, crying softly, bade his workers farewell in a voice choking with emotion. "Sure there's disappointment but the cause, the cause goes on. It's just one battle in a long war that is going on as long as we all live," Reagan said. With that statement, the *Yorkshire Post* reported, Reagan vowed that he would be heard from in the future. The *Times* stated, "It was a bitter morning after for him."

As the curtain lowered on the convention, the *Guardian* concluded that both President Ford and Reagan had lost their dignity and their public respect in the struggle for nomination. Jonathan Steele wrote that the Republican platform of 1976 was practically the same as 1948. The Republican Party had not changed with the times. It had missed the chance to go after votes of blacks and other minorities. As other reporters were editorializing, Steele, in the *Guardian,* declared that the convention had been a struggle between the Right and the Far Right or between the conservative and the ultraconservative. Patrick Brogan wrote with disgust that nothing was what it seemed to be at the convention; "there were only deceits practiced by politicians so transparent that they could not be taken seriously."

The *Herald* noted that the convention was one of mutual incomprehension and hatred. There was little to suggest that the Republicans had anything new to offer that was likely to prevent Jimmy Carter from entering the White House in January. The *Observer* declared that the Republican delegates were actually "middle-class anarchists who hoped to abolish all income taxes and who stated that all social welfare programs merely transferred money from those who earned to those who yearned." What distinguished Republican conservatives in attendance at the convention, reported Mark Frankland, was their reluctance to accept the forces of change in modern society and the need for government to regulate them.

The *Guardian* reported a British Foreign Office high official saying this was positively the very last convention he was ever going to attend: "It was such a waste of time and money for everyone." For years, the provincial newspaper continued, "many foreigners have been curious about who gathers around the bright lights of these political gatherings. They have come away bemused and mystified." Why was it necessary for thousands of men and women to travel an aggregate of millions of miles to cast votes for candidates for whom they were already committed both by obligation and by law? The television audiences, stated this source, "have declined seriously, prompting one network to cover events only on the merits of each segment." The day of constant live coverage, concluded the *Guardian,* was doomed. ABC had 500 persons working in the convention, NBC had 600, according to this popular paper, and CBS had approximately the same number.

In his widely applauded acceptance speech of thirty-six minutes, President Ford broke with all tradition and challenged Carter to debate with him face to face. The President said, "This year the issues are on our side. I am ready too; I am eager to have the right to know firsthand exactly where both of us stand." In Georgia, Carter accepted the unprecedented challenge quickly and with alacrity. One of the President's aides stated, "The President is challenging the wrong man at the wrong time." The *Daily Mirror* declared that President Ford had challenged the quick-witted Carter to a series of television confrontations. "It was a bold move for the President, and it could also prove a fatal one." The *Herald* stated that political experts agreed that the debates could be one of the most decisive factors in the election of 1976.

The *Times* contended that American political conventions were among the last and healthiest survivors of social customs of the nineteenth century, improved only by the introduction of microphones, amplifiers, and television lights. Conventions were therapeutic in that they enabled the delegates to remove extreme fatigue and tenseness from their systems. "The nonparticipating spectator was amused to see so many hundreds of respectable people—the great majority were well-dressed middle-aged men, standing on chairs, waving absurd banners, making as horrible a noise as they could manage. Conventions," concluded Brogan in the *Times,* "are marvelous fun and America would not be the same without them."

Emery saw the Republicans as bruised and bewildered, not at all exhilarated by the slugging match that finally knocked out Reagan. This energetic reporter found only seven delegates that President Ford won over from his arrival on Saturday at Kansas City to the voting for his nomination on Wednesday night. To Emery, it was quite clear that Reagan's naming of Schweiker as his running mate was the breakdown of his pursuit of President Ford. Had this decision not been made, Emery was convinced, Reagan might well have won.

Anthony Delano reported in the *Daily Mirror* that Reagan's hopes were shot to pieces when the Mississippi delegation broke its self-imposed unit rule and voted as individuals—all going for the President. Terence Lancaster, political editor of the London daily, wrote that Ford stumbled into the United States Presidency as a result of Nixon's criminality and had been falling over ever since—"notably on aircraft steps, ski-slopes and other places where photographers were stationed in force." Lancaster added that the nomination of Dole was Ford's biggest slipup. When only about one in five Americans was a hard-core Republican, a winning Republican ticket must appeal to the masses of independent voters, and Lancaster predicted the Ford-Dole ticket would fail to manage the necessary appeal. "If I were an American citizen," concluded Lancaster, "the Dole-Ford ticket would be the clinching argument for backing the Democrat Jimmy Carter."

Jon Akass reported in the *Sun* that the Ford campaigners were "running scared of peanuts." More than five hours of pandemonium were required to cast the evil spirits out of the Republican convention, Akass wrote, but the Ford forces solved the problem. The President, as a result, was a happy soul who radiated amiability. The message meandered about, wrote Akass, that President Ford was as nice a fellow as one would like to meet but that he was not a very bright person. A horde of people gave themselves to promoting the President's campaign. Akass felt assured that these people were nice folks with nice habits, but he thought that their efforts were of little appreciable value. The reporter saw them as cheated by agitators, by big government, by youth, and now, said the *Sun,* they were "threatened by an evangelical peanut farmer from Georgia." They were obviously jittery. "They frighten me!" concluded Akass.

Several British newspapers devoted editorials to the results of the Republican convention. The *Guardian* editorial, "Reliable Old Ford, Still a Good Guy," said the fact that the leader of the Western world was "driven to spend his working hours telephoning bakers, butchers, and hamburger broilers, begging for their votes, certainly reflected directly on the nature of the current Republican struggle." The editorial also redefined the nature of the Presidency at the end of that struggle: "The imperial American President was dead." Ford, who at first declared he did not want the Presidency, later decided that he liked being in the White House and in 1976 found himself seeking succor among the hairpins and powder puffs of his rebellious party. "Poor old Gerry," continued the *Guardian,* "who as a stumbling orator, also stumbled down stairs, exudes no confidence. He came to Kansas City, as the weakest President seeking reelection in modern times. If he is to be defeated in November, he, however, does not deserve to be humiliated."

The *Times* correctly editorialized that had the Republican Party nominated Reagan it would have placed itself in the hands of a group of extreme conservatives who would have dragged it to certain defeat in November. National elections in the United States were won by "flexible coalitions, not by ideologies or minority interest groups." President Ford had an uphill battle, said the London independent daily, "as he was seen as Nixon's legatee, as he was badly damaged by Nixon's pardon, as he showed bad judgment in naming Dole as his Vice-President candidate." Carter studied America carefully and was wooing the voters with systematic intensity and skill. The current candidates, concluded the *Times,* indicated that Carter must make some very bad mistakes to lose in November and that the President could not afford any mistakes.

The *Daily Telegraph* announced that the two contenders for the Presidency represented two different standpoints. Carter's preeminence resulted from the American desire for something completely different. "America will have to choose between Carter, an unknown quality, and Ford's two years in the White House which have not been brilliant by any means, but likable, solid, reassuring." The *South Wales Evening Post* discussed the BBC's broadcasting in Britain, and concluded that President Ford was just the President for a "yawning nation." The *Daily Post and Mercury* declared that the enigmatic Carter, "with his folksy style and brand of liberalism," held out to Americans the hope of a re-establishment of a link with her past in building a new future. Virtually unknown until this year (1976), Carter, "as the smiling, confidant newcomer offering a new deal," clearly came in with a strong appeal. But he had yet to be "tested in the hurly burly of political battle. His weaknesses were yet to be exposed." No one knew what the American mood would be when it finally came time to vote.

In the *Herald,* Richard Rose discussed a 93-page document issued by the White House in defense of Ford's administration. It emphasized peace abroad and declared that Ford "supports the diplomatic initiative started under the Kissinger regime." In two years he had held 121 meetings with foreign leaders and traveled 215,316 miles in pursuit of peace. The nation was at peace with itself. In the handling of the economy, the record was controversial. Ford claimed, however, that inflation and unemployment rates were falling and the economic productivity with real income was rising. President Ford's fact book claimed that the American economy was outstandingly healthy.

The *Scotsman* stated that the President survived at the convention by the "skin of his teeth in a skillful, professional and bitter assault from the right wing of his own party." Liberal Republicans attended conventions in 1964, 1968, and 1972, but none attended the 1976 convention. Wilmot Davies, in the Scottish paper, summarized the Republican strategy for the campaign: (1) Attack Carter's inexperience. (2) Attack the spending, wasteful Democratic Congress. (3) Attack the Democratic Party for the profligacy of its party program. Would the strategy work? Davies asked, "Was this the right road to the White House?"

In the meantime, in Chicago, the American Independent Party held its convention. Scarcely no mention of it was made in the British media. The party, founded by George Wallace in 1968, nominated Lester Maddox as its first Presidential candidate. The platform and the Chicago convention showed the American Independent Party to be anti-Semitic segregationists—claiming that all who disagreed with the party were either Communists or a tool of the Communists. Independent Party members discussed taking over the Republican Party for 1980. With Maddox's nomination, there were two recent Governors of Georgia now candidates for President—an unusual phenomenon—even in American politics.

Both of the Scottish newspapers, the *Herald* and the *Scotsman,* predicted that the Republicans would lose the election. President Ford, they stated, was hindered by the condition of his party, whose steady decline was only artificially halted four years ago by the folly of the Democrats in choosing George McGovern, a hopeless candidate, for President. The Republican Party, said the *Scotsman,* was too old-fashioned, not nearly black enough. To get itself growing again it needed someone much more enterprising than President Ford.

The *Herald* declared that the Democratic Party was united behind Carter, while the Republican Party was in complete disarray, with the President going limping home from the convention after scraping and fighting desperately for delegates sufficient to win the nomination. This condition did not hearten President Ford's supporters. His choice of Dole healed no schism among the Republicans, but Carter's choosing Mondale was excellent for unity. Carter must be well pleased with the outcome at Kansas City and "unless he was found to have been supplying peanuts to the Soviet Union it is difficult to see him stopped in his messianic progress to the Presidency." Brian Wilson predicted that there would be many bitter attacks on Carter because of his "born-again" religion and because Republicans claimed political fundamentalism for themselves.

The *Yorkshire Post,* in discussing the Republican convention, emphasized Ford's narrow margin of victory, continuing that the President had a reputation for humbling doggedness and ineffectiveness on a public platform. "The election of a President of the United States is a lengthy business and it appears tedious to many foreigners. But the United States is the leader of the free world." The identity of the next occupant of the White House was almost as important to the British, stated the eastern provincial paper, as it was to the Americans.

The *East Anglia Daily Times,* finding difficulty in accepting the carnival atmosphere that permeates American national party conventions, remembered that they were the preliminary round in electing one of the world's most powerful leaders. To the people east of the Atlantic Ocean, the American method of choosing a Presidential candidate was more of a game than a serious attempt to find the best man to compete in a Presidential contest. The pollsters were predicting that the Democratic nominee would win by a landslide. This would occur, not so much because President Ford had no record in the White House, but because he did not have the perceptivity to make the best of that record. Furthermore, Carter was clearly aware of criticism leveled against him by the President's supporters that Carter knew little about the workings of the national government, for he had gathered around him experts to brief him on domestic issues and on foreign affairs.

4

The
Campaign Begins

With the party platform adopted, the party nominations accepted, and the party conventions finished, the Presidential election campaign began. The *Irish Times* noted that a definite degree of paralysis had affected American decision making in the 1976 Presidential election year. In foreign relations, continued the Dublin daily, some governments already had made it clear that they were marking time until they knew who would win the election in November. Nevertheless, the *Irish Times* noted that international affairs have a built-in momentum, a knack for producing crises that do not permit delayed solutions. The condition of foreign affairs until after the election was most likely to be President Ford's trickiest problem, the *Irish Times* emphasized.

Domestically, the newspaper said, the President hoped economic conditions would improve, but unemployment was increasing and the conquest of the recession was further away than had been anticipated. On the other hand, the Irish newspaper wrote that Carter's relative youth was an attraction. The Dublin daily said rumors were heard that behind Carter's public charisma there was a ruthless and ambitious man but the rumors were harmless among a large sector of voters because the smiling charmer embodied the American dream in so many ways. The *Irish Times* said Carter would be difficult to defeat.

When Carter unveiled his proposed foreign policy, Sean Cronin was present to report it to the *Irish Times*. In summation, Carter stated the United States should withhold involvement in another country's affairs unless the United States was directly threatened; negotiate with the Soviet Union more stringently than Nixon and Ford had; refrain from influencing Europe in Communistic relationships; establish closer economic and political ties with European countries, because Europe could never become totally independent of the United States; assure continued

48

development of NATO through modernization and standardization of armaments, accompanied by a redeployment of American defense forces; subscribe irrevocably to the principle of majority rule regardless of race in relationship with African nations; accept completely the American principle of ensuring progress by peaceful means in foreign relations.

Jonathan Steele wrote, in the *Guardian,* that President Ford, a notoriously cautious man, suddenly turned gambler in that he made three uncharacteristically daring decisions: he named a relatively unknown Midwesterner as his running mate; he challenged Carter to television debates; he declared that Watergate would not be an issue in the national election. In admitting that he was an appointed President, Ford said, "To me the Presidency and the Vice-Presidency were not prizes to be won but a duty to be done."

The Republican Party, declared the *Daily Mail,* was in deep trouble. The party's passion had been dissipated on histrionic internal feuding, and postures of reconciliation were not convincing. The *Daily Mail* stated that American political conventions were totally media events. They were staged entirely at the convenience of the television networks and were programmed to hit prime time just after the cocktail hour. The President, confirmed the London newspaper, was a "pedantic, bumbling style speaker with a monotonous delivery that turns into a drone." Indeed, Ford's speaking style was his weakest spot, the newspaper declared, while Carter's charm and charisma were among his strongest assets.

The *Western Mail* chose the anniversary of President Nixon's resignation to editorialize on the nagging doubts about President Ford. Just two years earlier Nixon had resigned in disgrace after the greatest scandal in American political history. Since then, Nixon's nonelected and lackluster successor had led the country by keeping a low profile, the *Western Mail* explained. "Falling down aeroplane steps and slurring speech did little to inspire confidence in his leadership capability," the *Western Mail* wrote, adding that it was "churlish to deny that Ford had proved himself affable and decent and for these qualities America should be truly grateful." After the trauma of Watergate, the *Times* said, President Ford's dignity and sincerity, his honesty and lack of showmanship were important factors in helping America to come to terms with itself. Conditions, however, change; now other qualities were needed in the White House, the *Times* added.

In the closing days of August, President Ford returned to the White House after spending two days in Russell, Kansas, with Dole at homecoming festivities, which were followed by a week of skiing at Vail, Colorado. One of the President's first acts upon his return from the ski resort was to fire Rogers Morton as his campaign manager and to replace him with James Baker, a Texas lawyer. Earlier, the President had named Morton to replace Howard Callaway after Callaway was implicated in a Colorado property scandal.

Meanwhile, negotiators from President Ford's camp met with Carter's aides to arrange the details for the television debates between the two candidates. They assembled in the Mayflower Hotel in Washington. The workers uncovered several complex problems but they ultimately arranged for three debates between President Ford and Carter and one debate between the two Vice-Presidential candidates. While the debates were planned Carter told a large audience in Seattle that if he were elected he would issue a blanket pardon for all those who had evaded conscription during the Vietnam War. "I think it is time for the damage, hatred and divisions of the Vietnam War to be over."

To a group of American Legionnaires who were hostile to the "draft dodgers," Carter explained the difference between pardon and amnesty: "Amnesty means that what you did was right. Pardon means what you did, right or wrong, is forgiven. This is the single hardest decision I have had to make in this campaign." Amid shouts of "No," Carter stated that he was a Legionnaire and knew how they thought, explaining that his son Jack was one of hundreds of thousands who fought in Vietnam only to return to a bitter reception awaiting them when they got home.

At the Iowa Annual State Fair, the Democratic nominee stated that President Ford's farm policy did no more than "keep farm families from going bankrupt to produce the food which the consumers were trying to buy." He criticized the President's farm export embargo of trade with Russia.

Jane Rosen warned Washington, in the *Guardian,* that it faced a new "Georgia Invasion." She discussed at length the "little group of Southern country boys" who were not intimidated in the least by the prospect of governing the United States. Carter's chief advisers were, Rosen wrote, "soft-talking, easy-going Georgians, who also were tough, cool, smart, non-ideological strategists who have performed what most professional politicians regard as a miracle."

Hamilton Jordan headed Carter's headquarters staff of more than seven hundred men and women in Atlanta—the first time a Presidential candidate's national headquarters was ever placed in a former Confederate state. As manager, Jordan operated a decentralized, loose and open office, inviting both ideas and criticism. Jody Powell, Carter's press secretary, spent more time with the candidate than any one else. Powell, normally a quiet, lowly person, became shrewd and sophisticated in political life, and was dedicated to Carter, although, on occasion, Powell criticized the nominee. Charles Kirbo, the oldest of the Atlanta staff and a wealthy lawyer, reflected a moderate political conservatism. He, like Carter, was deeply religious.

As August ended, new polls were released, all of which showed President Ford closing the gap between him and Carter. Indeed, within the month the Gallup Poll found that the President's popularity ran from 33 percent to 39 percent, while Carter's strength declined from 56 percent to 49 percent; the gap between the two candidates had lessened from 23 percent to 10 percent. President Ford's new manager, Baker, was credited with creating the drastic reduction, and the President radiated confidence.

The *Daily Telegraph* declared that President Ford's greatest strength was in "being a nice guy with integrity but faulted in being too close to American big business." The *Daily Telegraph* reported the President describing his opponent as a person who, if elected, would be dominated by Congress in a wild, free-spending, liberal majority. Carter and Congress would unleash a new wave of inflation while, at the same time, slashing America's defense budget.

Cronin reported, in the *Irish Times,* surprise at the Republican Party—the party of privilege and wealth—being so afraid of Rockefeller. Cronin wrote that President Ford wanted to have John Connally as his running mate but the bosses refused because of Connally's alleged link with Watergate.

The *Guardian,* with complete confidence, predicted the type of campaign the two candidates would wage. President Ford would run a scare campaign by frightening voters with Carter's inexperience and fuzziness, emphasizing that Carter had been totally unknown two years earlier. In contrast, the Democrats would talk about the Nixon-Ford Administration and charge the President with the sins of eight years of Republican misrule, recession, unemployment, and scandal.

The *Daily Mirror,* after discussing the national conventions, concluded that no candidate would dare say that he would tamper with an economy controlled by just two thousand giant corporations or with a national budget in which approximately half of every dollar went to building more and more weapons to sell to military regimes in poor countries in return for favors for American corporations and for obedience to Dr. Kissinger's world order. The *Daily Mirror* observed that, after thirty primary elections, two party conventions, millions of dollars spent, thousands of hands shaken, countless babies kissed, delegates courted and deals made, there was but one issue—winning.

To win the election both parties would, as Cronin pointed out in the *Irish Times,* resort to the use of television, which had turned the United States into a village. Claude Cockburn contended that a great majority of Americans between the very rich and the destitutely poor believed that the Carter phenomenon was more than the rise of an immensely efficient, hard-working, hardheaded Democrat. Many saw Carter as assuring that the American capitalistic system guided by him—a man with a Bible in one hand and a computer in the other—could by a mixture of moral goodness and driving efficiency nearly abolish unemployment without increasing either inflation or government control. The *Irish Times* reemphasized that Carter was the first prominent white Southern politician who talked to the black masses in their own language, offering hopes that were literally immense to blacks of the South and throughout the United States.

On the other hand, an incident that occurred in North Korea in late August illustrated how President Ford would use America's military might. Several American soldiers with two officers advanced into Korea's demilitarized zone to cut down a tree that prevented the American command with its farseeing instruments from watching North Korea's military movements. The American officers were captured and killed by North Korean soldiers. Upon learning of the double murder, President Ford, the *Daily Mirror* reported, sent American troops, accompanied by heavy ground and air support, to chop down the tree. He also dispatched a 41,000-ton aircraft carrier with its 75 warplanes, 4 frigates, and a guided missile carrier to support the cutting down of the tree. North Korea sent a note expressing regret for the killings, which President Ford rejected. Why, asked the London paper, was the President playing the war lord role?—and proceeded to answer the question: "Because in a little more than two months, Americans are going to the polls to elect their next President." Opinion polls showed that massive demonstration of strength in national crises was a sure way to increase a President's popularity. The *Daily Mirror,* however, advised the President to confine his strength to America's many pressing domestic issues.

When Carter was asked to comment on the President's actions, he, according to the *Daily Telegraph,* replied promptly: "He's done a good job so far as I know. I think it would be a serious mistake for me to take an opposite position at a time of crisis when our national security might be involved."

Meanwhile, British journalists stationed in America pondered the results of the two national conventions in terms of British interests. The reporters were primarily interested in America's foreign policy. President Ford and Carter's differences over foreign policy were insignificant, the Britishers reported, although Carter's policy would have a more moralistic style than the President's. Nothing either candidate had said suggested in the least that American allies need fear if Carter won the election, the journalists concluded.

Anthony Delano, following an interview with Carter, wrote for the *Daily Mirror* that "Jimmy's the best for the British." According to Delano, Carter admired the British Parliament and had the greatest respect for the British health and welfare services. While Governor of Georgia, Carter and his wife had visited England in 1974; Carter described their brief stay in London. "We went to the House of Commons at question time. I found it intriguing. It inspired me and I learned from it. I was deeply impressed by the probing questions that were asked and the need for party leaders to be conversant with the details of legislation. I have pledged that members of my cabinet shall appear before joint sessions of Congress to answer questions about the workings of their departments. One of the things I am considering is that I should—like the British Prime Minister—appear there myself. I can't understand why your Parliament won't have itself televised. In the interest of open government I am in favour of televising Congress."

In Plains, where most of this interview occurred, Rosalynn Carter visited the old railway station where Delano and other reporters were talking to candidate Carter. As noonday approached, Rosalynn told several reporters, "I'd better go home and fix Jimmy a sandwich. No, not a sandwich of mountain oysters"—the local name for fried bull testicles—"to which Jimmy is very partial, but an eggplant sandwich. Jimmy likes eggplant sandwiches."

Meanwhile, in the British Isles reorganizational work among expatriate Americans increased as the Republican delegates at the Kansas City convention returned to their American homes. According to the *Guardian,* there were about 750,000 American voters living in Europe, including those 75,000 in the British Isles. The Republicans, unlike the Democrats, permitted no expatriate Americans to attend their national convention.

Furthermore, the Democrats dispatched Steven Cohen, a Boston lawyer and active Democrat from the Carter headquarters, to London, where Cohen began, with Robert Worcester, to raise $125,000 for the promotion of the Democratic ticket. As the first full-time party employee abroad for an American Presidential election, Cohen kept busy in his efforts to convince the majority of the 75,000 Americans in Britain to register as Democrats and later to vote. He found the golden peanuts that he distributed to the Carter supporters to wear in their buttonholes very popular.

In the meantime as the campaign in America officially opened early in September, the *Irish Times* editorialized favorably about the President's rapidly narrowing the margin that separated him from his Democratic opponent. In the White House, President Ford was aided by three veteran campaigners. Outside the Oval Office the President placed heavy vote-getting responsibilities upon Rockefeller in the East, Connally in the South, and Reagan in the West. Dole was scoring some excellent points, said the Dublin paper, in the Plains states. He was receiving front-page coverage, while any mention of Mondale's activities was found only in the middle pages. President Ford was performing his Presidential duties, staying in the White House, at the dictate of his campaign managers, the *Irish Times* wrote, to prevent him from making blunders like those that had marked the primaries. The Irish newspaper believed the outcome of the campaign would hinge on the televised debates. Betty Ford exclaimed to the *Irish Times* reporters that Ford would win because he is the "best equipped for the job," but a defeat would not leave her brokenhearted. "If he loses he'll go back to law practice and I'll win either way," she concluded.

Both contenders ignored the Labor Day tradition of opening the campaign on the holiday by starting their respective campaigns a few days later. Carter traveled south to begin his postnomination campaigning officially, selecting Warm Springs, Georgia, where President Franklin Roosevelt had died beside the restorative waters of the mountain springs. The *Scotsman* reported that Carter, standing on the front porch of the "Little White House" at Warm Springs, fired the first official shot of the campaign. "This year, as in 1932," Carter said, "our country is divided, our people out of work, and our national leaders do not lead." The 1976 choice was clear, Carter emphasized: "Are we Americans satisfied with a divided nation, one of timidity, confusion and mediocrity? Most of us believe we can do better." Carter added that President Ford, like Hoover in 1932, was "a decent and well-intentioned man who sincerely believed that there was nothing our government could or should do to attack the terrible economic and social ills of our nation."

The President journeyed to his alma mater, the University of Michigan, to initiate his postconvention race. On the campus where President Ford had played varsity football he was met with booing and jeering of student hecklers. Near the end of his "boring" speech, a firecracker exploded in the upper balcony of the sports arena.

Shortly before embarking for Warm Springs, Carter conferred with national Catholic leaders on the emotionally debated abortion issue. He admitted that he personally opposed abortion but would not support a Constitutional amendment prohibiting it. Upon emerging from the long conference, Archbishop Joseph Bernadine, head of the National Conference of Catholic Bishops, told the assembled press, "We continue to be disappointed with Governor Carter." But, added the ranking Catholic, "Personal opposition is not enough." In addition Senator Edward Kennedy, a staunch Catholic, had an hour conference with the Democratic nominee and emerged to announce his complete support of Carter.

Carter explained his Baptist views to the American Catholic leadership, as John F. Kennedy had explained his Catholic beliefs to many Protestant leaders in the campaign of 1960, but Carter's efforts were without dramatic results. In rejecting Carter's views on abortion, the Catholics promised Carter they would confer with President Ford in the hopes of securing a more acceptable opinion. The President told the Catholic leaders that he favored a Constitutional amendment leaving the abortion issue to each state, but his stand failed to satisfy the Catholic hierarchy. Eventually the U.S. Supreme Court left the decision of abortion largely to the women.

The President's advisers believed that Carter's disagreement with the Catholic leaders would influence millions of Catholics in industrial states to vote the Republican ticket. The industrial workers from New York to Wisconsin were largely blue-collar Catholic laborers. The *Daily Mirror* thought that these conferences were arranged by the Catholic leaders because of the decline in attendance at Mass, of a shortage of recruits for religious orders, and of a decisive decrease in Catholic Church contributions. The *Evening Standard* carried the Catholic reports to the press, as did the *Times* and the *Irish Times*.

Both candidates had expressed strong opinions on abortion. They agreed that regulating sexual conduct was no business of the President of the United States. Abortion was a matter about as irrelevant to a Presidential election as a subject could be. Failing to win the Catholics to his conclusion on abortion, Carter began successfully wooing influential Jews. He promised undeviating support of the Jews in Israel and insisted that support of Israel was derived from the Bible. Meanwhile, the *Evening Standard* announced that the Labor Federal Executive Board would give Carter its complete support. The AFL-CIO had a membership of approximately 13,500,000. However, Dole stated that the head of the AFL-CIO, George Meany, did not speak for the rank and file of the labor unions.

The *Times*, through its reporter Patrick Brogan, outlined Carter's campaign plan. He would campaign fifteen hours for five days weekly until November 2. His campaign managers, Brogan wrote, worked out the states in relative importance, listing the fifty states in the order of difficulty of winning them. The nominee would concentrate action in the states with the largest number of votes, especially where the battle was the closest. President Ford's White House aides publicized his campaign plan. The President would not go on the political stump as Carter planned to do, but when President Ford did leave the Oval Office he would speak in the most heavily industrial states—New York, Pennsylvania, California, and the populous states around the Great Lakes.

Political flaps marked the early campaign. The *Daily Telegraph* noted that Clarence Kelley, the recently appointed chief of the FBI, had used public funds to decorate his home, permitting some agency employees to fit and hang curtains there. Only when this incident became known did Kelley refund to the FBI the cost of the services and materials used in his home. Carter denounced President Ford for not firing Kelley. On another issue, the *Daily Telegraph* reported that, in Brooklyn, New York, Carter denounced President Ford's refusal to come to the aid of New York City when it was on the verge of bankruptcy.

The *Time*s reported the President's promising a noble effort to bring peace to Africa. He explained that America's policy would prevent any escalation of violence; realize popular aspirations; guarantee minority rights; ensure economic progress; resist intervention in Africa of outside forces. Domestically, the *Times* said, the President sought to capture the spotlight and the initiative from his opponent by emphasizing the improving economic conditions and the increasing number of jobs Americans had. Carter countered that inflation was the highest priority and that he, if elected, was determined to decrease the rate of inflation.

While the candidates argued, Mark Frankland discussed, in the *Observer,* why so many Americans did not vote. They didn't vote because they didn't care, Frankland said. The American voter realized that he was not voting for issues anymore but only for politicians who would decide the issues. Thus, Frankland concluded, there was spreading apathy and a real cynicism growing in America. Indeed, neither Carter nor President Ford really stirred the people's interest.

After watching the campaign develop for a short period, President Ford left the Oval Office and began speaking in the Midwest, stating that "Americans want specifics, not smiles. It is not enough for anyone to say, 'trust me,' trust must be earned. The question for the 1976 campaign is not who has the better vision of America but who will act to make that vision a reality. The American people will demand specifics not smiles, performance not promises." The American people, the President continued, "are ready for simple truth, simply spoken about what government can do for them and what it cannot and should not do for them." He emphasized massive education when he shouted, "In my Administration the education of America's middle-income families will neither be forgotten nor forsaken."

Carter, said the *Times,* promised universal literacy in America. Following endorsement by the American Federation of Teachers and the National Education Association, both of whom were endorsing a Presidential candidate for the first time, Carter announced that he would send his eight-year-old daughter, Amy, to a public school.

In an attempt to win favor with expatriate Americans in the British Isles, Carter gave an extended interview to William Lowther of the *Daily Mail.* An article, "Why I Want Closer Ties with Great Britain," reported the first interview with Carter in the executive cabin of his 727 campaign jet, "Peanut One," while flying at thirty thousand feet from one speaking engagement to another. It was a rare first and wide-ranging interview. The *Daily Mail* quoted Carter as saying, "I want closer consultation with the leaders in London and I anticipate frequent meetings with them." During the interview, the Democratic nominee sat hunched in a wide armchair, with his shirt sleeves rolled up to his elbows. "There is a definite need for us to share a closer consultation before our nations make major decisions," Carter continued, explaining: "I will make sure that in all instances members of Congress in both parties and also the people of our country are involved much more deeply than under this [Ford's] Administration in the evolution and consummation of our foreign policy."

Lowther explained that Carter's statement reflected his Southern background, for most Southerners are of British descent and have a strong emotional link with the old country. Lowther, noting Carter's fierce independence, wrote that the Democratic nominee insisted on taking care of his personal details and wanted to be seen carrying his own compact leather grip in his left hand and the two extra suits in a garment bag over his right shoulder when leaving or boarding his chartered campaign jet. Above mountains on a flight from Oklahoma City to Phoenix, Arizona, Lowther discussed with Carter how disarming it was to see a politician of such status carrying his own luggage.

Naturally, Lowther questioned Carter about his ideas on foreign policy. With Russia he would encourage peaceful competition, Lowther wrote, and with America's natural allies Carter would build a stronger basis of cooperation, consultation, and commitment than presently existed. In all deliberations, Lowther said, Carter would keep in the forefront the assurance of human rights. "We must be careful not to interfere in the internal affairs of countries and respect the results of democratic elections with the right of countries to make whatever free choices they like," Carter told the *Daily Mail* reporter.

Lowther marveled at Carter's ability to drop one subject completely and give his total attention to another in less than a moment's notice. The candidate showed no signs of the grueling campaign pace, Lowther said, except late at night, when his eyes became puffy and his temper short. The reporter noted that Carter had no great interest in food when on the campaign trail and "during the long day eats almost every meal aboard the aircraft. His lunch is usually composed of a small green salad, a corned beef sandwich and a bowl of chili. He seldom ever drinks, except for a single jigger of Regal Scotch, served straight before dinner on Saturday nights. He may on occasion allow himself a single Bloody Mary with a twist of lime. However tired, Carter, at the end of a long enduring seventeen-hour day, never forgot to go to the flight deck and thank the crew for a safe journey. Nor did he ever omit to shake hands with the Secret Service agents who were his constant guards."

Lowther was convinced that Carter was dedicated to his church and a firm believer in prayer, for Carter concluded the interview, lasting nearly two hours with "I don't favor government trying to impose any sort of religion or spiritual standards on their citizens. As a Baptist, I believe very deeply in the complete separation of church and state. I do think though that there is a search among our people for a recommitment to basic moral principles of honesty, integrity, truth, brotherhood, compassion, and love."

As the only foreign reporter to accompany Carter in the first ten days of his campaign, Lowther described walking through volatile ghettos, a ride in a torchlight parade, singing hymns in a revival in the little white wooden Baptist church in Plains. For Lowther it was a memorable assignment in reporting historic travels.

From a speaking tour in the Midwest the President, the *Daily Telegraph* announced, once more abandoned his stay-in-the-White-House strategy by launching an aggressive and colorful campaign tour through the South and a trip down the Mississippi River.

While President Ford was touring the mid-South from a ship drifting down the mighty Mississippi River, stopping at cities along the river, making well-received speeches to hastily assembled crowds, Carter and Mondale were making a one-day whistle-stop tour in a train in the Northeast. Carter enjoyed his brief appearances from the rear of an open platform on a glittering aluminum train, dubbed "A Train for a Change." Unlike the Harry S. Truman "Give 'em Hell, Harry!" train in 1948, which ran for a week, the "Train for a Change" left Newark at 6:30 A.M. and ended its journey at Pittsburgh that night. According to the *Times,* Carter, closely protected by tight security, appeared fit and relaxed. Never a stirring speaker, he was excellent at simple, important sermonettes and sent the people away glad they had come.

The London *Illustrated Daily News* wrote that in a year when millions of Americans apparently sought divine intervention in the affairs of their nation, the Democratic challenger for the Presidency seemed to be the best available substitute for the Messiah. The *Daily News* said that thus far Carter had made no errors in his campaign, worked out four years earlier and documented in a lengthy memo for Carter to follow to win the Presidency. "He has followed it to the dotting of the *i* and the crossing of the *t,*" stated this paper. "The David from Georgia who would challenge the corrupted and incompetent Goliath in Washington, was the man whom Americans could trust, and who would bring love and compassion to the White House."

The *Daily News,* noting that in the last year Carter had made more speeches and shaken more hands than any other politician in the world, quoted the Democratic nominee as saying, "When I shake hands with them, for that instant, I really care about them individually in a genuine way and I believe they know it a lot of times. Quite frequently, they put their arms around my neck and say 'God bless you.' " The *Daily News* said that Carter was helped by change: the decline of George Wallace; the disarray of his rivals; the misjudgment and vanity of Hubert Humphrey. Carter perceived that the political rule of the establishment could be broken, and the *Daily News* declared that a man from the South could challenge the system and break it.

In Washington, Jonathan Dimbley wrote in the *Illustrated Daily News,* "The establishment shakes with apprehension at the prospect of Carter in the White House." The old party bosses in Washington, Dimbley said, would find out that he was tougher than his soft voice and less amiable than his gentle smile. "Certainly, he must know that to get to the White House his rhetoric won't be enough. Does he realize that the race to the White House is a race from the starting gate, not merely the finishing post? For the sake of America," Dimbley concluded, "we must hope that he can and that he does." The *Economist* saw lifted spirits in President Ford's campaign, while in the Carter headquarters the advisers were troubled.

Both candidates endeavored to improve their campaigns by using members of their families.

Nicholas Von Hoffman reported in the *Economist* that the election campaign was a family affair for both President Ford and Carter; never had the families been used in a Presidential campaign as they were in 1976. John Pilger stated in the *Daily Mirror* that Carter was inspired by his mother, Miss Lillian, "a rare Southern lady with fiercely held liberal views on race." She and her family sought racial integration in Dixie years before the U.S. Supreme Court, in 1954, declared racial segregation in public schools unconstitutional. Although seventy-seven years of age, Miss Lillian accepted a schedule of appearances in behalf of her ambitious son. Rosalynn found her place on the campaign trail as a daily speaker. She enjoyed campaigning for her illustrious husband, because she was free to say things she wanted to say. She continued speaking regularly on a personal schedule until the election in November. The *Times* said Mrs. Carter was in the campaign limelight on several occasions. The *Daily Mail* described the Carter women as being sensitive and slim, as well as tender. These ladies were all from Scarlett O'Hara country, the *Times* said, "where they're sweet as honey and tough as men."

Helen Lillie wrote in the *Herald* that Rosalynn in fourteen weeks of campaigning spoke in thirty-four states. "This little forty-eight-year-old 'Georgia peach' made speeches, shook hands, and smiled charmingly from early morning till late at night, five days a week, often staying with politically strong families and always sending a handwritten note of thanks for the hospitality she received," Lillie wrote. On weekends she relaxed with her husband and their eight-year-old daughter. Mrs. Carter, the *Herald* continued, was greatly respected as a political strategist. She persuaded Carter to campaign in every primary instead of only the safe ones. She proved right. She reinforced the folksy family image.

The *Daily Mail* said that, at home, Mrs. Carter mended the family clothes as well as "washing and ironing Jimmy's shirts. She frequently buys her husband's clothes."

Born in a very poor family, she had worked hard all her life—as she says. "Her slow drawl hides a personality," explained the *Daily Mail* reporter Lowther, "that has been geared to a single-minded pursuit of Carter's ambitions. Naturally shy and introverted, she has forced herself to tour the nation alone, campaigning for power. She avoids parties and playtimes. Happiness to her is sitting at home with her family, going to church, fixing her words to suit her husband. She works eighteen-hour days to perfect her style, to promote her position. What she lacks in warmth and spontaneity, she makes up with work and courage. She has the steely determination and the quiet strength to deal with anything. In more than seven months of campaigning she has gone out on her own to meet people in far-flung places her husband was not reaching." An *Evening News* reporter, Elizabeth Speier, upheld Lowther's opinion that Rosalynn had the charm and the poise to fill the post of America's First Lady "with perfection."

Ann Simpson described Carter as being surrounded by women, especially Rosalynn, whom Simpson called a "magnolia made of steel." All women in Carter's life possessed an archaic, disconcerting mixture of Pollyanna charm and fierce Deep Southern ambition, according to Simpson, writing in the *Herald*. "The Southern Belle syndrome was developed to trap a man with sweetness, then resolutely, but still with coyness, manipulate him towards the highest goals," Simpson contended. "Carter both exploits and learns from the wiles of Southern Belles," Simpson said. "He knows the value of their drawling, persuasive pleasantries and he knows that the womenfolk in his family are extremely politically astute, sensing electorates' oncoming moods with uncanny precision." Thus, if Carter were elected President, Simpson and other reporters predicted that his Administration would be a family affair.

Were women the key to Carter's success? He was a man who, according to the *Daily Mail*, actually preferred women's company to men's. "A very unusual trait in a politician," the *Daily Mail* said, "for men who prefer women to men usually have, in psychological terms, a deep feminine streak in their own natures—subtle, complex and highly initiative." The *Daily Mail's* summary description of Carter shows his confidence in his ability to win with a smile what he could not obtain by either force or reason. He grew to adulthood in a family of unusually strong women. Lowther wrote: "His woman, Rosalynn, is extremely important to him and highly influential. She is of the Deep South, and the Southern Belle is the only living example of eighteenth-century femininity left in this world. Southern Belles are developed to control and manipulate their plantation-owning, fox-hunting, gambling husbands, the last of the true English squires."

Lowther contended that Carter's women had not dominated or controlled him. Instead, they had taught him their wiles and developed that deep feminine intuition in his character. "He is neither henpecked nor shackled; though he has adopted the mind and method of his women he has kept intact his own masculine authority." He was more willing to trust talented women with power than were his predecessors. The *Daily Mail* reported that Carter, if elected, planned to have women in his Cabinet and hoped to put a woman on the U.S. Supreme Court. Furthermore, he would give Rosalynn important governmental duties in her role as First Lady. The *Daily Mail* pointed out that Rosalynn was the daughter of an auto mechanic who lived on the wrong side of the tracks and who died leaving a wife and four daughters when Rosalynn, the oldest, was only thirteen years of age. The *Daily Mail* said she capitalized on "her one great asset, her almond-eyed beauty, and at nineteen married the richest guy in town. Thirty years later, in 1976, a millionaire with economic security and a happy family of four children, Rosalynn never let go of her traditions of a dutiful, loving wife."

Until the campaign ended, Rosalynn and her husband continued to meet on weekends wherever they were campaigning at that time. This joint plan they began sharing in the primary weekends and continued it until the election. The first chore she did upon their meeting was to check her husband's clothes carefully. She mended, darned, washed, and ironed all of his clothes and had them ready to wear the next week. The *Daily Mail* explained that she did not do any of this from a sense of insecurity or uncertainty about herself, but rather "she contends this is a part of her role and her strength and determination to permit nothing to change despite her demanding place in the campaign. When she appears with Jimmy publicly she is transformed into the partner-perfect traditional wife. With her hands folded placidly in the lap of her dress, right leg crossed perfectly behind the left."

What was the campaign status of the family of the first appointed President? They, like the challenger's family, were active campaigners. President Ford said that his wife, Betty, was a much better campaigner than he. With great charm, obvious charisma, with courage and candor, Betty Ford, declared the *Daily Mail,* was continuing to prove why she was one of the most popular women in America. At fifty-seven, Mrs. Ford was well known as a fun-loving beauty who could dance all night, as one who loved to go out for a good time, whose spirit and exuberance spilled over into every aspect of her busy life. She assumed a regular speaking schedule in behalf of the President's election, though she did not appear on the political platform as frequently as did Rosalynn, nor was she given the "independence of expression" shown by Mrs. Carter, the *Daily Mail* added.

From any realistic viewpoint, the Presidential campaign of 1976 was much more a two-family contest than ever before in American history. In support of this conclusion, each Presidential candidate and his wife had four children. Seven of these eight had recently reached adulthood, and all of them were active in their fathers' campaign. (Amy Carter was only eight years of age and inactive in the campaign.) The British agencies of public opinion noted this significant change and kept their readers informed of this interesting phenomenon.

In addition to this significant change in the 1976 Presidential campaign, several British newspapers, including the *Daily Telegraph* and the *Evening Standard,* emphasized the contrast between Carter's meteoric rise to gain the Democratic nomination and his "unfortunate political judgments" following the nomination. "He had failed to get a firm grip on his campaign organization, which was badly split by rivalries among the staff members," the British papers wrote.

Ill-thought-out political judgments played an important role in Carter's decline in popularity as registered in the Gallup and Harris polls. Furthermore, Carter was condemned in the British press for his errors of political judgment. President Ford's gains among American voters were such that the outcome of the election was actually in doubt for hours after the election was held.

Among the bad decisions the Democratic nominee made was the calamitously candid interview given to *Playboy* magazine. In this interview Carter admitted that he had lusted after a number of beautiful women, noting that the Bible stated that those who lust after women have committed adultery mentally and have sinned against the Mosaic law. He added that those of us who have not violated marital vows but only lusted after women should not condemn those who have forsaken their vows and have bedded with other women. Confessing his sins, Carter stated: "I've committed adultery in my heart many times. This is something God recognizes I do and have done and God forgives me for it. But that doesn't mean I condemn someone who not only looks on a woman with lust but leaves his wife and shacks up with somebody out of wedlock." He added a second error in political judgment when he stated that "I don't think I would ever take on the same frame of mind that Ex-Presidents Nixon or Johnson did of lying, cheating and distorting the truth" to the American people.

The publication of the interview certainly must have embarrassed Mrs. Carter and shocked many sincere Christians throughout the country, especially in the Southern Bible Belt. The *Irish Times* was among the part of the press that reported a brief interview with Rosalynn Carter: "He's a good husband. I trust him completely and absolutely.

We have a great marriage—thirty years of it." She admitted that her husband had never discussed that matter with her and added: "He doesn't have to explain it because we have a very close relationship."

The *Sun* called the *Playboy* interview a "very silly mistake." The *Sun* said Carter's "flawless image has been greatly marred by the confession of a major sin. . . . Carter's views and language will cause a political storm in the campaign for the Presidential election in November." The *Daily Express* concluded that, despite Carter's "piercing blue eyes, his immaculately coiffured hair and his gray hand-pressed suits . . . his blend of brotherly love and brutal determination leading to the most phenomenal rise in American political history," the *Playboy* interview was naive and, worse, distasteful. Some newspapers thought the Carter interview was a major election blunder because he had established a close link between the Bible and the ballot. The *Sun* editors declared that Carter had faltered and was in "serious danger of getting himself regarded as some kind of oddball." Indeed, Carter's reputation as the mystery man from the South who can do no wrong was damaged. However, in the end, concluded the *Sun,* he would win the election.

The *Times* described Carter and Rosalynn, after campaigning separately for a few days, meeting before a huge crowd in Pittsburgh. "They kissed and hugged effusively and repeatedly as the crowd cheered and hurrahed," the *Times* reported. This independent paper claimed it was "incredible" that the candidate should have granted an interview to the nude-girlie *Playboy* magazine "as if the public wanted the President to deal with such private matters publicly and in such plain language."

The *Daily Mail* quoted extensively from the interview, including Carter's accusation that Johnson and Nixon had lied, cheated, and distorted the truth to the American people. The London daily also lamented Carter's remarks about finding an American Ambassador in Europe who was "a fat, bloated, ignorant, rich major contributor to a Presidential campaign" and who "doesn't even respect the language of the country in which he serves and knows practically nothing about American history." "It was," concluded the *Daily Mail,* "an insult to the American people and to the people of that country in which the embassy was located."

Jon Dressel, in the *Western Mail,* described Carter as "a beaming, sandy-haired man in a rumpled Palm Beach suit, who walked up to people, extended his hand and said, 'Hello, I'm Jimmy Carter. I'm going to be your next President.' " Dressel characterized the introduction as "abrupt and arrogant." Carter, stated the *Western Mail,* seemed neither "flashy nor nervous but absolutely cool and confident, more like a person in authority making a rather obvious announcement than an underdog, boondocks politician struggling for the greatest prize against incredible odds."

The *Herald* noted that Carter's interview with *Playboy* provoked disgust throughout the conservative Southern fundamentalist Bible Belt and quoted several persons to prove the conclusion. W. A. Criswell, pastor of the largest church in the Southern Baptist Convention, declared, "The whole thing is highly distasteful. I'm very hurt by it." Back in Washington, Senator Robert Byrd of West Virginia expressed himself plainly: "I don't think it's terminal, by any stretch of the imagination [but] I don't think this particular interview should have been given to this particular publication." Senator Hugh Scott, the Republican leader soon to retire, theorized, "Carter has used this in a rather exotic springboard for his candid views of morality which will probably gain him some sympathy among the ultratolerant and shock the generality of the good people of this country."

Another Scottish newspaper, the *Scotsman,* reported that Carter would not have much trouble in being elected the next President of the United States. Reporter Frankland wrote that the Democrats outnumbered the Republicans two to one, with about as many independents as there were Democrats, and, Frankland asserted, Carter should take half the independent vote. Surveys showed, Frankland said, that, in contrast to President Ford, "who was about as stimulating as a glass of milk," Americans wanted their President to be a strong leader. On the other hand, the *Scotsman* reporter noted that some voters said that Carter had no sense of humor, while others thought he was entirely too ambitious. Some along the northeastern coast disliked Carter's staunch conservative fundamentalist Baptist religion and his Southern background. There was a widespread suspicion, Frankland wrote, that Carter spoke out of both sides of his mouth, saying one thing one day and another the next. And, finally, the *Scotsman* concluded, the way that Carter set out to become President was not entirely melodramatic; it was the closest thing to a coup d'etat that was possible in a democracy.

Meanwhile, Carter left the campaign to prepare for his first debate with President Ford. A whistle-stop train carried Vice-Presidential candidate Mondale, Mrs. Mondale, and Mrs. Carter on a visit to small towns across the golden corn heartland of Ohio, Indiana, and Illinois. Rosalynn gave her single brief speech on the uniqueness of her husband's campaign at each stop. She repeated that Carter had shunned special interest groups and was not obligated to any group.

Mondale, said the *Times,* was a good up-and-at-'em orator, who could be a humorous speaker. Of Carter's *Playboy* interview, the Vice-Presidential candidate repeatedly told the small-towners that Carter speaking in candor was refreshing, and might prove quite beneficial. "If you ask Carter a question he will answer it," Mondale said. "That is one of his characteristics which is admirable and rare in a politician."

At each train stop Mondale showed the crowd a newspaper with a picture of President Ford and a cow. He said that, as a Minnesota farm boy, he and all farmers knew that cows were stupid. "While Carter was out meeting with the people, where was President Ford when the unemployed needed him?" Mondale asked, and invariably someone in the audience would shout, "With the cows!" "That's right," roared Mondale as the crowd responded in gales of laughter.

Mondale found the people in mid-America worried about unemployment and inflation. The voters wanted the Democrats to increase employment and lower inflation. Fred Emery wrote in the *Scotsman* about Mrs. Carter walking through the train to speak to reporters and to answer questions by Betty Friedan. "Did not women have the same rights as men to lust and commit adultery without being condemned for it?" Friedan inquired. Mrs. Carter replied, "Men and women all have rights." Friedan prodded Mrs. Carter: "Have you ever lusted after a man in your heart?" Mrs. Carter snapped back, "If I had I would never tell you." That ended Friedan's interrogation of Mrs. Carter, the *Scotsman* said.

The Edinburgh paper reported that during the entire trip from New York to Chicago the train schedule was adhered to closely, the comforts of the brand-new rolling coaches were marvelous, and the weather was perfect. The *Daily Express* declared that Carter's *Playboy* interview turned the Presidential election upside down. The *Evening News* averred that Americans have a habit of talking openly about religion and love. "In Britain we never talk about such things like these because we regard both subjects as very private," the *Evening News* wrote. The British, more and more, were believing that Carter was the biggest fraud and showoff of all American politicians, the newspaper added.

The *Economist,* as did several other publications, wondered what Carter's views on sexual intercourse had to do with the Presidential election. It was doubtful that he really intended to indicate a connection between the two. The *Irish Times* asked if Carter's *Playboy* interview kept the campaign from being too dull. Mrs. Mondale, when questioned about Carter's interview and asked if she secretly lusted after men, scoffed, "I do it all the time," and the large audience laughed heartily. This Dublin paper concluded that "most of the news media viewed the interview as a major blunder but not an irredeemable one."

5

The
Debates

As previously noted, President Ford in his acceptance speech at the Republican convention challenged former Governor Carter to a nationally televised debate. Carter, at his home in Plains, accepted immediately. Subsequently, a group of aides, representing the combatants, met in Washington to arrange the details for three ninety-minute debates and an additional ninety-minute debate between the two Vice-Presidential candidates. The location of each debate and the subjects to be discussed were agreed upon, as well as the dates on which the debates were to be held.

This series of debates, said the *Evening Standard,* would control the whole election "because it focuses on the important questions of economics and jobs." British reporters estimated that a hundred million people would watch the first debate in Philadelphia on September 23 in the hope of seeing where Carter really stood on matters affecting the future prosperity of the country. The *Economist* predicted erroneously that Carter would throw "the Nixon saddle over Ford's back and fasten the girth tight."

Meanwhile, Mark Frankland, stationed in Washington by the *Scotsman,* wrote that most Americans believed that the debates would decide the election—a conclusion with which Frankland disagreed. The debates, he argued, were not an important part of American political life. The whole idea of the two Presidential candidates, the nominated leaders of the two great parties, meeting head-on was an unusual political phenomenon. Many political experts in Britain, contended Frankland, agreed that a Presidential debate was not the best way to win an election. Neither President Ford nor Carter was likely to debate the basic issues confronting America, Frankland said. They would not speak as the leaders of their respective parties for the very good reason that forty percent of the American voters were independent. There were, however, benefits in holding the debates: they would give voters a chance to make a choice based on their interest and emotions; they would help voters make a more knowledgeable decision; they would interest, possibly, some of the millions who, though of voting age, had never participated in elections.

Frankland added that debates could well end in a free form of political commercials—"one for a President who is athletic and pleasant and sensible in a conservative way, the other for an ex-Governor . . . who is brighter and would make a far more imaginative and tough leader than his opponent but suspects it may be safer to convince the people that he is just a reliable moderate." Carter, Frankland said, had to be able to reassure many people who had not yet made up their minds.

The *Times* was one of the few British newspapers that informed its readers about the details of the debates. The sessions would not be interrupted by commercials. Three journalists would ask the questions, in turn, under the direction of a television reporter acting as moderator. The *Daily Telegraph* announced that the British Broadcasting Corporation would broadcast all of the debates live throughout the British Isles. The debates would also be heard over the British radio national hookup.

The *Daily Mail* said the fierce political battle between the plodding Ford and the pious Carter could be decided by the debates. More attention, wrote William Lowther, would be devoted to imagery than to the issues. The *Irish Times* stated that Ford had asked the voters to choose between performance in office and Carter's promises. Carter answered that Ford had accomplished nothing positive—except avoiding another Watergate scandal. Carter promised to bring new leadership to unite the country again.

Sixteen years earlier, the Presidential debate of 1960 marked the first time in American history that a sitting President had ever debated a challenger. Carter began the debate with an obvious timidity but recovered within thirty minutes and continued more confidently throughout the rest of the argument. He discussed inflation, unemployment, the lack of a coherent energy policy, and the general belief that the federal bureaucracy was in a mess. The President replied that the mess had been caused by the Democratic Congress and that Carter, as a Democrat, was in part responsible. Carter declared that if "my opponent accuses me of being responsible for the Washington mess, and I was not a part of it, he was responsible for the Nixon Administration of which he was a part in its entirety. Moreover, my opponent pardoned Nixon unjustly."

The *Daily Post and Mercury* regarded the first debate as crucial, but the discussion tended to deteriorate as both candidates kept up a seemingly interminable barrage of figures and percentages. For example, the *Daily Post and Mercury* quoted the President as saying, "I think the record will show that in four years in which Carter was Governor of Georgia that spending increased more than fifty percent, the number of state employees jumped more than twenty-five percent, and government indebtedness through bond issues went up over twenty percent."

The *Evening Standard* noted that the Carter camp was worried about the crucial first debate. Both of the debaters acquired huge notebooks on the economic issue and other domestic problems, but no notes were allowed on the stage during the debate. The *Sun* noted that Ford, a celebrated bumbler, was "forceful and unfaltering whereas Carter momentarily lost his famous poise and swallowed hard mid-sentence, showing his tension." A quick Harris poll showed that thirty-nine percent thought Ford won the debate and only thirty-one percent granted Carter the victory. Thirty percent considered the debate a draw. A further disappointment to the Carter camp was that President Ford seemed to be closing the gap between the two candidates. According to the Harris poll the President received thirty-seven percent and Carter only forty-two percent, with twenty-one percent of the registered voters undecided.

The drama of the occasion occurred when the power went off. The sound system broke down and for twenty-seven minutes the candidates stood there silently facing each other before the electricity was restored and the debate continued. After the debate Ford joyously announced that the "momentum is now on our side." The *Daily Express* declared that the showdown to sell a President revealed that Carter was "definitely in a political slump." The *Irish Times* noted that both candidates took the debate seriously but that it proved to be long-winded and mostly laborious. If there was an overall difference in the candidates, the *Times* said, it was that "Carter emphasized compassion with the poor and underprivileged in society when Ford managed to appear unnecessarily insensitive."

The *Irish Times* stated that both sides claimed victory in the debate. Carter declared, "I feel good about it [the debate] and I'm looking forward to the next one." President Ford reported, "We did all right. The momentum is on our side." The debate aided the President in deciding to enter the campaign more actively than previously, when he had feared he might make mistakes that Carter had been making for a month campaigning almost alone. The independent *Times* described Carter's nervousness at the beginning of the debate, but the paper added that he recovered his poise and finished better than Ford, who, by the end of the debate, had lapsed into his more "familiar woodenness."

As the month ended, the *Evening Standard* quoted some Carter workers as saying the challenger had blown the election. He was slipping badly in the important states of California, Illinois, Michigan, and New York. The Carter campaigners, the *Evening Standard* said, were very sad that he had eroded the Democratic lead in early August to a bare plurality at the end of September.

In a leading editorial, the *Times* described the contrast between the American and the English political systems. It was "much easier in America with a decentralized system of power than in a centralized system of the British type," the *Times* wrote, "for a power-seeking, ambitious person who wants the top job without working his way up through the party apparatus or grinding legislation through the Congress at the Capitol." The newspaper added that Carter, if elected, would find himself in some "very intractable" situations. The Congressional Democrats who should show him party loyalty were jealous of their privileges, increasingly capable of drawing up their own budget, assertive in the country's foreign affairs, and intimately enmeshed in the interest of the bureaucracy and of business. As President, the *Time*s said advisedly, Carter could find the Democratic Congress "very difficult to influence and still more difficult to change." Having been an insider for a quarter of a century, President Ford knew the workings of the system and did not bang his head against its limitations. The paper said that Ford, although not an ideal or an imposing President, had been a "safe, sensible, sound and decent one and is trusted abroad." The final result, concluded the *Times,* at its simplest would be determined by how many Americans wanted unpredictable change more than continuity.

The *Irish Time*s considered the American comments on the first debate and concluded that a great many Americans were not excited about either Presidential candidate. The *Daily Mirror* contended that the debate was so completely planned in advance that neither candidate would make a fool or a hero of himself. The London daily stated that American politicians did not experience the real debates of their British counterparts, for what "counted in television was one's personality, not one's prose; personality would always show through." The *Daily Mirror* explained that President Ford was much the "larger man; he looked powerfully solid." Carter seemed quite slight by comparison and was fidgety; he was prone to smile nervously. Carter's face, thought the *Daily Mirror,* looked more lively, while Ford's face seemed to be "puddingly." Neither candidate gained a complete victory in the debate; the commentators and the opinion polls called it an obvious draw, the *Daily Mirror* concluded.

The *Daily Express* and the *Daily Telegraph* were among the British papers that informed their readers of President Ford's visit to Alabama, where Governor George Wallace introduced him: "I want to say, Mr. President, that all of the people of Alabama appreciate your coming to our great state." From Mobile, Alabama, the President went to Mississippi, where he stated in Biloxi, "I don't believe law-abiding citizens should be deprived of the right to bear arms." To a conference of the National Association of Chiefs of Police the President shouted, "The first hundred days of my new Presidency will be devoted to a war on crime." In short, the *Daily Express* exclaimed, President Ford was "looking more like a winner." Carter, meanwhile, was appearing on the extreme West Coast, the paper said, "complaining like a loser." Carter called Ford a Republican who stood for the tradition of Harding, Hoover, and Nixon. Carter scolded President Ford as a person who was "insensitive to the suffering of the poor, the handicapped, and the aged," the *Daily Express* noted. Maurice Quainstance, in the *Herald,* thought that the television duel had failed to stir the voters or create any excitement among the millions of Americans who had watched it. Neither candidate could claim a clean-cut edge over the other.

While the *Herald* saw neither side winning the debate, the *Daily Mail* contended that President Ford had won narrowly, ensuring "this year's race for the White House being one of the closest political battles in recent American history." Ford's aggressive, forceful performance gained him support simply because it was such a vast improvement over his usual dreary efforts, the *Daily Mail* said. Unknown to the public, including the Carter people, experts from the Hollywood film industry were flown to Washington to spend a week with the President to provide him intensive training in dramatic speech delivery, body movement, and, most important, facial expressions, the *Daily Mail* reported, adding, "clearly President Ford was drilled to hide his sheepish gainless grin—it made him look foolish. He was brilliantly made up to look tough and rugged." Close-up, however, the *Daily Mail* explained, "one could see that thick pancake makeup had been plastered over his face and high into his thinning hair." It stopped the light reflecting on the President's balding head and cast him as a heavyweight boxer. No one could doubt, continued the London paper, from President Ford's overall image that "here was a man ready to smack anybody in the mouth at a moment's notice, a man who would back away from no fight. Furthermore, that was the type of a person most Americans wanted for their President—a man who would stand up to anyone, who was afraid of nothing."

By contrast, the *Daily Mail* said, Carter was very much himself. He had undergone no special training for the debate but had spent much time studying the facts and figures of the government. Like other British sources of public opinion, the *Daily Mail* noted Carter's nervousness, his stumbling over words, his sweating, and his seeming unsure of himself. "Within one half hour he conquered his fright and, once he gained his stride he equalled his opponent in presentation and authority," the *Daily Mail* said. Both men gained their objectives. The President successfully projected himself as more than a "Courtier President appointed by Richard Nixon." He looked like a man firmly in charge of his job. Carter proved that he had full command of the details of government and was well prepared and able to take over the occupancy of the White House, the *Daily Mail* concluded.

The *Evening Standard* informed its readers that the debate had become a duel, with statistics as a weapon of choice. Both men kept up a barrage of figures. As the evening wore on, the debaters began to throw fully loaded innuendos at each other. President Ford charged that, with Carter in the White House, there would be greater budget deficits, more spending, and more unemployment. Carter's mouth tightened as he answered, "It's not a matter of Democrat and Republican. It's a question of leadership or no leadership. Eisenhower worked with Congress very well. Even Nixon worked well with Congress because he was a strong leader," the *Evening Standard* quoted Carter. This London afternoon paper added, nevertheless, that the President was more aggressive and Carter was more on the defensive throughout the debate.

Discussing the debate, the *Times* stated that American businessmen felt that the economy was safe in President Ford's hands. They were fearful of Carter and admitted that their fears arose from the vagueness of what they perceived to be Carter's economic policy proposals. Comparisons between President Ford's and Carter's economic policies amounted to differing rhetoric and style rather than policy difference, the *Times* stated. In terms of the U.S. economy of 1976, the London paper contended, the differences between President Ford and Carter were minimal. "The many fears of the businessman," concluded the *Times,* "seem unwarranted if not ungrounded."

Eugene McCarthy, former U.S. Senator from Minnesota, the *Times* told its readers, ran as an independent for President, attacking both of the chief political parties in his campaign. Neither the Republican nor the Democratic Party had a God-given right to represent the American people, McCarthy said. The Ford-Carter debates McCarthy deemed completely ridiculous. They were another event from which he was excluded and for which he denounced the parties. McCarthy lost in his efforts to obtain equal time from the broadcasting corporations to tell the American people about his platform. He had another legal battle to get his name on the ballots of the states. "After dogged litigation," the *Times* announced, "he succeeded in getting on 29 state ballots, which accounted for 318 of the Electoral College's 538 voters." He was the Don Quixote of American politics, the *Times* said. To solve the unemployment problem he advocated American labor working shorter hours and accepting less pay so that all of the unemployed would be accepted into the labor force. He could, concluded the Times, attract enough votes from Carter to assure the election of President Ford.

Meanwhile, President Ford was accused by Charles Ruff in the *Daily Mirror* of pocketing contributions given to his reelection campaign as a Congressman—a charge that was investigated when Congressman Ford's designation as Vice-President was being considered by Congress. Ford had endorsed the checks from two labor unions over to a county in his

Congressional district and apparently had had no control of the money after that endorsement. Subsequently, when he was a candidate for President, this charge was repeated. The President urged a rapid and complete investigation, saying, according to the *Daily Mirror,* "I'm very proud of my personal integrity. It's more important to me than the election."

Yet another charge against President Ford was his acceptance of four vacation trips to golf links from corporation lobbyists. On these trips the President admitted that he talked politics with his hosts "informally but with no impropriety," adding, "I do not consider these infrequent weekends a violation of the rules of the House [of Representatives] on any ethical standards." President Ford's election chances suffered yet another setback, said the London daily paper, when a secret probe of his income tax filings showed that the President and his wife lived on $3 to $8 weekly pocket money during 1972. In that year Ford earned $40,000 in Congressional salary and $20,000 for lectures and public appearances. The President explained the meager cash incident by stating that his living expenses were paid by the group to whom he made speeches. Furthermore, his tax returns showed that he had paid $500 for clothes and $700 for a Vail, Colorado, skiing holiday. When the Internal Revenue Service refused to accept these figures and their explanation, the President paid a fine of $250 for the first offense and returned $700 to the fund from which the money for the Colorado holiday had come.

The *Evening Standard* ran a story about a trip Carter had taken to Brazil while Governor of Georgia, in a Lockheed Jet Star of great luxury and comfort, as the guest of the Lockheed Corporation, during which he had offered to aid his host corporation in any way possible.

Answering the charges, both candidates kept busy making speeches until the time for the second debate arrived. As previously agreed, the second debate was held in San Francisco on October 7. On the eve of this debate a Gallup poll showed that Carter's lead over President Ford had been cut to eight percent—a new low for the Democratic nominee. According to the *Evening Standard,* the drastic shift in contrasting percentages resulted from Ford's inroads in the South, from the President's gaining the support of the Reagan faction of the Republican Party, and from the Republican nominee's lead in attracting independent voters—a very important group in 1976. In the South, Carter's lead was down from thirty-five percent a month earlier to seventeen percent.

The *Economist* called the Democratic candidate "Calamity Carter" in accusing him of "having had a bout with foot-in-mouth disease." As public speakers, the journal thought, both candidates were uniformly dull. President Ford was more so. In fact, as a stump speaker, "his words came from his mouth in awkward and often incoherent bursts." His clichés could be easily misplaced. The *Economist* contended that the difference between the two candidates was one of style and personality. Their policies were remarkably similar. On the basis of known performance the periodical preferred the President, citing "a feeling of being more comfortable with the devil it knew." President Ford's Administration was the most open, candid, and straightforward Administration in recent years, the *Economist* said. In his views on the issues, Carter, like the President, was a "conservative, cautious, and prevaricating man." In fact, the ancient distinction between the American political parties, thought the *Economist,* was less clear in 1976 than earlier.

The *Times* noted the similarities of the two candidates, concluding that there would not be much change in the stock market whether Ford or Carter was elected President. The *Observer* noted that both President Ford and Carter were ignoring the real issues facing Americans—the economic conditions, especially unemployment and inflation. Furthermore, as Mark Frankland put it, "The candidates liked to think of themselves as racing, galloping knights with the winner determined by brilliance and speed." Voting patterns in the United States showed that for the last twenty years Americans had cast their ballots for the candidate whose character they liked best rather than for his stand on the issues. The present election, on the basis of historical forces, looked like the speed of a mouse, the *Observer* stated, terming the campaign "the mouse race to the White House."

John Gillingham, in the *Daily Post and Mercury,* urged American voters to cast their ballots for "Mr. Nobody for President." From his listening post in Washington, this English reporter wrote there were more than a hundred and fifty people in the United States running for President. Some of the candidates were serious, such as independent McCarthy, and Gus Hall, the perennial candidate of the Communists. Eddie Collins, another candidate, campaigned for nudity. As reported in the *Daily Post and Mercury,* Collins said, "I believe that nudity will kill peoples' drive to love money and clothes; that will save our national resources. I see nudity as an ecologically sound movement."

Stephen Banker wrote in the *Economist* that independent voters held the key to the White House. Neither the Democrat nor the Republican campaigns had caught fire. Such apathy and noninterest or excitement was disappearing as political tempers began to flare. A large majority of independents were sitting comfortably on the fence of indecision. They had not yet bestirred themselves to make a choice. These held the balance of election power; they would decide the election. "It looks as if the victor," concluded the *Economist,* "would be the man who falls flat on his face least frequently in the next three weeks." Political mud was flying thick and fast.

Both Carter and President Ford had made mistakes in their first national campaign. Carter suffered from having "peaked" too soon. He gave too many interviews, especially the one to *Playboy;* he made too many speeches, accepted too many engagements. His campaign team suffered from personal tension and from narrow provincialism. The relations between his campaign headquarters in Atlanta and the Democratic National Committee in Washington left much to be desired.

According to the *Guardian,* Carter suffered most, perhaps, from the increasing popularity of McCarthy. The Gallup and Harris polls were showing that McCarthy would receive seven percent of the votes and in some of the Northern industrial states a higher percentage. When informed that he was drawing more than three times as many voters from the Democratic Party as from the Republican Party, McCarthy, as reported in the *Guardian,* said, "I don't see why the Democrats have to win. They don't stand for anything anyway. It is wrong to claim that moral leadership is one of the functions of the Presidency. The real question in this country is the bankruptcy of ideas. Bad ideas have more impact than corruption and immorality at the top. There is no debate on unemployment, which is becoming structural. The only way to deal with unemployment," continued McCarthy to *Guardian* reporter Jonathan Steele, "is to redistribute work. Have a shorter work week, eliminate overtime, and share work out among more people."

President Ford was having great difficulty in recovering after the exhausting preconvention fight with Reagan. As Nixon's appointee he was the first nonelected national executive. As Nixon's pardoner, the *Daily Telegraph* informed its readers, he suffered general condemnation. For permitting Kissinger to take complete control of foreign policy and to practice secret diplomacy, President Ford was misunderstood. He was surprised by a report of a long study by the General Accounting Office, issued by the House of Representatives, in which the President was severely criticized for his role in the *Mayaguez* rescue operation off Cambodia in 1975.

The American freighter *Mayaguez* and its forty-member crew were seized by the Cambodian *Khmer Rouge,* a Communist ship, on the high seas. The U.S. rescue of the ship was hailed as a military triumph. Nevertheless, President Ford, according to the *Daily Telegraph,* unnecessarily caused the killing of forty-one American boys in an uncalled-for, ill-planned military rescue. The *Daily Telegraph* said the tragedy was the result, according to the General Accounting Office's published report, of a hasty Presidential decision based on poor intelligence. But the President boasted of America's military triumph over Communism, the *Daily Telegraph* emphasized, never mentioning the needless sacrifice of forty-one American lives. A significant segment of American voters agreed with President Ford in his "imperialistic military display," the *Daily Telegraph* wrote.

The *Guardian* reported that, according to a White House source, the President became angry upon learning of a tragic and uncalled-for statement made by his vulgar-mouthed Secretary of Agriculture, Earl Butz, on a jet flying from the Kansas City Republican convention. It happened in this way, the *Guardian* reported: Pat Boone, "angel-faced heartthrob and dedicated Christian, sat beside John Dean, one-time White House legal adviser to President Nixon and subsequently sensational witness before the United States Senate Watergate Investigating Committee, on a plane for California." Directly across the aisle from them sat Sonny Bono. The three of them were discussing the lack of successful appeals by the Republican Party to the black voters. Sitting in a seat immediately in front of them, Butz stuck his head between the two seats and told Boone that "the coloreds only want three things. Do you know what they are?" Answering his own question, Butz continued: "The coloreds only want a tight pussy, a pair of loose shoes, and a warm place to shit."

Dean attended the Republican convention as a reporter for *Rolling Stone,* and reported the conversation in the popular magazine. In the *Irish Times,* Dean's statement appeared in an expurgated form, as it did in *Rolling Stone,* "as a tight copulation, loose shoes, and a warm place to defecate." Only a few British newspapers, including the *Guardian,* published the statement as Butz actually made it. Dean's article, moreover, did not mention the author's name. A *New York Times* reporter heard about the statement and, through successful sleuthing, traced the statement to Butz. However, before publishing an article containing the statement and attributing it to Secretary Butz, the reporter phoned Boone to get his affirmation of Butz as the correct author.

Democrats and Republicans demanded that Ford fire Butz immediately, but the President remained silent. He spent several days weighing whether to retain the Nixon-appointed Secretary of Agriculture or fire him. The *Guardian* thought that, with friends like Butz, President Ford had little need for political enemies. Bob Dole, attempting to defend the President, linked Butz's statements and Carter's *Playboy* interview, suggesting, as stated in the *Irish Times,* that the public was "getting fed up with stupid statements." Fritz Mondale declared the statement "poisonous," and Carter said it was "disgraceful." The Republican Ambassador to the United Nations, William Scranton, was certain that it would "seriously hurt" American relations with the black African countries.

The *Times* informed its readers that Butz had boasted to Barbara Walters (who, with a five-year, five-million-dollar contract, was making her debut as a member of the ABC evening news program) that he had told that black joke many times to groups of white farmers throughout the American farming states. The *Daily Express* concluded that President Ford had been gravely embarrassed and that the incident probably would rob him of the votes of millions of outraged black and white Americans alike—especially clergymen.

Vice-President Nelson Rockefeller, in London to exhibit a collection of North American Indian art and to aid in organizing the expatriate Americans for the Republican ticket, labeled Butz's remark "tragic—both in terms of the impact on America's black conservatives and on the former Secretary of Agriculture's career as a trusted public servant." Winchester reported in the *Guardian* that Butz was a national hero among the farmers who lived on the back forty, and gave examples to prove his point: One woman farmer in Pennsylvania stated publicly that Butz should not be forced to resign—"he was not Secretary of the blacks but Secretary of Agriculture of the United States." The Farm Bureau of Illinois declared that Butz's resignation would be "bad news for America."

The President's campaign was put in a tragic condition by the way he handled the Butz affair, concluded the *Guardian,* and other sources of British public opinion echoed that conclusion. The *Scotsman* quoted Butz as having publicly apologized for "an unfortunate choice of language." After two conferences with President Ford, the Secretary tendered his resignation. Apparently, Secretary Butz had never worried about the enemies he made so long as the white farmers continued to be his friends. The *Economist* declared, with apparent delight, that at last Butz's "loose tongue and mindless vulgarism" had proved his undoing. In submitting his resignation, the Secretary said, "This is the price I pay for a gross indiscretion in a private conversation."

The *Scotsman* reported that, in accepting Butz's resignation, the President stated, "Butz is a decent and a good man. I accept his resignation as one of the saddest moments of my Administration." He praised the former professor of Agriculture at Purdue University as "wise enough and courageous enough to recognize that no single individual, no matter how distinguished his past service, should cast a shadow over the integrity and goodwill of the American government by his comments." The *Herald* ran an editorial on the Butz debacle. It stated in part that normally such an offensive remark about the black people would "be no more than a storm in a teacup." However, President Ford's main "stock-in-trade was his reputation for reliability and common sense in high office." His handling of the Butz dismissal, the *Herald* said, gave his political opponents the opportunity to accuse him of dithering. The President was aware of how Nixon's popularity among the rank and file of "Middle America" had depreciated as a result of the bad language exposed by the White House tapes and their deletions. President Ford was just plain angry over the whole debacle and was well aware of the necessity for renewed effort to gain support. In fact, Dole, recently dubbed by the *Herald* "Dobermann Dole," stated publicly that he believed the Butz incident would defeat the Ford ticket in the election to be held in only a month.

With the passing of the Butz incident the British press turned its attention to other phases of the American Presidential campaign, including the status of American labor in the election. The *Guardian* told of a letter that George Meany had written to President Ford, urging him to move forcefully to aid the British to recover from the collapse of the pound. The British people, continued the national president of the AFL-CIO, had "accepted burdens, conditions, and constraints in a manner which warrants general praise rather than carping criticism." Learning of this letter, Dole declared in a speech, "I understand Carter is going to have two hot lines if he's elected President—one with Russia and one with George Meany's office. Thus he can get his orders, and if the phone rings from Russia, he'll know what to say." The *Guardian* quoted the letter, while the *Economist* told of Dole's reaction.

While Dole was linking the national labor leader with the Carter campaign, the Mondales were on the Boeing 727 "Minnesota Fritz," touring some industrial states, speaking usually to different groups in the same city. Fritz, said the *Economist,* leavened his partisan denunciations with a dry wit and a good sense of timing. For example, when addressing a tremendous crowd of laborers in a northern industrial city he stated, "For a working man to vote Republican is like chickens voting for Colonel Sanders." Joan Mondale, said the *Daily Mirror,* was talking at the same time to a tremendous audience of women in the same city. She was asked to explain the difference between Watergate and Democratic Congressman Wayne Hays's conduct with Elizabeth Ray. She replied, "The Democrats do it to their secretaries; the Republicans do it to the American people."

Meanwhile, Jonathan Steele took issue in the *Guardian* with members of the British press for being extraordinarily fickle with Carter. The Democratic nominee's trouble was not of his own making. He was ridiculed unmercifully, Steele wrote, "as a secret lecher, or a hopeless square or both." Carter's basic theme was to restore American self-confidence when American values were dreadfully thin. His call for openness and decency in government had won him the nomination. He should go back to them now, advised the *Guardian* reporter. There was absolutely no need for the Carter campaign to panic as a result of the first debate or the *Playboy* interview. His best hope to win the election was to hammer away at the solid and genuine issues—unemployment, urban decay, tax reform, and corporate irresponsibility. This sound and logical advice was being followed completely, concluded the *Guardian*.

This was the political atmosphere when the second debate between Ford and Carter was held in San Francisco on October 7. As previously agreed upon, the chief subjects of the debate were foreign affairs and defense. The *Times* suggested that, in the first debate, when everyone thought Carter would cut President Ford to pieces, the President had emerged the winner. This time, when all thought that President Ford would win easily, Carter emerged the victor. The *Irish Times* reported correctly, as did other agencies of British public opinion, that Carter turned the tables on President Ford and won the debate easily.

"Ford astonished millions of Americans," declared the *Herald,* "and pitched his campaign for reelection into deeper trouble with a double blunder in this television debate." In response to a question the President answered, "There is no domination by the Soviet Union in Eastern Europe and there will never be under a Ford Administration." The President, given an opportunity to clarify himself, sank far deeper into his quagmire defense of the past year's Helsinki Agreements on East-West relations. Smiling happily at his opponent's tragic gaffe, Carter did not miss the golden opportunity for the kill. "I would like to see President Ford convince the Polish-Americans and the Czech-Americans and the Hungarian-Americans in this country that those countries don't live under the domination and supervision of the Soviet Union."

Ford's other lapse of accuracy was his assertion that "this Administration overthrew an elected government" in Chile. Carter permitted this error to pass unchallenged. The President, said the *Irish Times,* muddled the current American policy toward China when he incorrectly stated that the 1972 Shanghai Communiqué contained an agreement that the differences between China and Taiwan would "be settled peacefully." Peking never agreed to anything but its own right to liberate Taiwan in any way it saw fit. Carter pledged the preservation of independence and freedom of the people of Taiwan. President Ford, said the Dublin paper, seemed "to wince under Carter's aggressive scathing attack and spent much of the ninety minutes in defense, making several clear mistakes."

The *Herald* noted that Carter's aides were elated over President Ford's mistakes and promised to raise the Eastern European issue every day until the November 2 election. A member of Carter's campaign strategy group, Stuart Eizenstat, exclaimed that President Ford's remarks "belie every statement that he is knowledgeable in foreign affairs." Editorially, the *Herald* labeled President Ford's remarks "astonishing and disturbing." It was the "purest sophistry to claim that the Soviets do not dominate their satellites." The *Daily Telegraph* contended that President Ford's egregious errors were sure to haunt him for the rest of the campaign. There was great wrath in the American ethnic communities over the President's statements.

Ross Mark stated, in the *Daily Express,* that President Ford's gaffe left his campaign floundering dangerously as White House aides tried desperately to find a way out of the dilemma and Carter's aides pounced on the mistakes with glee. The *Times* predicted that Carter would certainly exploit the President's errors to the hilt. The *Scotsman* stated that President Ford had pitched his campaign into deeper trouble by his double blunder in the television debate and would have to reestablish his constructive image before the election. According to the *Daily Post and Mercury,* "The crowd gasped in amazement and millions in the television audience were stunned when the President declared that the Soviet Union did not dominate Eastern Europe."

The *Times* stated that Carter had scoffed at Ford's leadership in foreign affairs: "As far as foreign policy goes, Dr. Kissinger has been the United States." President Ford replied, "Mr. Carter has indicated he would look with sympathy to a Communist government in Italy. I think that would destroy the integrity and strength of NATO and I am totally opposed to it."

To this his opponent stated, "Mr. Ford's words unfortunately are not true. I have never advocated a Communistic government for Italy. That would obviously be a ridiculous thing for anyone to do. This is an entrance of deliberate distortion of the facts." And, the *Times* added, "so were the President's words on defense cuts."

The *Evening Standard* quoted Carter as saying that all of the horrible mistakes in foreign policy made in Ford's Administration arose because the American people and the Congress were excluded from the process of decision making. The *Daily Mail,* as did other members of the British press, noted the President's blunders on foreign policy and concluded that "Jimmy Carter was one step closer to the White House thereby." Not only did Carter "dominate the second debate but President Ford walked into a very nasty and destructive political trap," the *Daily Mail* said, noting that foreign diplomats stationed in Washington were stunned by the President's statements. The *Daily Mail* quoted one foreign diplomat of high rank describing the President's gaffe as "It's crazy. Isn't it what NATO is all about?" The London daily paper concluded that the debate was a much livelier and more revealing confrontation than the first one fourteen days earlier. To the *Daily Mail,* "Carter emerged as more relaxed and more assured. His responses were crisper and he projected himself as well informed and in charge." Finally, the provincial *Guardian* concluded that "by managing to cram both his left and right foot into his mouth during the televised foreign policy debate President Ford appears to have brought his once accelerating campaign effort to a complete halt."

From San Francisco, the President journeyed to Beverly Hills, where he enticed Reagan to the same platform for their first joint appearance since the Kansas City convention. Speaking at the University of Southern California, the *Guardian* quoted the President as saying, "I am very much aware of the present plight of Eastern European nations. It is our policy to use every peaceful means to assist the countries of Eastern Europe and their peoples to become less dependent on the Soviet Union and to achieve closer contact with the West and, of course, the United States of America."

From the second debate Carter traveled to Salt Lake City, where he called the President's blunders on foreign policy "ridiculous, a disgrace and a major political blunder." He reserved his most unkind cut, said the *Guardian,* for a Democratic rally in Los Angeles only a few miles from where President Ford was speaking. There the Democratic nominee pointed out that in the television debate the President stood alone— "not able to consult Dr. Kissinger." Mr. Ford, continued Carter, "made a statement which outraged America's allies and disturbed the people of the United States." Ford's blunder, stated the western provincial paper, was a double blow to himself. "He upset the large Polish-American community; traditionally Democratic just when he recently seemed to be making inroads," the *Guardian* said. The Polish vote was concentrated in Chicago and in Pittsburgh. These two cities were located in two important industrial states; in each state the Polish vote was an important factor. The remark, concluded the *Guardian,* made Ford look incompetent.

The *Daily Express* reported the President's summoning to the White House the brain power of the Republican Party, including Mrs. Anne Armstrong, the United States Ambassador to Great Britain, and his running mate, Robert Dole, for a strategy meeting. One result of the meeting was that President Ford should gain the initiative by hard slugging against Carter. Since the President's blunder in the second debate, Carter was "jumping all over him," said the *Daily Express.* The Democratic candidate, as reported in the *Times,* spent two days campaigning in or near Chicago. He spoke to the various ethnic groups—the Polish-Americans, the Irish-Americans, the Italian-Americans, and the blacks and, finally, to the members of the powerful Democratic Party committee headed by Richard Daley. Wherever Carter went those days he was accompanied by Boss Daley, who always spoke briefly of Carter before the candidate spoke. Carter seemed much more confident since the second debate. His staff told Peter Strafford of the *Times* that Carter now had wind in his political sails.

One result of the White House strategy conference, wrote the *Times,* was the President's admitting publicly that he had made a mistake about Russian domination of Eastern Europe. He invited sixteen or seventeen ethnic group leaders of Eastern European origins to the White House for a conference that lasted almost an hour. These ethnic leaders, said the *Times,* were already Ford supporters. The success of the exclusive meeting was attested to by one of the leaders, stating to the press upon emerging from the conference, "The President put the record straight and we forgive him." President Ford issued a forthright statement: "The countries of Eastern Europe are, of course, dominated by the Soviet Union. Were it not for the presence of more than thirty Russian divisions there now, the countries of Eastern Europe would long ago have achieved their freedom. The United States never has, does not now, and never will recognize, accept, or acquiesce in Soviet domination of Eastern

Europe. The peoples of Eastern Europe yearn for freedom. While their countries may be physically dominated, their spirit is not. Their spirit has never been broken and never will be. Someday they will be free."

Another result of the White House strategy conference was reported by Ross Mark in the *Daily Express* and resulted in the American Presidential campaign being thrown into great turmoil by allegations that Carter had had adulterous affairs with several women when Governor of Georgia. Carter angrily denied the charges: "I have never engaged in extramarital relations. I believe the American public will show its good sense by not responding to these baseless allegations." It was an open secret in Washington, continued the *Daily Express,* that the rumors of Carter's alleged affairs emanated from the Washington headquarters of President Ford's Republican election committee. Perhaps, personally, the President had nothing to do with the attempt to smear Carter's reputation. The charges, however, threw the Democratic candidate, who was billed as "Mr. Clean from the South," off balance. Jack Anderson, America's foremost investigative reporter, investigated the rumors thoroughly before declaring them completely false. Carter thanked the American and the British newspapers, which had withheld publication until Anderson filed his report, for not publishing the lie. "The attempts to smear Carter," concluded the *Daily Express,* "have further lowered the tone of Ford's sorry Presidential campaign."

The campaign continued in a mudslinging atmosphere as Carter relaxed at his home in Plains for a few days. There Carter read the latest opinion polls with consolation and satisfaction. Shortly before the second debate he had led President Ford by only two percent. Since the President's fantastic goof about Eastern Europe, Carter's two percent had bounced up to a ten percent lead over his opponent. Would President Ford slip further in the opinion polls? Some members of the British press, including the *Daily Express,* predicted that he would. At that time the President, in search of Jewish votes, made a crucial decision to sell Israel devastating weapons—a conversion bomb that exploded with the power of a mini atom bomb called the Full Air Explosion (FAE). Israel received a hundred and twenty American-built heavy tanks, the M60.

The President's goof about Eastern Europe was discussed by Dole in an interview with a reporter from the *Evening Standard*. The Republican Vice-Presidential candidate expressed the convictions that the President could easily lose the election. Ford's gaffes were a fatal mistake that would cause him to lose conservative support. With more confidence than his running mate, the President announced that if he were elected Dr. Kissinger would continue as Secretary of State. Furthermore, President Ford stated to Campbell of the *Evening Standard* that he had made only one slip in the televised debate of ninety minutes "while Carter was guilty of more than fourteen distortions in the same time."

The President's gaffe over the conditions in Eastern Europe was continually brought to the attention of the British people as the British press repeatedly discussed President Ford's remark about the Soviet Union in Eastern Europe. Winchester wrote in the *Guardian* that the effect of the mistake rumbled and reverberated across the European nations like "a funeral bell." Winchester explained that "rarely has a full-grown Presidential race ever turned around so suddenly and so decisively. Last week the British were watching the 'I-told-you-so' steady overhaul of the Atlanta hare by the Grand Rapids tortoise, as Carter made mistake after misjudgment, after error. But now the tortoise had flipped over onto its carapace and the jubilant rodent goes merrily on while Ford aides do the best to right their candidate and get him lumbering on the race against the finishing line which looks awfully close. Indeed, Ford had spent the last few days trying to explain what he meant when he said what he said."

The *Daily Telegraph* told its readers that both Carter and President Ford had removed the gloves and were using tougher language and making more personal attacks on one another while the public appeared to continue apathetic. The President visited Dallas, the first President to do so since President John Kennedy in 1963. Both President Ford and his host, Connally, wore bulletproof vests in the parade and in all public appearances. It was obvious to some British reporters, including Richard Burton of the *Daily Telegraph,* that the President was reeling from the most disastrous week of his election campaign as he sought to overcome the self-inflicted damage in the television debate and the Carter attempts to portray him as an incompetent Nixon.

Back in Washington, Ford once more sought the advice of his running mate and other advisers on ways to rectify the incredible mistakes about the Soviet Union's control of Eastern Europe. Again, the President was urged to restrict himself mainly to the White House and to display his "Presidential image" to the voters, leaving the brunt of the campaign to the Vice-Presidential candidate. Again, Ford ignored the consensus of opinion of those attending the White House conference and immediately renewed his active campaign; this time in New York, New Jersey, and Illinois. Furthermore, he arranged for a three-hundred-mile whistle-stop tour through several Midwestern states. Stella Winter reported in the *Evening Mail* that Carter and President Ford were like "two highly strung racehorses thundering toward the finish line in the United States Presidential election race" and that both were conducting last-minute blitz campaigns. Both candidates were striving strenuously to put their ideas before the voters amid increasing criticism of their failure to deal with the real national issues and problems.

Both candidates, as reported by Jane Rosen in the *Guardian,* were continuously active in New York City with parades, speeches, and conferences in their continuing competition for the Jewish support. From New York City the President rushed back to the White House for a long and fruitful conference with Israel's Foreign Minister, Yigal Allon, who, upon emerging from the White House, told reporters that his talk with the President was very constructive and that the response to Israel's request for more monetary loans and military weapons was "most satisfactory." No new secret arms agreement was reached, but the President promised to expedite the delivery of some military weapons on which the Pentagon had stalled.

President Ford's decision to speed weapons shipments, stated the *Guardian,* obviously was intended to influence Jewish voters in the key states of New York, New Jersey, Illinois, and California. The Jews, said the *Guardian,* held "a special dimension" of voting strength in those states. In the San Francisco debate, Carter had attacked President Ford for failing to give Israel adequate support. Of the total American military weapons sold to the Middle East, Carter stated, the Ford Administration had shipped to Israel only twenty percent, while eighty percent went to the Arab states. The President replied sharply that his Administration had sold Israel more than $4 billion of military hardware and that he was dedicated to the survival and security of Israel.

Meanwhile, as President Ford conferred with the Israeli Foreign Minister, Carter was meeting with many Jewish leaders in small groups and individually. His performance, declared the *Times,* was undoubtedly impressive. The candidate parried such questions as he preferred not to answer in a straightforward way. A rabbi informed Carter of an anecdote that was going the rounds in New York City: "Young Jimmy was asked by his father whether he cut down the peanut plant. 'Father,' said young Jimmy, 'I cannot tell a lie. Maybe I did, and maybe I didn't.' "

As reported in the *Guardian* and the *Herald,* John Dean reappeared in the Presidential campaign when he gave an interview on NBC in which he stated that Richard Cook, a White House aide to President Nixon, had talked with Congressman Ford several times about a pending vote in the House Banking and Clearing Committee, which had been endeavoring to launch an investigation of the Watergate break-in before the 1972 Presidential election. The vote, said Dean, would have given the committee the power to compel witnesses to attend its hearings and to be put under oath to testify. Congressman Ford, the Republican House Minority Leader, was in charge of lining up Republican votes on the committee, which were eventually able to turn down any inquiry. Ford stated that he had no recollections of talking via telephone or otherwise with anyone in the White House about stopping the House Banking and Currency Committee's investigation of Nixon campaign money and its relation to Watergate. (Wright Patman of Texas was chairman of this important committee.)

October 12, Columbus Day, found Carter back in Chicago and, as earlier, the guest of political boss Daley. They, said the *Guardian,* attended mass in the Church of Our Lady of Pompeii in the heart of the Italian-American area. Speaking to an American audience, composed largely of Italian-Americans and Polish-Americans, Carter, referring to Russia's position in Eastern Europe, stated, "We will never accept permanent domination over countries that want to be free." The *Guardian* emphasized Carter's and Mondale's activities as they flew about the country jubilantly exploiting the President's blunder by attending every ethnic parade, festivity, and banquet they could find, never missing an opportunity to denounce Ford's "ignorance of foreign countries." However, the *Guardian* reported that leaders of the Eastern European ethnic groups, who were infuriated by the President's gaffe in the debate, were slowly returning to the Republican fold—especially after the affable White House conference. The newspaper explained that, although no other politician could equal Carter's personal commitment to Israel, many Jews mistrusted his politics and found fundamentalism alien.

Nevertheless, Ford was further embarrassed by a rumor, very popular in Washington, that the President would issue a pardon to all those who were in any way involved in Watergate—including John Mitchell, John Ehrlichman, and Robert Haldeman. The *Irish Times* was among the papers that quoted the President as saying there was absolutely no validity to the pardon rumor. Despite President Ford's denial of the rumor the *Guardian* published the latest Gallup poll, which showed that Ford was slipping. Carter had a comfortable lead in the South and in the Midwest. The two candidates were about even in the West, and Carter was losing in the Northeast. He was using populist issues, charging that the Ford Administration was running the country for the benefit of the "fat cats" and that his Administration favored special interests.

President Ford was further embarrassed politically, announced the *Herald,* when he secured a Congressional appropriation for a national immunization program against swine flu and thirty-three persons in sixteen states died after having had the flu shots. The President, amid much publicity, took a swine flu injection to allay a scare throughout the nation.

But not all news concerning the President's campaign was embarrassing. The *Herald* and other British newspapers announced that President Ford was cleared of all charges of illegally using funds. Charles Ruff, special Congressional Watergate investigator, announced that, after several weeks of investigation, nothing was found that showed Congressman Ford had acted illegally in any way in regard to the donations of the labor unions to his Congressional campaigns.

With charges of earlier illegal use of money in his campaigns found to have been false, the President left the White House on a speaking tour. Speaking at Yonkers, a suburb of New York City, President Ford brought international attention to the occasion by signing a bill into law in the Yonkers City Hall. The law transferred money from the federal government in Washington to the states and the cities. Yonkers, on the Hudson, was a step toward decentralization. The President stated that he trusted the local bureaucrats on the Potomac. President Ford's followers, said the *Times,* cheered at the appropriate places. His crowds, neither large nor enthusiastic, were composed mostly of schoolchildren who were obviously happy to get away from school. The President appeared to be relaxed, at ease, and smiled frequently. He turned most questions that he did not want to answer aside with laughter, the *Times* reported.

At a Liberal Party dinner in New York City, Carter, as Campbell wrote in the *Evening Standard,* sent a New York City crowd "into a spasm of cheering when he made a sarcastic reference" to the fact that President Ford had twice refused to say whether he had tried to head off a Congressional investigation of the Watergate burglary as early as 1972. Ian Ball reported to the *Daily Telegraph* that Harlem was moved by Carter's exuberance of a Southern revivalist at a camp meeting. The Democratic candidate gave a large audience of blacks exactly what they wanted, reported the *Daily Telegraph.* CARTER: "I need to covet with you. I need your help. Will you give it to me?" It had been eight years since a candidate for the Presidency had visited Harlem.

As the third debate approached, both the *Irish Times* and the *Economist* were outspoken in their criticism of the American Presidential campaign. President Ford blundered along, said the *Economist,* explaining, "Popular enthusiasm for Ford and Carter continues to be sluggish and volatile at the same time." The campaign was soggy and sour; the public was visibly uninspired by either candidate. No Presidential campaign in America since the 1920s had been as uninteresting, declared the *Irish Times,* and "certainly none in which two leading candidates were less loved or less hated. More would vote against Carter because of his religiosity or against Ford for his stupidity." Indeed, the majority of the voters had to choose between two men about whom they knew little and cared less, concluded the Dublin paper. The press and the media, reported the *Economist,* were watching despondently for the next verbal goof by one side or the other.

The President was determined to go out in the country from airport to whistle-stop and from Elks lodge to church social, but his advisers and his staff, who were no great shakes, were stubbornly opposed. Betty Ford was talented, spirited, and loyal, but her health was a persistent worry. Luckily, President Ford's opponent was no wonder campaigner. Carter's performance on the political stump was equally circumspect and narrow. To get the electorate to vote in respectable numbers and to vote for one of the two candidates, neither of whom had yet shown a good reason to get to the polls, was going to be a real problem, thought the *Economist.*

The Scottish *Herald,* in an editorial headed "Nobody's Favorite," said the American Presidential campaign in the Bicentennial year was negative and futile. Solid issues facing the American people had vanished into a void of silence, and interesting proceedings were enlivened only by the speculation as to whether President Ford or Carter would make the next gaffe, lamented the *Herald.* To the Glasgow paper an alarming number of American voters seem to be reluctant to go to the polls. This would produce the lowest turnout for a Presidential election in decades. Some United States voters, concluded the editorial, were ready to vote for nobody rather than for somebody in November.

The *Daily Telegraph* predicted, with an appreciable degree of accuracy, that, if Carter were elected President, his family would become roving envoys as he sent the Carters abroad, one by one, on one excuse or another. In essence they would be roving ambassadors. They would hold conferences with leaders in foreign countries to say, for the President, we in America care about you. Returning to the White House, they would report to the President on what we should do to correct the mistakes of the past and to strengthen an alliance of friendship.

The *Economist* described the American Presidential campaign as the "battle of the dwarfs," adding that the way President Ford "handled *l'affaire Butz* let the voters know that he was challenging the Reverend Peanut in the race for the election." The most sophisticated Americans were dumbstruck, the *Economist* said, that the Secretary of Agriculture could be so unguarded in front of "John Dean, the sneak with the tape recorder memory, who had sunk Butz's old boss Richard Nixon's American Society's well-being kings into political oblivion." In all likelihood, said the journal, "Ford was too stupid to see that, which was why he could go through the official ritual of denouncing what his secretary said without having to fire him." Some people, thought the *Economist,* were deciding to vote for Carter on the basis of his being "a better devil." Millions more, the *Economist* thought, were taking another look at the third-party candidates or even confirming their decision to boycott the election entirely. "In fact, murmuring questions were heard about a political system that offered such dwarfs epigones in the place of genuine destruction," the *Economist* added.

The *Times* was among the British papers that witnessed Carter's clearly aging during that last year—all of which he had spent campaigning—but the crowds to whom he spoke loved him more than they had in the youth of his campaign.

If Carter looked unusually fatigued, President Ford appeared refreshed and in good campaign spirits as he traveled aboard a whistle-stop train. President Ford repeatedly attacked Carter from the back of the "Honest Abe" train as it sped through the Midwest. The *Times* quoted the President as saying, "Jimmy Carter will say anything anywhere to be President of the United States. When he's in California, he sounds like Cesar Chavez; when he's in Chicago, he sounds like Mayor Daley; when in New York, he sounds like Congresswoman Bella Abzug; when he's in Washington, he sounds like my old friend George Meany and when he comes to Illinois, he sounds like a little old peanut farmer. He wavers and he wanders, he wiggles and he wobbles and he shouldn't be President of the United States." The *Times* noted, as so many others had done repeatedly, that President Ford was not an inspiring speaker, and Patrick Brogan, the *Times* reporter who accompanied the President, was convinced that the President gathered only a few voters in Illinois when he traveled whistle-stop through the state. Furthermore, President Ford several times announced he was happy to be in "A" town when he was actually in "B" town.

If the *Times* did not believe that the President was gaining many votes in Illinois, it was convinced that Carter's interview with *Playboy* continued to worry the Democratic campaign and to jolt its hitherto unshakable confidence. Mayor Daley was well aware that no Democrat had ever reached the White House unless he carried Illinois. Therefore, Daley was leaving no leaf unturned to deliver the Illinois vote to the Democratic nominee. While Daley was obviously firmly scornful of his party's nominee, the Democratic machine would roll out the red carpet for his support. Carter's *Playboy* interview had caused "a gale of hilarity to sweep the country from coast to coast." One political writer noted, stated the *Times,* that from now on Carter was in dead trouble with every woman he met because of his lustful eyes. "In his [Carter's] heart he knows your wife" was common gossip in many cities in the United States.

As a speaker, Steele wrote in the *Guardian,* Carter appeared actually more attractive than his opponent, but he was not another Kennedy, though his style was desperately imitative. Steele remembered that a Democrat told him, "The American voters could end up preferring the blockhead they know to the one they don't know."

The enterprising reporter assigned to the "Peanut Two" jet to accompany Carter in his "Peanut One" wrote an interesting article for the *Guardian* on a day with the Democratic candidate. The journey, which began in the Deep South, moved rapidly northward, with the two 727 Boeing jets landing two hours later at Albany, New York. In a brief speech, Carter emphasized preserving an intricate relationship with the voters, but, added Steele in the *Guardian,* "he is really more interested in exposure in the media than he is in face-to-face encounters."

From Albany the candidate and the press flew to Rochester for a second speech. There Carter promised never to raise the income tax on the wage earner; he would only close the loopholes of the rich. "You can depend on me for that," he assured the audience. For months, Steele reported in the *Guardian,* Jimmy and Rosalynn Carter had traveled around the country, meeting people at factory gates, in barber shops and at farmers' markets. "We talked a little and listened a lot," explained Carter. His entire campaign organization was not built up on professional politicians but composed of "people like you who don't want anything selfish out of government but just want to be treated fairly." At Rochester the candidate made sure that the albatross of Ford's Eastern Europe error never unwrapped itself from the President's neck. Next to Carter on the platform, the *Guardian* reported, sat a woman translating his words into sign language for any in the audience or among the television viewers who were deaf. The candidate concluded his remarks by calling attention to the woman and held up his left hand with just his forefinger, his little finger, and his thumb outstretched. "I only know one expression in sign language. Does anyone know what this means? 'I love you.' "

In Syracuse the local campaign workers elbowed their way too close to the candidate. "The fat-bellied, puffing policemen," the *Guardian* stated, became panicky until the "Secret Service men took over and bands began to play 'Happy Days Are Here Again.' " Introduced by the local party chairman, Carter began his speech with a series of questions: "How many of you believe it's time to have a CIA and an FBI obey the laws? How many of you believe it's time to have a fair income tax system?" By his interrogations, Steele concluded in the *Guardian,* Carter had aroused "four emotions in a brilliantly controlled sequence; impatience for change, anger at the status quo, plus pride in the country and faith in himself." Shortly before five o'clock the Boeing 727s, "Peanut One" and "Peanut Two," lifted off the ground at Syracuse for New York City, where Carter made two more speeches that evening and night.

The following morning Carter flew to Detroit, where, said the *Guardian,* he addressed the Economic Club at noon with a well-prepared speech on crime. In an excellent example of Carter's strength he stated, "When I was Governor I visited Georgia prisons many times—talked with inmates to learn about what their problems were and what we could do to help them. We found black people there and white people there, well-educated and illiterate people. Thirty-five percent of all inmates of our prisons—perhaps of yours—are mentally retarded. We found young people and old people. We found poor people but we didn't find rich people. The corporate criminal, the white-collar criminals too often get off with a slap on the wrist. This can only cause contempt for the whole concept of equal justice." White-collar crimes cost this country dearly, yet there had not been a felony indictment for price-fixing since Ford took office. A few radical souls, Steele reported in the *Guardian,* clapped noisily while the rest of the Economic Club sat silent.

Carter outlined his proposed plans, as stated in the *Guardian,* for keeping the Attorney General out of politics, for appointing federal judges on merit, for eliminating double standards in justice, for shortening the long wait before cases came into court, for enlisting citizen volunteers to help in high-crime areas, for introducing and improving recreational facilities in areas where juvenile crime was high, for prison reform, and, most important of all, for a stronger economy and more jobs for the minority and ethnic groups.

This was a major speech for the Democratic nominee. The *Guardian* summarized Steele's experiences of those days on "Peanut Two" with Carter: "For all one doubts about his hawkishness in foreign policy, his inexperience in economic management, his deliberate obfuscation on some issues, his blatant trimming on others, this man has a gift of intellectual application, a willingness to abandon prejudice and to accept the complexity of things, and a sense of anger about injustices at least at the margin of society which one cannot help but welcome."

Unlike Carter, President Ford was hindered somewhat by public remarks made by General George Brown, Chairman of the Joint Chiefs of Staff. Public remarks, which may have been true but which the General showed poor judgment in making, were his criticisms of the British military establishment as composed of nothing but generals and admirals and bands. Furthermore, Brown said, the British government had not equipped either part of its military establishment adequately.

The Chairman of the Joint Chiefs of Staff made more trouble for Ford, as related in the *Guardian,* when he stated that Israel and its military forces were a strenuous financial burden on the United States. Brown claimed that he expressed the consensus of the Pentagon opinion when he declared that Israel was given too many military arms at times when the United States actually needed the equipment for its own defense. The President reprimanded the General but did not fire or demote him— as a number of Americans urged the President to do. Ford stated that the General was ill advised in some of his remarks. The *Herald* said that General Brown's remarks were another campaign headache for President Ford. The General's latest vocal outburst was that he doubted that the United States had the stomach to face up to the Soviet Union. Brown was highly respected for his military competence, despite his reputation for bluntness.

With the advent of September's cool nights and warm days nearly all members of the British press began to make predictions on the outcome of the election. The *Guardian* was among the first to do so. Winchester, reporting for the *Guardian,* had been in the United States for several years. He was convinced that the Democrats were set for sweeping gains in both houses of Congress. With the nation plunged into a trough of apathy, the *Guardian* stated, it was the local races that were attracting most attention. "The campaigns for the principal state legislative bodies show the mood of the nation far better than does the race for the Presidency," Winchester wrote. Americans were turning more to the left again as the Democrats were winning more elections to the Senate, the House of Representatives, and the state legislatures. An unprecedented number of Congressmen would not return to public office, correctly predicted the *Guardian*—some because of scandal, or sex, or senility. Not returning were Senators Hart of Michigan, Mansfield of Montana, Scott of Pennsylvania, and Symington of Missouri, leaders who had dominated the Senate for nearly two decades. In the House of Representatives twenty-seven were gone—led by Wilbur Mills and Wayne Hays. The Democrats, concluded the *Guardian,* had only one worry—money.

Brian Vine reported in the *Daily Express* in mid-October that there were only fourteen more days before the American voters must decide "whether to trade in their old Ford for a new Model C or to keep their old Ford for four more years." Vine added, "With a face full of teeth, a voice full of hope, a Plainsman reaching out for the American dream which a bewildered post-Watergate public was easily tempted to make true, Carter still was a mystery man, a farm boy with a suspicious amount of guile about him." What really intrigued the American voters, the *Daily Express* reported, was a matter that had appeared previously in the British press—the men behind the man Carter. They were called the Carter clique, the Atlanta Mafia, the Front Room Boys.

"Never had such a motley bunch emerged to carry, with such ease, an obscure politician to the steps of the White House. Who were these muscle workers?" asked Vine in the *Daily Express* and then answered: Hamilton Jordan, brilliant political science graduate of the University of Georgia, campaign manager; Jody Powell, the leading campaign strategist and press secretary; Pat Anderson, who said he got through college with the help of "booze and broads"; Dr. Peter Bourne, a British psychiatrist, proconsul, and the original Capitol Hill contact; Charles Kirbo, a corporate lawyer for the Coca-Cola Corporation, honorary Chief of Staff and trusted adviser; Lawrence Klein, chief economic adviser; Gerald Rafshoon, who molded the candidate's image on television commercials and who once worked as a Twentieth Century-Fox publicist. Vine, describing the aides as Carter's "little liver pills to Washington," said that they could begin a new brand of government, which would "blow through the stagnant corridors of Washington with the freshness of a morning breeze across the peanut country."

Meanwhile, the British, unknown to most Americans, were conducting public opinion polls. President Ford, said the *Daily Express,* was shocked when he learned that a British opinion poll showed that only thirty-four percent of the British had a good opinion of the United States. This, stated the *Daily Express,* was the lowest in twenty-two years, or since

1954—and could cost the President the White House. The polls undermined President Ford's comments that Carter was slandering America's good name and "giving our allies doubts about us and our policies." The President placed Dr. Kissinger on alert to be ready to answer Carter on any foreign policy statements. And the recent Harvard professor told a *Daily Express* reporter how difficult it was "to drive information into Ford's head." Furthermore, Kissinger told others that State Department men spent many hours with the President giving him pat responses for his television foreign policy debate with Carter in San Francisco. But this resulted, concluded Kissinger, in "the right responses coming out at the wrong time and on different subjects."

The *Yorkshire Post* editorialized on President Ford's unpopularity. It stated, with tongue in cheek, that the President must have had some difficulty with the English language to say that Eastern European countries were free to conduct their own internal and external affairs in the way that Western European countries were. "No rational person could argue otherwise." Furthermore, the President stated that the Pope had signed the Helsinki Agreement and that he would never have done so if the Agreement meant that Eastern Europe was dominated by the Soviets. This blunder would not win Ford a single Catholic vote, thought this member of the British press. Indeed, many in Washington expressed utter dismay at President Ford's remarks.

The *Economist* discussed another phase of the American election and predicted erroneously that one important casualty of the Presidential campaign could well turn out to be the Electoral College—that "shadowy body" through which the indirect election of a new President was performed. The present arrangement had been in vogue since the adoption of the Twelfth Amendment to the Constitution in 1804. "Three times in the nineteenth century," the *Economist* said, "this ill-taken system had installed a President who came in second in popular vote." In 1968 the imperfection of the American Electoral College system was adequately illustrated, the *Economist* stated, "when an elector in North Carolina chosen to vote for Richard Nixon actually voted for George Wallace."

The postelection Congress considered a Constitutional amendment to abolish the electoral college by substituting direct popular election of the President and Vice-President. The proposed amendment enjoyed wide support. President Nixon publicly urged its adoption, and the House of Representatives passed it by an overwhelming majority. A Senatorial filibuster killed it in 1970. Senators from the Southern states, supported by a few small-state Senators elsewhere, defeated the proposal. Apparently, they feared the erosion of states' rights and were willing to forgo the principle of having a larger say in the election directly of the nation's two most important executives. The *Economist* believed that the disproportionate allocation of the election strength, the greatest defect of the

Electoral College method, gave the leading candidate all of a state's votes, with no regard to the narrowness of his margin.

Organized labor, the *Economist* stated, was supporting Carter, not because of any great genuine enthusiasm for the Democratic candidate but largely because of labor's "utter disgust" with the Ford Administration. In the opinion of organized labor, nothing could be worse for America than another four years with Ford as President. Under the federal election laws, the AFL-CIO was prohibited from contributing money to Carter's campaign fund, but it did have two other contributing factors to offer—a vote registration drive among the millions of union members and a large group of canvassers, the *Economist* explained.

Other agencies of British public opinion, including the *Evening Standard,* discussed adversely the American Electoral College in the choosing of the President and Vice-President. Campbell reported in the London afternoon paper that the total number of votes each candidate received was immaterial to the outcome of the election. "What matters," stated Campbell, was "winning a majority in the Electoral College, that creaking eighteenth-century anachronism which allows each state a certain number of electoral votes according to its size [the number of Congressmen and Senators it has]. Consequently, the grand prize of the Presidency goes to the individual who puts together the winning combination of states giving him the magic number of 270 electoral votes."

As reported in the *Daily Mirror,* a televised debate previously agreed to by representatives of President Ford and Carter, between the two Vice-Presidential candidates, never before attempted, was shown in Britain and America. Senators Dole and Mondale were the first opponents for the Vice-Presidency to engage in a televised debate.

Dole's first wife, Phyllis, met him when he was recovering in a hospital from a military wound and massaged his right arm until he had some use of it—and became the mother of his only child, who, in 1976, was twenty-two years old. Phyllis, who had remarried, told reporters, "I hate to see Bob wear out the seat of his pants in that second-place chair. He'd like to be President and I think that's where he's going." Dole had also remarried. His second wife, Mary Elizabeth, was, the *Daily Mirror* stated, "unchallengeably one of the brightest and the most beautiful of Washington's political ladies." Some twelve years younger than Dole's fifty-two years, she was a talented lawyer and an excellent civil bureaucrat.

Mondale was happily married to Joan, an intelligent woman who was the mother of their three teenage children. Mondale had arranged his public life so as to spend more time with his family than Dole did. The *Daily Mirror* said these two men sharply contrasted in the types of campaigns they were waging: Dole was the sharp critic of Carter, a "sock it to 'em" challenger, whereas Mondale was more of a humorist, a less bitter critic than his opponent. When Dole challenged Mondale to state where the Democrats stood on the issues of the campaign, Mondale, smiling in disbelief, smoothly ran down the list: "more jobs in the economy, lower prices, fairer taxes, better hospitals, more houses and stronger leadership." Dole, the *Daily Mirror* continued, accused the Democrats of creating World War II and condemned them for causing war casualties in World War II, and in the Korean and Vietnam Wars, equal to the total population of Detroit. In answer Mondale stated that "such remarks showed Dole to be a hatchet man."

This debate, held in the Alley Theatre, Houston, Texas, the *Times* reported, made dismal television. It was a sharp-tongued exchange between the two members of the United States Senate and delivered with customary blunt edges. Mondale, the more knowledgeable, seemed to be extremely nervous. Dole, in exact contrast, was more relaxed and, the *Times* said, played the role of the television comic until he ran out of jokes. The debate, won by Mondale, did wonders for his campaign, concluded the London independent popular newspaper.

The *Observer* reported that the debate was "almost a straightforward confrontation between the traditional Democratic and the Republican views on how to manage the economy, how much and whom to tax." Dole, the conservative Republican, scarcely mentioned unemployment and social problems. He charged the Democrats, the *Observer* said, with not caring about inflation—the cruelest tax of all. Mondale promised better health care. He came "across as intelligent and concerned but without the passion he sometimes gets before a live audience. He displayed a touch of sanctimoniousness," never smiling or cracking a joke.

Dole's big advantage, continued the *Observer,* turned out to be his damaged right arm. He remarked that the Vice-Presidency was not such a bad job. It was "indoor work and included no heavy lifting." Most noticeable, the *Observer* maintained, was the way these two Senatorial stars appeared to be so weak and subdued. The curse of the Vice-Presidency, an office that was so close to power, yet so ignominiously powerless, seemed to have already possessed them.

The *Observer* expressed a widely accepted British opinion when it wrote that the Presidential election was a nationally recognized bore: "Ford was a pleasant bore; Carter was a boring puzzle." The two major party programs did not reflect the growing complexity of American life, with its inevitable drift toward a more loosely knit democracy in which there was a greater popular participation in government of all sorts and at all levels. Instead, Carter and President Ford endeavored to give the impression, the *Observer* noted, that if elected they would be able to do everything necessary to make America a happier place to live for America's growing population. The signs of the time, the *Observer* concluded, were that more and more of the American people simply did not believe that sort of promise any longer.

Anthony Shrimsley reported in the *Sun* that he had seen two characters who were riding in "Peanut One," which was painted white, orange and blue-and-red-striped. One of the characters was a competent farmer, former Governor of Georgia, ambitious to live in the White House, and the second character was a peanut farmer from nowhere with a talent for capturing "ordinary men's suspicions and resentment of Big Government." Carter rejected rides in Cadillacs or Lincolns, the *Sun* said, because they were the "luxury limousines of the big shots." He had an instinct for the gut anxieties of voters and the ability to take an emotional charge from the people.

Carter's speech style, the *Sun* stated, was curious—full of midsentence pauses and sudden spurts typical of the Southern Bible preacher he was; his speaking style was proudly pedestrian. Upon seeing a friend, Carter remembered the friend's name and where they had been together. The *Sun* argued that Carter's face, "which was usually gray, was now pink and alive. His hair, which had looked gray, began to appear more tawny."

Among the several stops made by "Peanut One" and "Peanut Two" was Kansas City. From the airport, the *Sun* informed its readers, Carter and his entourage made their way to the City Hall, where a large crowd awaited them. In front of the Kansas City Hall, the *Sun* said, Carter discussed the production of corn and soybeans and the Kansas City people loved it. "We have been farmers in my family for two hundred and ten years. I believe in balanced budgets. In my family, we've had some hard times, but we always had the budget balanced. If I'm elected President we're going to have balanced budgets again. You hear a lot about Great Britain and her problems—our unemployment is higher than theirs, and it is higher than Germany's and Japan's." The crowd, Shrimsley wrote in the *Sun,* was with him, a country boy millionaire against the politicians from Washington. "You help me in November," the candidate concluded, "and when I'm inaugurated President in January I'll help you, if I'm elected President, and I don't intend to lose."

The final debate of the campaign was held in Williamsburg, Virginia, on October 22. The *Irish Times* noted a different tone of campaigning at the third and final debate. Both candidates were polite to each other, apologized for their previous mistakes, and promised that neither would make an attack on the other in the last eleven days of the campaign. Carter looked relaxed as he stated that if elected he would put people to work and would lower unemployment. In foreign affairs he promised to never become militarily involved in the internal affairs of another country, "unless our own security was directly threatened." President Ford, continued the *Irish Times,* appeared grim and tense as he stated that, if elected, he would ask the people to tighten their belts and to support increased military defense expenditures to maintain peace. He would eventually reduce the taxes for the middle-income wage earners.

Millions who watched the third debate on the television screen agreed with the opinion polls and the British press that Carter won the final debate. It was Carter's greatest performance, said the *Times*. Some Americans thought that each debate became more boring. Mark Frankland wrote in the *Observer* that, as tedious as the debates have been, anyone who has ever heard great oratory might doubt that these "wooden exercises in monologue ought even to be graced with the description of debate."

These debates were remarkable not so much for what they were as for what they promised. For the first time, the President of the United States agreed to face his opponent in a series of television debates. From now on, the *Observer* predicted, television debates would become a significant part of all future American Presidential elections. This year's debates, so unsatisfactory in many ways, would certainly be refined and improved, the paper said, explaining that "the electronic revolution is upon us and can scarcely be stopped." President Ford, the *Observer* stated, sincerely believed that the American Bicentennial Celebration in July bestowed a "heavenly cachet of approval on his Administration." There were public doubts about both candidates. In the President's case the doubt concerned his ability to lead and his competence, and, particularly, his intelligence. While Carter displayed a good mind on all public occasions, the *Observer* declared, he also revealed his calculating ambition to win the Presidency, which made many Americans pause before endorsing him.

The debates were not exciting, but they gave ample opportunity to learn President Ford's and Carter's ideas on public issues. The debates forced attention on the President and Carter rather than on the Republican and the Democratic Parties. President Ford offered the role of a passive President, with a minimum of federal programs and leaving things alone. Carter would be an active President—reorganizing government to make it more efficient and help less-well-off Americans—average Americans—to develop more confidence in the Presidency.

6

The
Campaign Ends

In late October the President left the White House, reported the *Times,* amid the applause and best wishes of the employees who staffed the White House, and promised them that he would not return until after the election. He promised the staff that he would "pull the political surprise of the century" on November 2.

President Ford's last foray into the South began in Raleigh, North Carolina, where he addressed a crowd, said the *Irish Times,* of more than ten thousand. The President's speech was vibrant and his spirits were high. He repeated to the Tarheels his call for a "mandate for limited government, for fiscal responsibility, for rising prosperity, for lower taxes, for military strength and for peace throughout the world." From Raleigh he flew to Richmond, Virginia, where he repeated his clarion call. Some of President Ford's aides insisted that he would win without the South, but they knew that his chances were much better if he could gain states in Carter's native Dixie.

Meanwhile, Carter was also campaigning in Virginia. He spoke to an estimated ten thousand enthusiastic supporters at Alexandria—just across the Potomac from the national capital. Rosalynn Carter created an innovation when she introduced her candidate husband to this large audience. Many professional politicians, stated the *Irish Times,* would have received compensation to deliver the sort of speech Mrs. Carter delivered with ease. Both Carters were in fluent form as they delighted thousands of loyal followers. Rosalynn drew a loud round of applause when she said, "We need a working man in the White House and Jimmy is a working man." She received even louder applause when she exclaimed, "Jimmy produced a budget surplus every year he was Governor of Georgia." In fact, said the Dublin daily newspaper, Mrs. Carter did such an excellent job at introducing her husband that he could have said almost anything and he would have won the full support of the large emotional and excited

96

crowd. The Democratic candidate delivered his familiar speech, racing swiftly through the Watergate episode, denouncing government secrecy, revealing the plight of the minorities in America, showing the dreadful state of unemployment, and then concluded by once more declaring his love for America and his great respect for all Americans. His last sentence was a plea for assistance: "Help me in the next ten days and together we will make this country great once again."

Now that the President had taken a short coffee break, as it were, before his grand finale, while the challenger was resting his feet in his home at Plains, it is fitting to digress a moment for a few comments not directly involving the political issues of the campaign.

As previously noted, on occasion, bits of humor and wit were introduced into the campaign that largely ignored major American issues but stressed personalities. John Pilger wrote in the *Daily Mirror* that the American political system, following a "pregnancy, constipation, indigestion and boredom was about to give birth to a new President—a President Gerry or a President Jimmy." The *Daily Mirror* quoted President Lyndon Johnson's statement when he was President and President Ford was leader of the Republican minority in the House of Representatives: "Gerry Ford is actually so dumb that he cannot chew gum and fart at the same time." The London daily paper said, "If the American voters cannot accept Carter's Bible-totin', born-again religion, or continue to retain Ford's dumbness, there are more than two hundred other candidates running for the Presidency." These candidates included Ernie Whitford, who was campaigning on a single-issue platform, namely, to wipe out constipation. "I say," wrote Pilger, "let's hear loud applause and a big hurrah for President Ernie."

Another diversion from the main issues of the campaign and the two chief Presidential candidates involved former Senator McCarthy. When "Clean Gene" McCarthy was informed that a recent Gallup poll had given him six percent of the nation's vote and that the press had called him a potential spoiler, McCarthy said, "Me a spoiler! What is there to spoil?" The *Daily Mirror* explained the quote, indicating the complicated and antique inner workings of the American election process—the Electoral College.

Jonathan Steele reported in the *Guardian* on the unusual mother of Jimmy Carter, Miss Lillian, who was very active in the campaign, though she was in her late seventies. She, according to Steele, gave a standard introduction: "My name is Miss Lillian and my boy is running for President." She made more than six hundred speeches for Carter, and Steele quoted her boasting, "And I couldn't have made that many without being good. When Jimmy was coming into Madison Square Garden to accept the Democratic Presidential nomination I had such a feeling of awe that I wanted to weep. I believe it was the first time I realized what Jimmy was doing and that if he was elected he would be the most powerful man in the world." She had been so busy campaigning that she had never thought about it, Steele said, but then she talked out loud: "Oh, Lord, this is the truth. That is my son." He was almost like a cathedral to her, the *Guardian* reporter stated. He was a part of the Carter peanut warehouse and the water tower, which was painted in the Bicentennial red, white and blue. Steele wrote that she reflected on the white frame Plains Baptist Church, saying, "One of its Sunday school teachers was on the verge of becoming President—but the church remained impervious to change." The church, Steele explained, dominated the life of the white community of Plains and reflected the social habits of the town.

Steele wrote that once, during the campaign, Miss Lillian saw four blacks wanting to attend the church. "I went over to speak to them," Steele quoted Miss Lillian. "I was praying, 'O Lord, please let them come into the church.' I couldn't invite them in. We have to keep the door locked until ten minutes to eleven, because we have such huge crowds. I told them I was glad to see them. They said they had come to attend church. I said, 'That's just fine.' " Later, Steele wrote, when she was in her pew her son Jimmy came in. "I whispered to him, 'Jimmy, there are four blacks outside and I hope to goodness they let them in.' " He said, "I think they will." He went to the front to join the Sunday school. As the service started she looked up and saw four blacks being given seats in the front row. In Plains, as in so many other Southern communities, Steele said, the church has defined the lives of generations of people.

Miss Lillian, the *Guardian* continued, had lived in a simple world of personal morality and loyalty to the way of life that surrounded her. "In her lifetime an astonishing liberation of the South had occurred," Steele wrote. "The main beneficiaries have not been the blacks but the silent members of the whites." The Carters, concluded the provincial paper, were good, religious people, God-fearing, law-abiding, charitable when they could be, cautious when they felt they must be. The *Daily Express* also reported that Miss Lillian was out lecturing or speaking to the elderly, promising them that she would look after their interests if Carter won the White House. "If he doesn't, he's gonna catch the Devil from his Mamma," the *Daily Express* quoted Miss Lillian as promising with a wink.

Louis Heren published a Carter family article in the *Times* simultaneously with Steele's article in the *Guardian*. The greatest contrast was that the *Guardian* article dwelt on Carter's mother, whereas the Heren article emphasized the candidate's religious background and experiences. Heren's article explained the American system of choosing a President more than did the Steele article. "Americans' great faith in renewal helped to explain their intense interest in Presidential elections and in slogans such as the New Deal or the New Frontier," Heren wrote. "The inauguration of a new occupant of the White House could become a new national rebirth. For a few brief weeks everything could be magically new, nearly everything possible and because of that belief many things were possible."

Heren added the belief that helped in the success of Jimmy Carter— the Jimmy Who?—the relative unknown who came out of the Southern piney woods to run for President. He was the Democratic nominee in part because he believed that he was born again. Carter's rebirth, or what psychologists would describe as a conversion experience, did introduce him to a large constituency, perhaps the largest silent majority in American political history. Heren wrote that "clearly Evangelicanism had become a potentially powerful force in the land since morality in government became an issue. The majority, however, still see secularism as appropriate for a modern pluralistic society such as the United States." Carter made known his religious background, Heren noted, when he stated that "my wife and I were born and raised in innocent times when the normal thing to do was to go to church."

The few days of rest, reading, and relaxation soon ended and the candidates renewed their active campaigns.

In New York City, Carter spoke of Terence Cardinal Cooke having given him some good advice. "If I ever give another interview on the biblical sins of pride and lust," he said, "it will be to a reporter from *Our Sunday Visitor.*"

Meanwhile, the *Evening Standard* declared that President Ford was pinning his hope on a "car salesman," explaining that the President was depending on a "razzmatazz time" though a half dozen of America's largest states with the balding sports broadcaster, Joe Garagiola, who sold cars on a television commercial. The *Evening Standard* reported that in California the President sat down with Garagiola, who asked the President well-rehearsed questions on politics and foreign policy designed to show Ford in the best possible light, eliciting such answers as "Well, Joe, when you have dealt with the representatives of a hundred and twenty-four nations, allies as well as adversaries, you gain confidence and strength." Ford was so delighted with the broadcast, the *Evening Standard* said, that he was going to trundle Garagiola through Illinois, Ohio, Pennsylvania, and New York in a "frantic effort to close the gap," as reported in opinion polls, on Carter in the last nine days of the campaign.

The *Daily Express* declared that President Ford was chased by the Watergate ghost, in that suspicions continued that Ford had obtained the Presidency in exchange for saving Nixon from going to jail. The astonishing backlash from Watergate days, wrote Ross Mark, could damage President Ford's already fragile chances. The President, conscious of this potential danger, was endeavoring to put distance between himself and Nixon.

The *Economist* thought that President Ford would be severely hurt by the economy turning sour just a few days before the election. The American economy was not worse really, the *Economist* said, it was only improving more slowly. Unemployment was up; the Dow-Jones was a hundred points below the high of January, 1973. "Seemingly, the pause that refreshes had become the pause that depresses," the *Economist* summarized.

The *Daily Post and Mercury* announced the President's hitting the campaign trail for the last week of the race and the decisions by the Committee for the Election of the President to spend more than $3 million. The budget decisions, wrote this far western provincial paper, were a last-ditch publicity campaign to try to wipe out Democrat Carter's lead. This huge expenditure was at least one-third of President Ford's media advertising budget for his entire campaign. The President had contracted for fourteen special television and radio programs, which would cost an estimated $4 million.

The agreement entered into mutually between President Ford and Carter at the final debate that no further attacks would be made on each other for the rest of the campaign was disregarded when the President resumed a personal attack on Carter. He accused the Democratic candidate of inexperience and of inviting foreign aggression, when Carter discussed appropriations for the military and of not using military force to prevent Russia from expanding into Yugoslavia upon Marshal Tito's death. Carter answered the President by declaring that it was time to stop bluffing with America's military might. President Ford's campaign headquarters distributed paper cartoons that poked fun at Carter personally; other cartoons showed Carter's sons smoking marijuana. Speaking in South Carolina, Carter stated that these cartoons and story sheets were a "kind of slanderous attack on me and my family members that causes me concern. President Ford ought to be ashamed of it—it's possibly going to hurt him more than it will me."

The *Daily Post and Mercury* reported that, if all of these personal attacks were for the purpose of creating voter enthusiasm, they failed completely, if the pollsters were correctly interpreted. This western provincial paper said that, because interest was negligible and enthusiasm was invisible, the new President would be elected by thirty percent of the electorate. The whole concept of government by the people, the cornerstone of American democracy, was in jeopardy. Professional political analysts were seeking plausible reasons for such a staggering lack of interest in the country's democratic process, wrote Andrew Borowiec, a reporter for the *Daily Post and Mercury*. In attempting to explain the flight from the polls, Borowiec reported that the voter was more mature while sophisticated campaign methods remained unchanged. Electronic media were bringing to America's living room the stereotyped images of smiling candidates promising anything under the sun and indiscriminately attacking opponents on every conceivable issue. "This was clearly not what the post-Vietnam and post-Watergate American expected," Borowiec wrote.

The *Daily Post and Mercury* reporter said one public opinion poll showed that sixty-eight percent did not intend to vote for any candidate who didn't live up to his campaign promises, because the caliber of candidates Ford and Carter did not warrant the effort to vote. Statistically, the United States had the lowest voter turnout among Western democracies and it was diminishing steadily. In the 1964 election only 61.8 percent voted; 1968—60.8 percent; 1972—53.6 percent, and 1976 was estimated at 46 percent. Borowiec contrasted these statistics with the West German vote in 1972—91 percent; in France, 1973—82 percent; in Great Britain, 1970—71 percent. Borowiec said the apathy toward voting was the result of an increasing disillusionment with the American political system.

Were the criteria for electing the President of the United States still valid in the latter half of the twentieth century? Borowiec asked, explaining that the television screen had turned American Presidential candidates into actors. For example, a *Times* reporter described Carter, dressed in a denim jacket, khaki jeans and old boots, in his brother Billy's office in the early morning sipping a cup of black coffee and chatting. Outside tractors hauled trucks piled high with peanuts, and yellow school buses carried blacks and whites together to the same public school. Carter never ceased to emphasize, said the *Times,* how his roots were in Georgia, and how he liked, as well as needed, to recharge himself by contact with his home and business. Thus, the distance that Carter had gone from the heart of Dixie to the threshold of the Presidency was all the more overwhelming, the *Times* said, as one drove through the seeming back-roads of Georgia.

Ross Madden asked the significant question, in the *South Wales Evening Post,* was the American Presidency too tough for one man? Had this, the most powerful job in the world, become too demanding for any one person to perform? There was a growing body of opinion in America that it was no longer fair—or safe—for one man to shoulder a crippling burden of responsibility that grew heavier with each passing year. The *South Wales Evening Post* said President Johnson became a frail shadow of the man he was before taking on the Presidency. Nixon, who spent $50 million to assure himself a second term, in 1976 led a life of semi-invalidism. It was hardly surprising that American political pundits, wrote Madden, were saying openly that the winner of this election could be the last man to tackle the world's number-one job single-handed.

On October 26, the *Guardian* announced that the frenzied battle of the airways had already begun and that both candidates were unleashing a blitz of television and radio commercials paid for out of carefully husbanded campaign checks, now that there was a legally imposed ceiling on election spending. The President was relying heavily on a series of half-hour commercials in five of the key industrial states: California, New York, Illinois, Ohio, and Pennsylvania. These prime-time commercials, showing President Ford with Garagiola, began in California and moved eastward. The thirty-minute film opened with some carefully edited film footage of Ford's rallies during the day, complemented by a good deal of canned applauding and cheering. The commercial then switched to a studio where Garagiola was seen seated with President Ford, Ford's best-looking son, Steve, and Edith Green, a former Democrat who was director of the California Citizens for Ford. Garagiola asked questions and President Ford responded with answers carefully selected and rehearsed several times. The President utilized saturation coverage, the *Guardian* said, with five-minute radio advertisements as tens of thousands of commuters drove to work.

Finally, President Ford included a series of shorter television commercials, which were used during the day at selective times to catch the largest number of viewers. These, said the *Guardian,* included street interviews with voters, who, in answer to a carefully phrased question, always criticized Carter for his vagueness on the issues. Despite these skillfully planned, well-financed commercials on radio and television, the *Guardian* had its own prophecy on the election returns: "Ford will lose the White House."

The *Daily Telegraph,* in a leading editorial, announced its selection in the Presidential race: "With Respect, Ford." This was a most important election whose results would have significant effects, the *Daily Telegraph* said. "It was a contest between something old and something new. In President Ford the Americans would recognize something very familiar. The well-tested way of doing things. Carter was a new phenomenon—a new political animal. An alluring figure, he had a tremendous knack for making liberal policies appear conservative—and vice versa—depending on his audience." The *Daily Telegraph* added, "Carter may well win the election but if he does we believe America has made a mistake." There was an uneasy similarity between Carter's approach to economics and that of the British Labour Party. It was clear, stated the London paper, that Carter would want to spend and spend—to spend on blacks, on health, on education, on housing, on environment, and on practically everything else one can think of except defense, which he would like to cut.

Carter had stated repeatedly that unemployment was the United States' greatest problem but, the *Daily Telegraph* added, he gave only a courtesy nod toward inflation. In contrast, the President brought inflation down to five percent, which he considered entirely too high. "A second reason why we hope Carter will be defeated," the paper concluded, "is that he has had no experience in foreign affairs. We believe that Carter would be soft on European Communism and that he would be a 'me, too' to the softy Democratic Congress in foreign policy instead of offering some creative tensions."

The *Daily Express* agreed with the *Daily Telegraph,* editorializing "For Gerry with love—America's favorite person." Although the article dealt more with Mrs. Ford's speaking talent, her unusual rapport with her audience, her shrewd political ability than with the President himself, the final conclusions were Ford "for continued amicable relations with the British."

Another London paper, the *Daily Mail,* dwelt on Carter's ambiguity under pressure and had doubts about his political judgments. The long and arduous campaign had slowly but unmistakably exposed Carter's soft center, the *Daily Mail* said, in his unthinking readiness to be all things to all men. Yet, the newspaper noted, Carter remained an attractive candidate. He might yet come to offer Americans responsible and energetic leadership. But, to the *Daily Mail,* he looked risky, and the riskier he looked the more the unquestionable honesty of Gerald Ford came into favor. "That's why this newspaper, by a narrow but definite margin, prefers President Ford."

The Scottish papers—the *Scotsman* and the *Herald*—were not as vocal in their choices as the London papers in announcing their respective candidate for the American Presidency. The reporters, housed in the United States, chose to discuss the American election from an international point of view rather than on the basis of personalities. Frank Frazer in the *Scotsman,* for example, predicted with accuracy that "the next Administration to have a significant impact on the life style of the average United States citizen may well be led by neither Jimmy Carter nor Gerald Ford. There is a very strong probability that it will be Arab-dominated and that it will wield its influence upon the people of the world's richest industrialized nation through the supply and the pricing of oil."

The United States and other nations had had a foretaste of what could be in store for them when the Organization of Petroleum Exporting Countries (OPEC) cartel imposed a temporary embargo on petroleum supplies in 1973 in its bid to influence events in the Middle East. The United States created a crash program to reduce its dependence on outside sources of energy. The plan became known as Project Independence, which the Nixon Administration promised would make the United States completely self-sufficient in fuel by 1980. In the election campaign, however, said the *Scotsman,* "American energy problems have been given low rating and emphasis has been on *Playboy* interviews and wealthy golf trips." The Nixon and Ford Administrations, the newspaper added, had bogged down in no decisions as forty-five percent of the United States' oil continued to be imported. "Basically, the Republicans want all restrictions off—for a free market," the *Scotsman* said, and "the Democrats do not trust the oil companies and want some controls retained."

In an editorial, "America's Choice," the *Scotsman* stated that a great many Americans found themselves unattracted by either candidate. There had rarely been a national election in America that aroused so little enthusiasm. The instability of Carter in the public opinion polls showed that the voters were unsure of the Democratic nominee. "One thing that seems certain is that election day will be a great day for apathy," the *Scotsman* wrote, because "Carter was frustrated, if not angry, over a very personal sordid and slanderous attack on him. But he did not blame President Ford himself personally for the nasty example of American election practices."

The attack Carter complained about appeared in a four-page paper called *Heartland*. A cartoon on its cover showed Carter standing in a pulpit holding up a Bible in one hand and a copy of *Playboy* in the other, with the caption "All things to all people." Carter labeled this a "sordid attack" and said that the President should be ashamed to circulate such "trashy political propaganda," the *Scotsman* reported.

The newspaper said it was difficult to make effective attacks on President Ford, except on the grounds that his kindly and bumbling ways made him unstable for the highest office in America. Carter's ambitious, thrusting character, continued the *Scotsman,* did not inspire unusual affection from the voters. Obviously the differences in personality and style played a large part in getting Americans to make up their minds to go to the polls on Election Day or in failing to vote.

The Scottish *Herald* supported the *Scotsman* in believing that the undecided, wavering voters held the key to the American election. According to the latest Gallup poll, as many as three in ten American voters could still vote either way, the *Herald* said, showing interest in the attitudes of groups of American voters and how they were affected by the approach of the election. The highest undecided group, according to the *Herald,* was among people over fifty years of age, with women tending to be more uncertain than men. The *Herald* reported that high school graduates and the upper-income brackets had a higher percentage of uncommitted people, but probably the highest percentage was in the independent voters. Catholics, continued the *Herald,* were concerned about Carter's born-again evangelical faith. Both candidates, said the Glasgow paper, were not very different on many issues. Approximately one-fourth of the supporters for Ford or for Carter were considered switch voters. These undecideds, concluded the *Herald,* held the key to the American election, and where they would go no one knew.

The *Irish Times* withheld picking a Presidential winner but continued to give its readers daily information about the approaching election. Unlike the other sources of British public opinion, the Dublin paper gave attention to statements by the Vice-Presidential candidates. Bob Dole was quoted as having said that "the Democrats, 'the party that gave us George McGovern,' used to believe in a strong America, but no longer. Veterans, in particular, should shudder at the thought of a man like Walter Mondale being only a heartbeat away from the most powerful job in the free world. For, while Governor Carter's proposal to slash defense spending by fifteen billion is irresponsible, the prospect of Senator Mondale sitting near the seat of power offering advice and counsel on defense policy is more than just bad. It's downright frightening."

The next issue of the *Irish Times* carried more about the running mates of Carter and Ford. A few days earlier, Dole, speaking publicly in behalf of the Republican ticket, stated that World War I, World War II, the Korean War, and the Vietnam War were the responsibility of the Democrats. Reporters subsequently confronted Dole with his statement and he denied having made it, whereupon the reporters played a tape of his speech, including the statement, the *Times* noted. Even when hearing his own words, Dole denied them, but later was forced to admit the statement and withdraw his denial. Mondale stated that anyone who had said that the last four wars in which the United States had participated had been caused by the Democrats was "totally irresponsible and despicable," the *Times* added.

Meanwhile, President Ford and Carter were attacking each other's statements on foreign policy. Before the Economic Club in Pittsburgh the President declared that Carter's statements on foreign policy were potentially dangerous, in that they strongly favored isolation. The election, President Ford declared, was a choice between the known and the unknown. Carter, said the *Irish Times*, had been on the defensive the last few days. The newspaper reported Carter-produced quotations from the President's previously made public statements that he would not send United States troops to hot spots in Africa, Europe, and the Middle East. The *Times* quoted Carter saying in Illinois, "I think the world is tired of bluff and blustering where you insinuate you're going to send troops to some country when you know our people won't let you do it." The paper said Carter added that the billions of dollars he would save in the defense budget would be obtained by stopping the administrative waste in the Pentagon rather than by cutting back on armaments.

In the meantime, the *Evening Standard* published an editorial, "A Tawdry Choice," which said that the "American Presidency has lost nothing of its glitter; the problems that confront the President remain matters of vital interest to most of the world but the two men who were appointed gladiators by their respective political parties have succeeded in inspiring little more than a general form of public indifference from all but their most immediate supporters." The *Evening Standard* said that Carter had done his best to spice things up by his *Playboy* interview and that his efforts at being nice to the Irish and to President Ford had raised an occasional roar of laughter by forgetting which state he was speaking in and by dropping the famous Eastern European charges. "But the laughter and the controversy have had a hollow sound as an electorate thirsty for a serious choice of leadership and vision at a time of considerable uncertainty has failed to discern the qualities it seeks in either of the candidates," the *Evening Standard* concluded.

Seen from the eastern side of the Atlantic, the *Evening Standard* continued, news reporters thought that the very nature of the American contest itself was the reason for a tawdry choice. "When the personalities of the individual contenders were submitted to such cruel and increasing scrutiny is it surprising that the result was a computerized package in which the need to be all things to all sections of a variegated electorate was overriding?" the *Evening Standard* asked. The paper added that in the last hectic week the public was seeing the "anything he can do . . ." syndrome in full swing. The President promised to reduce the income tax the minute he was returned to office. His rival, Carter, instead of wondering what had stood in the way of the tax measure during the President's time in office, felt impelled to follow suit.

The campaign was nearing its conclusion. President Ford had only four more days to let the right word swing more in his favor. If the political shift moved fast enough to give him a second term it would be a matter of some relief in Britain. "President Ford may not be a whirlwind of intelligence but he is a sane and straightforward man and a stabilizing influence," the *Evening Standard* said. "Carter has engendered as much doubt about his capabilities as enthusiasm for his freshness. His ill-judged remarks about Ulster were proof of his inexperience, which could prove a dangerous handicap in the most powerful elective office in the world."

And what were the ill-judged Ulster remarks? In Pittsburgh in an Irish St. Patrick's Day parade someone pinned a badge on the lapel of Carter's coat that read "England, get out of Ireland." Photographers rushed up and took pictures of Carter wearing the badge. Only then did Carter read the badge and remove it from his coat—too late to prevent wide distribution of photographs in America and Great Britain. Later, in a speech, the Democratic nominee told a cheering audience, composed mostly of Irish-Americans, "The Democratic Party understands the special problems in Ireland." It was a mistake, the *Herald* quoted Carter as saying, "for our government to stand idle. I know how heartsick you feel to see bloodshed and disharmony in Ireland." A Carter aide stated that "Carter certainly did not mean that the United States should send troops or arms or economic aid to take sides in general," the *Herald* added.

The British press and political leaders answered Carter's speech with general condemnation. The *Daily Mail* declared that a storm raged as Carter called for a united Ireland. The candidate implied that England was standing in the way of justice in the Irish problem. Carter had no sympathy with the Irish Republican Army (IRA) but agreed completely with England that negotiation was the only way. The Birmingham *Evening Mail* reported Carter's receiving the endorsement of the Irish National Caucus, which was a coalition of Irish-American organizations. The Ipswich *East Anglia Daily Times* published Carter's remarks, causing anger in both English and Irish political circles.

Immediately after Carter learned of the distribution of the photograph and of his speech he cabled the Dublin and London governments: "I do not favor violence as part of a solution to the Irish question. I favor negotiations and peaceful means of finding a just solution which involves the two communities of Northern Ireland and protects the human rights which have been threatened." The *Evening News* declared that "Carter shocked the British ministers by his blatant support for the Irish Republic cause." The *Daily Express* stated that the "American peanut politician Jimmy Carter should mind his own business."

These members of the British press collectively quoted several British and Irish politicians' replies to Carter's statements. A Tory member of Parliament, Mrs. Jill Knight, overreacted perhaps: "Good God. This appalling gaffe outdoes Ford's in the Communist influence in Eastern Europe by 100 to 1. One's mind boggles at the implication of a man with views of this kind becoming President." Ulster Unionist Harry West stated that "Carter's remark was senseless, disgraceful. It is despicable that an American Presidential candidate should stoop to such a level." Mrs. Betty Williams, a leader of the Irish Women's Peace Movement, said, "Carter should stick to his electioneering and leave the Irish problems to those who know it best." James Malyneaux, leader of the Ulster Unionists, told reporters that the "irresponsible opportunism of this peanut-politician" had undone much of what had been achieved in per-suading Americans to stop the supply of arms to the IRA. Nevertheless, a Conservative group of the members of Parliament tabled a resolution "to ask the United States office seekers to cease playing politics with the lives of British citizens." Enoch Powell, a member of Parliament, said, "During the American election it is kind to ignore everything that happens there, or is reported to have happened, while that country suffers its quadrennial illness."

Shortly before the election the *Guardian,* in a leading editorial, "The Peanut and the Shamrock," discussed the conditions in Ireland and Carter's mistake. The editorial noted that on a Pittsburgh platform Carter sat with Sean Maestrofain's confessor, pledging himself to a united Ireland, a redress of Irish grievances, and a commission on international human rights. Only the IRA could take heart; Carter's foreign affairs policy was to put human beings before power politics and not to be afraid to intervene on the side of the righteous minority.

"This was a most lamentable result of Carter's strategy to be all things to all American voters," the *Guardian* said.

The *Daily Express,* in evaluating the American election only three days away, stated that there were three factors undermining Carter:

1. He had antagonized many black voters by not espousing their cause.
2. He had failed to seize the East Coast liberal vote, which had eroded to Senator Eugene McCarthy.
3. His high-gear campaign had stumbled and failed to catch the imagination of the voters.

As a result, the *Daily Express* said, President Ford was within grasp of the most stunning upset in twenty-eight years. Recent opinion polls, said *Daily Express* reporter Ross Mark, showed the President "closing with a rush on the peanut millionaire Jimmy Carter from the snows of New Hampshire to the Rio Grande and way out West in California—a lack-lustre campaign had suddenly caught the imagination of the nation." Mark quoted President Ford as exclaiming, "I'm not only pleased but amazed at the kind of progress we've made."

The *Irish Times* characterized the Presidential race as one of stark contrasts, with the President sprinting to the finish line and Carter looking over his shoulder at President Ford gaining on him. Carter stated to a cheering crowd that the economic indicators meant that the economy was headed downhill in the months ahead. "The Republicans have had eight years and failed. We cannot depend on those who have created this economic mess to clean it up. It's time for new leadership with new ideas," the *Irish Times* quoted Carter.

Pierre Lesaurd reported in the Dublin newspaper that most Americans were bored by the Presidential race. Only one thing that was certain, Lesaurd wrote: "Less than one-half of the American voters would go to the polls." The latest polls, he said, showed that about seventy million United States citizens would not vote—because of the lack of luster in the campaign and the deep-seated cynicism that had gripped the body politic. There was an increasing disenchantment with the United States' political institutions. Lesaurd found nothing in the campaign to reverse the increasing apathy. The greatest indifference was among the youngest potential voters.

Louis Heren wrote in the *Times* that what the American voters wanted was a political party it could believe in. American society and politics had undergone enormous and abrupt changes. Cities, reported Heren, had lost much of their old cohesion and raison d'être. The golden age in American cities had arrived when politicians and government officials could get on with the job of governing. In that era American political parties flourished as loose coalitions in a political climate. Public indifference made for stability. The United States, stated the *Times,* was dangerously divided in the 1960s and old political loyalties were sundered as blacks and young whites sought change by violence. "American political parties," continued Heren, "played a little or no role in these political convulsions. The national conventions, which were never very powerful, had become flabby and weak."

Heren added that the American two-party system had survived strongly enough; it was no longer threatened by the rise of a third party like the Thurmond Dixiecrats or the Wallace Independents, although dissatisfied voters represented the largest voting groups. There was a dilemma in political enthusiasm, with some obvious dangers. The American political pessimists, Heren thought, believed that the personality of the candidate and his ability to perform on television were as important as the campaign issues. Issues and candidates could be packaged and sold by the media. Indeed, the media, the *Times* reported, in American political campaigns could create and manipulate the issues. The old, easily controlled electorates had been replaced by a newer, more responsive and involved electorate determined to do its own thinking and making its own decision regardless of party labels. To an increasing number of American voters issues meant more than party labels.

Optimists, continued the British reporter, claimed that a more vigorous democracy had emerged from the turmoil of the sixties and early seventies. Millions of Americans, argued Heren, were dissatisfied with their political process, which they regarded with suspicion, if not cynicism. The electorate was less predictable and more volatile than formerly. Only political parties could provide political stability and a consistent and developing program or ideology. "The great need in American politics," concluded the Washington-based British reporter, "is for political parties to become representative and responsive."

According to the *Daily Telegraph,* President Ford feared a world crisis with Carter's advocated policy in American foreign affairs. In the past, the President said, our Presidents had never stated in advance what course of action they would take in event of an international crisis. When a potential adversary knew what one would do in advance, one's flexibility was limited and his opponent's was increased. The *Daily Telegraph* quoted President Ford as saying, "It was with some surprise that I learned recently of a specific proposal for total economic warfare against the Arabs in the event of another oil embargo." Statements of that type, the President explained, invited conflict instead of serving the cause of peace. They actually invited aggression, thought the President, rather than deterred it. The American voters, declared the *Daily Telegraph,* had "a choice between keeping tradition based on strength and peace, or venturing into the unknown with a doctrine that was untried, untrusted and potentially dangerous." This policy deviated substantially from the solid principles of the bipartisan foreign and defense policies of the past thirty years, the *Daily Telegraph* said. It had a strong flavor of isolationism, which was affirmed by President Ford.

Meanwhile, Peter Strafford, a *Times* reporter stationed in Washington, described the triumphal drive Jimmy and Rosalynn Carter made along Fifth Avenue in New York City in the crisp autumn sunshine. There was no apathy in that crowd. In fact, in their enthusiasm many observers broke through police barriers and ran alongside Carter's open car. Strafford wrote that the Carters were elated over the reception, with the Carters making several speeches through the city.

"Mrs. Carter, a deceptively frail-looking woman, was given a big role in this New York City visit," Strafford said. She made the first speech in the garment district. It was a rousing speech, declaring Carter was experienced in the art of government, for he had experience in the Georgia Senate and as Governor of Georgia. He would reorganize the federal government in Washington. "He is needed," Strafford quoted Rosalynn saying about her husband, "to provide the leadership and new spirit for the country."

The *Daily Telegraph* provided some humor involved in the Carter visit to the garment district in New York. As the crowd gathered along Fifth Avenue and Forty-second Street where the Carter motorcade would pass, venders barked, "Peanuts, get your Carter peanuts. One dollar a bag for Carter's peanuts." Each bag held ten ounces of peanuts and was distributed by "Carter's Nuts, Inc." Each bag had a symbol of Carter with the familiar toothy grin. Carter had nothing to do with the company, a large nut emporium in Manhattan known as the "Nut Hut." The Republicans, the *Daily Telegraph* added, said, "Carter's Nuts! And everyone's happy."

Jane Rosen wrote in the *Guardian* that in the northwestern states the wealthy and the middle classes feared Carter's economic policies and were going for the President, "the lesser-evil candidate." However, Carter had the blue-collar vote and the black vote. Rosen said that Carter, with his Southern provincialism, his twice-born-again religion, and his vagueness on issues, had left so many New Yorkers politically cold toward him that the Republicans were encouraged. Realistically, Rosen concluded, "there was very little excitement about either President Ford or Carter." The *Daily Telegraph* thought that the "battle for occupancy of the White House left the voters yawning."

Many regarded New York as the most populous corner of the most boring Presidential campaign in memory, the *Daily Telegraph* added, and President Ford was now spending federal money generously in New York City, in complete contrast to his policy of a year earlier, when he had refused to support a federal plan to pull New York City out of bankruptcy. "Suddenly hundreds of millions of the American taxpayers' money had become available for things for which New York had begged, such as highways and street improvements; treatment plants and housing mortgages," the *Daily Telegraph* reported.

From Washington, Helen Pick reported to the western provincial *Guardian* that, if elected, President Carter would find racial tension in the national capital city, where the largest block of blacks in the Western world resided. Given home rule in 1974, Washington had elected a black mayor and blacks to thirteen of its fifteen council seats. Indeed, wrote Pick, Washington had become more like a developing African country than the capital of the United States. The population of Washington was seventy-four percent black; the public schools ninety percent black. As a black middle class developed, the middle-class whites moved out to the suburbs, leaving the city to the blacks and poor whites. "Carter may integrate the North and the South," concluded Pick, "but he will find it very difficult to integrate Washington, D.C."

The *Scotsman* noted that the efforts of Carter and Mondale to link the Ford Administration firmly with the Nixon Administration caused President Ford increasing uneasiness. In an effort to counteract these charges, the President explained the differences between his Administration and that of his predecessor. In Illinois, the *Scotsman* quoted President Ford as saying, "My administration has been very fundamentally different from that of President Nixon." During Ford's occupancy of the White House, the *Scotsman* said, there was no imperial White House as during Nixon's occupancy. President Ford abolished pomp, forbade rigid formal ceremony, and prohibited all dictatorial authority.

Anthony Shrimsley reported to the *Sun* that, if the United States woke up, Carter would win. "Ford," Shrimsley said, "has begun to wobble like a beaten man." America did not have a strong President in the White House. Apathy, which had gripped the country, Shrimsley wrote, was partly the result of the length of the campaign. If those voters who really wanted a change, the *Sun* stated, would simply summon up the courage and take the time to vote, the Democratic nominee would win.

The *Sun* described an attack President Ford, supported by Dr. Kissinger, made on Carter's statements on foreign policy. President Ford stated that Carter had declared that, if Russia invaded Yugoslavia, he would not send American troops to support the Yugoslavs. That announcement, said the President, as stated in the *Sun,* actually promoted war and was very dangerous. Yet, as Carter replied, President Ford himself had declared that he would not send American boys into Lebanon, Angola, Eastern Europe, or Rhodesia.

Dole, asked if he would send United States troops in Yugoslavia, answered emphatically, "No!" Carter's coalition, the *Sun* reported Dole as saying, was composed of the old coalition of 1936. According to the

Sun, the Franklin Roosevelt coalition of the 1930s was composed of the South, the big Northern cities, blacks, the young, low-income groups, union members, Jews, and liberals. This coalition, stressed Dole, comprised, in 1936, sixty-five percent of the American population; today, 1976, it comprised only forty-five percent.

Steele wrote in the *Guardian* that the American national election was the "Greatest Democratic Show on Earth," but, as the election moment drew near, "there came the ritual moment of doubt. Why didn't the candidates discuss the issues?" The end of every political campaign left the voters with three choices: to vote for *A,* or for *B,* or not vote at all. The American campaign ending, said the *Guardian,* was more issueless than ever before. Neither Carter nor President Ford commanded enthusiasm from large sections of their parties. The President had barely squeezed by Reagan. Carter had just concluded a tour of New York without much excitement among the liberals or the labor forces, the *Guardian* reported. The debates had been more stage-managed and rehearsed than the rest of the campaign. A trivial slip of the tongue in casual conversation, which ordinarily would have gone unnoticed, became as dramatic on television as an actor forgetting his lines. The one noticeable change in the campaign, Steele said, was fewer bumper stickers and buttons, much less razzmatazz by both parties—all made necessary by legalized restrictions on spending. Steele added that the removal of hoopla only made the population more quickly bored.

The thrust of both President Ford and Carter was definitely conservative rather than innovative. Serious controversy was avoided at all costs. Both candidates held practically identical philosophies. American politics, as the *Guardian* viewed the scene, "when filtered through an elite Congress and an establishment-minded press, especially when corporation interests dominated, became the most ideologically cohesive in the world." The basic American crisis, concluded the *Guardian* reporter living in Washington, was that the country's "dominant ideology had fallen too far behind reality. Pressures for more government controls grow as corporations' true empires more and more eliminate competition and centralize the national market."

The *Spectator* said on October 30 that the debates, for lack of anything better, might have become the most important element of the United States Presidential campaign. In the third debate Carter gave the impression that he was interested in the people's problems, while President Ford seemed angry at the people for having any problems. Given the Butz affair, the *Spectator* contended, it would have been more honest, though perhaps less political, for the President to have explained that he would fire everybody in his Administration guilty of making racist remarks. Members of the American press, concluded the *Spectator,* took issue with President Ford and Carter for not addressing the issues.

The *Economist* predicted that only about half the electorate would vote. If the race between Carter and President Ford turned out to be as close as some were predicting, the next President of the United States would be the choice of about one-fourth of his fellow Americans. "Why?" the *Economist* asked. "Were the political institutions of the United States voting on an increasingly soggy foundation of public apathy as of positive discontent with the whole system?" The main issue of the past twenty-five years, continued the *Economist,* was whether the pluralist democracies of the West could hold their own against the authoritarian one-party systems of the Communist world and even decrease the advancing tide of authoritarianism. The Western democracies, predicted the *Economist,* with an increasingly massive dropout of resentfully disillusioned nonvoters, would not win.

What were the reasons for the prevailing and increasing nonparticipation of the American electorate in national elections? The *Economist* answered: General belief that all politicians were crooks. Candidates invariably said one thing and did another. Government was too secret. Scandals, such as Vietnam, Watergate, and Lockheed, wrought ill effects. Both Ford and Carter were practically the same in conservative ideas; the voter had no real choice in voting.

The conservative, liberal, and independent members of the British press were in sharp contrast with the views expressed in the London *Socialist Standard* on the American Presidential election of 1976. This socialist monthly magazine, in viewing the American national election, said that with President Ford or Carter the object was power. Why did such supreme power exist and did its continuation serve the welfare of the majority of society? In the United States, continued the *Socialist Standard*, "The Presidency was a political cloak for the operation of big business, capitalism. The turmoils of capitalism, the economic crisis, unemployment, poverty, et cetera could be blamed on the ineptitude of the President or the government's erroneous policies."

The *Socialist Standard* said, "The falsehood that capitalism can work without creating social problems was kept going by the repeated appearance of making a fresh start. A new President? A new Government?" The socialist monthly contended that to think in terms of liberal versus conservative was "really not to think at all but to swallow the cut-and-dried concepts of the pundits." According to the *Socialist Standard,* with President Ford and Kissinger in charge of policymaking, America in 1975 sold more than $11 billion worth of war-making hardware around the world, while Carter wanted a ceiling on the yearly amount sold and a case-by-case review to see whether the sales furthered American objectives.

The *Socialist Standard* said that Americans who fondly regarded themselves as liberal regarded Carter as a liberal, and those who considered themselves conservatives thought he was one of them. "The balancing trick of appearing to be all things to all men was the essence of the capitalistic politician," concluded the *Socialist Standard.*

Since the differences in the Ford and in the Carter policies, argued the *Socialist Standard,* needed to be searched for with a large magnifying glass, "personality" became the only means to "tell the other from the which." The choice by the American political parties of a running mate was a "shabby bit of expediency aimed at balancing the ticket—into vote catching." Any capitalist politician in power who refused to endorse a war involving the "national interest" would be forced out of his office.

A provincial independent paper, the Cardiff *Western Mail,* entitling its lead editorial "Why Ford Must Stay at the White House," wrote on the eve of the election that, despite the importance of the American election, "most voters were disappointed in the two candidates"; the turnout at the polling booths promised to be unusually low. Neither candidate created excitement or fostered genuine interest or attention for the massive electorate. Both candidates, the *Western Mail* said, were trying to win support from the widest possible cross section of the American public, and the images they projected were carefully formed by a team of highly paid researchers, and were, to a large extent, an effort to be all things to all people.

The provincial newspaper thought Carter the better candidate. He was young, attractive, untarnished by gutter politics and promised to bring a fresh approach to the Presidency. But President Ford had been a reliable and trustworthy occupant of the White House for the last two years. "He also managed to heal many of the wounds created by the outgoing Nixon Administration. And, at a time when America was full of self-doubt and uncertainty about her future, he kept his own country and the Western Alliance together," the *Western Mail* said. Admittedly, the *Western Mail* editorial contended, the most controversial decision that President Ford made was the pardon of Nixon, but the appointed President had acted with needed compassion. The President had earned the respect of many hundreds in America and abroad. "America and her allies would be the poorer if Gerald Ford is no longer in the driver's seat after Tuesday," the *Western Mail* concluded.

Steele wrote in the *Guardian* that the American "bicentennial election" was a cliffhanger and very definitely up for grabs—Jimmy Carter's lead of thirty-three points in July had almost totally eroded. Political-minded Americans, Steele said, were in for "a long night of nail-biting and anguish." Pick wrote in the *Guardian* that "Carter has only himself to blame for reducing his massive lead last July to one percent in the Harris opinion poll." The size of the turnout could be a decisive factor. The American people were in tune with the Democrats in believing it was time for a change, but the problem, concluded Pick, was to translate that belief into the candidacy of Carter. Simon Winchester reported how President Ford and Carter had replaced all Monday night television programs to publicize their campaign extravaganza—at a cost of more than $4 million for the two candidates. A major problem in this campaign was the general apathy of the people—a problem that, thought Winchester, was largely the fault of the candidates. "The voting public has been served up with a mixture of incompetence and unfairness," Winchester concluded.

Shrimsley, describing the last moments of the campaign for the *Sun,* condemned in strong terms President Ford's last campaign night television sales pitch. "It dredged the depths of advertising technique," wrote Shrimsley, explaining, "It was a drooling documentary style eulogy which made this very ordinary politician into a heroic combination of Gary Cooper, John Wayne and Dwight Eisenhower. Everything was dragged in—even Betty Ford's breast cancer operation was weepily recalled. A man with any self-respect would have read the script and thrown it away."

The President ended the scenario with a sweeping pledge that if he were elected no American soldier would fight on foreign soil for the next four years. It was a promise of such towering dishonesty, Shrimsley said, that even Nixon would have envied it. "If the President really meant what he said, he was effectively demolishing every American Alliance, including NATO. If he did not mean it, he was telling a barefaced lie."

"Carter's biggest hurdle," thought the *Sun,* "and astonishingly his least difficult was to capture the Democratic Party." The Democratic nominee disguised his racial moderation and courted the "blue-collar vote with a crude anti-establishment, anti-Washington appeal." Shrimsley contended that Carter campaigned poorly—he dodged and weaved and evaded any detailed policy statements. "On wooing the big labor and the big city bosses' votes, he joined the system and ceased to fight it," the *Sun* reporter said. "The message that a new Administration was better than the discredited Nixonites gradually seeped in and the American voters lurched out of apathy and voted for the Carter-Mondale ticket."

Editorially, the *Guardian* expressed itself in a "Lesson on How Not to Choose a President." "This election," the editorial read, "should be universally condemned for its boredom and platitudinous disappointment. The whole campaign has been adrift with the candidates, but more surely in the system and the trappings of that system." For example, the *Guardian* thought the debates were "tedious, confusing and deadly dull." The pathway of both candidates had been strewn with mistakes, the editorial explained. Neither candidate was an oratorical giant or possessed a taint of chauvinism. President Ford, for all of his limitations, was a sensible, honest, and stabilizing influence. Carter demonstrated achievement in his sharp rise from obscurity to promise a new tenancy in the White House, which might be better attuned to America's real needs. "Our preference has long been a Carter Presidency," the *Guardian* continued. An American government with a Republican President facing Democratic majorities in Congress produces immobilization and tends toward a fracturing of the Presidential structure, the editorial added.

The *Guardian*'s editorial discussed at some length the American state primary system, which it denounced as entirely too long. In fact, "its length brings self-destruction, that which is alive at the start is crushed by boredom at the end. Politicians are trapped in a box of suspicion and totally unreal aspirations, shot at from so many different positions, denigrated so persistently from so many new, different platforms that no man entering the contest can think he will survive whole," the *Guardian* explained. "In just two and one half years the whole grotesque juggernaut will begin to grind forward again; and whether it be Ford or Carter who hears its first stirrings, it will signal the death of trust and the death of decisive government—unless the American people, brooding over the tedium and the exhaustion of 1976, decree that enough is enough."

The *Irish Times* editorially sought to answer the significant question "Ford or Carter?" According to the Dublin paper, many Americans were less than inspired by the campaigns and the personalities of the two candidates. "However unexciting the two men may be, the election is of tremendous importance for the rest of the world and for Western Europe in particular," the *Irish Times* said. "The man elected will lead in the defenses of the balance of power between Eastern and Western Europe and in the type of economics that will prevail over the major nationalistic economies in the Western world."

The Scottish *Herald* in an editorial, "The Race for the White House," thought the race was a squeaker: "This strange United States Presidential election has resulted in a cliff-hanger." The Belfast *Telegraph* declared that the election "balanced on a knife's edge." The *Daily Post and Mercury* expressed the same sentiment when it stated that the election was "one of the closest Presidential races in American history," for President Ford had trimmed Carter's lead to a mere sliver.

The London newspapers were in agreement with the members of the press elsewhere in the British Isles. The *Evening Standard* announced that the American election was "up for grabs," as the Harris poll showed Carter only one point ahead of President Ford, and the Gallup poll showed the President one point ahead of Carter. London betting bookers reported heavy betting, more than $3 million, with support for President Ford growing in the betting.

The *Sun* declared that "if tomorrow [November 2] the American voters do, by design or default, reject the Democrat Jimmy Carter for the bumbling figure of Gerry Ford it will be a victory of the first magnitude for political cynicism. It may be, however, that President Ford's ponderous amiability is what America needs to heal the wounds." The metropolitan paper was specific in its statement as to the real issue of the American Presidential election. "The true issue as America makes its choice is not whether Gerald Ford is a nice guy, nor is it Jimmy Carter's smile, his Southern background. . . . The issue is not foreign policy or defense or taxation—the real issue is integrity," the *Sun* explained.

It was a choice between "one from the outside and one of the party which became submerged and saturated in the worst attempt to subvert the Constitution which has yet come to light." The *Sun* said, "It's bumbling Gerry versus smiling Jimmy," adding, "If Ford and Dole are elected it means that a vital opportunity to cleanse the politics of the free world has been spurned." Although Carter's talents were not spectacular, the *Sun* said, they were substantial. His major asset was that he owed no great debts. "The choice for the Americans is between a new man, untried but committed to uphold the better things America stands for, and the nomination of a party whose most recent leaders now languish in prisons in disgrace or in detested political exile." The *Sun* concluded that "if justice gets the vote tomorrow the Republican Party will now serve its beneficial term of four years in the wilderness."

Stephen Barker wrote in the staunchly conservative *Daily Telegraph* that Carter was the voice of political reform with a Southern accent. He was a devout Southern Baptist, which worried some people of other religious persuasions, but it seemed to give him an inner calm. Carter's opponents called him "fuzzy on the issues," the *Daily Telegraph* said, but he had been quite specific. His staff had taken a position on every issue of the campaign. The trouble, contended the London daily paper, was that Carter's positions were unorthodox. Carter's programs, according to the newspaper, was to streamline the government and make it more efficient; to make the United States less dependent on foreign oil; to create more dynamic leaders in the national government and to devise a more moralistic approach to foreign policy as America began her third century. Finally, the *Daily Telegraph* continued, "if Carter wins, the great civil war will at last be over." The same paper, in another article by another reporter, spoke of President Ford as the "kindly epitome of American virtues." He was not brilliant, the *Daily Telegraph* said, but he was decent and kindly—even his opponents liked him personally. He was a good family man with an amiable wife and a happy domestic circle. Finally he, as President, had restored calm and trust to the American people in the office of the Presidency.

The *Daily Mail,* through reporter John Edwards, quoted President Ford as saying, when he was shown the latest polls in Houston, Texas, "Gee, I feel good." As the President began to work the crowd, shaking hands with each person, he shouted, "Didn't I tell you that I would not give in?" The *Daily Mail* believed that many American people wanted as their President "somebody homely and old-fashioned." Perhaps they even liked a guy who fumbled and stumbled a bit. "It made them think that he was one of them," the *Daily Mail* explained. According to the *Daily Mail,* President Ford stayed clear of the cities, knowing that they belonged to Carter. He was obviously most happy when among the rich whites in the suburban areas.

From his station in Washington, D.C., Patrick Brogan declared, in the *Times,* that the American election would be as close as those of 1960 and 1968. Carter's declining percentage in the South signified to the reporter the likelihood that President Ford would carry one or more Southern states. The *Times* took the President to task for promising that "the first priority of my next Administration will be an additional cut in federal taxes." He failed to state, said the independent London newspaper, that any tax cut was contingent on "matching reduction in government spending and that any cut in public spending would have to be confined to nondefense sectors, most notably welfare and unemployment assistance programs."

Furthermore, *Times* reporter Frank Vogt wrote, the President's statement "I have sought and successfully obtained the biggest tax cut in our history" was "totally inaccurate and untrue." Vogt supported his challenge of the President's statement by summarizing the economic conditions in the United States: "Given the present circumstances, the sluggishness of the economy, the low rate of industrial capacity utilized, the severe financing problems of many cities and the extremely high rate of unemployment, a severe cut in public spending, which President Ford desires, would probably be disastrous."

The *Daily Mail* pronounced the American campaign race "neck-and-neck" in large block letters across its front page. Ironically, the *Daily Mail* said, the campaign throughout had been marked by lackluster and dullness; only now, at the very end of the race, had it blossomed into excitement. The *Daily Mail* reporter, William Lowther, had watched Carter closely "as lines around his eyes grew deeper and his tombstone smile began to fade." The Democratic nominee was a phenomenon peculiar to American politics. He held out to the American people two prospects: he offered imagination, vision, and the promise of a better tomorrow, and he promised everyone a job and the nation a new pride.

Lowther wrote that "Watergate and Vietnam capsized the American Ship of State. Ford was able to put the ship back on even keel but he could offer only a fairly steady anchorage—an uninspirational but safe leadership." Carter, on the other hand, Lowther added, "wanted to put up sail and move the old Ship of State. Instinctively the people wanted to follow him but they were frightened that he wasn't able to handle a storm." Lowther contended that the people had faith in Carter's morals but doubted his means. "If Carter is defeated it will be because America is too timid to gamble on a dream that seems too good to be true," concluded the *Daily Mail.*

The *Daily Mirror* spoke of Carter's last-lap effort as a grueling continental marathon as the candidate sought to win the California vote. Carter was riled about the relentless disappearance of a twenty-point lead over President Ford since August. In California he wooed the huge but poor labor force by backing the revolutionary farm union organizer Cesar Chavez.

Fred Emery asked in the *Times,* "It looks like Carter, but will he make a better President than Ford?" and discussed the impending election only twenty-four hours away. The outcome might turn on something as old-fashioned as getting the voters out, or the weather, Emery said. A year of great policy choices, differences, possible consequences, underpinned by an urge for change, had finally come down to a personality contest. This, said Emery, hurt Carter, as "all uncertainty lies with him." He was so different from the norm of American politician—Southern background, style, ultrasincere personality. Emery wrote that Carter had great vision and personal commitment to efficiency and compassion, while President Ford had done nothing during the campaign to suggest untapped resources of leadership. The President had warmed his image as a genial stumbler. Indeed, he had Carter to thank for the colossal distance he had already caught up—from thirty-five percent in July to about even now.

"The campaign was trivialized by slips of the tongue, bumps of the head and a string of impolitic remarks and interviews," Emery wrote. Events were magnified beyond recognition by television. The Democrats had everything going for them. Eight years of Republican rule had climaxed in a recession and continued high unemployment. Why Carter, obviously a capable man, had failed to inspire confidence was a puzzle to Emery. One of the main threats of the campaign, if President Ford were elected, would be his vetoing of most of the bills a Democratic Congress would send him. Personally, Emery concluded, "I believe Carter will win." He quoted Carter as saying, "I want to be a Better president than I am a candidate," and Emery added the admonition, "He had better be."

The British media did not take a vacation on November 2—the day America elected its President. Quite the contrary, the daily newspapers were prolific in their discussion of the United States national election— the candidates, the issues, and some of the last-minute efforts to sway American voters.

Several papers, including the *Daily Telegraph,* the *Daily Mirror,* and the *Herald* discussed an incident that embarrassed Carter. On Sunday, before the election forty-eight hours later, black clergyman Clemon King of Albany, Georgia, who, as a Republican, had been a candidate for public office four years earlier, went to Plains seeking attendance at morning worship services. King was accompanied by three other blacks—all from Albany. The Plains Baptist Church, the Carter family's church, was informed of the incident and voted not to hold services that Sunday morning.

In the early 1960s, and over the opposition of all members of the Carter family, who were affiliated with the church, the congregation had adopted a resolution to prevent "niggers and civil rights agitators" from worshiping in that church. Those supporting the Reverend King had photographers and television crews on hand to capture the scene for broadcast in the evening to the American people.

In California, Carter heard of the incident and declared that it was politically motivated. The local pastor, Bruce Edwards, explained the incident as "an attempt by the enemies of Governor Carter to sabotage his campaign." Learning of this incident, President Ford, scenting a breakthrough, told his last-day rallies, "We're going to win and win over-whelmingly." The *Daily Mirror* was convinced that in the Democrat camp a lot of sad people were beginning to believe Ford's political statements. The *East Anglia Daily Times* declared there had never been anything exactly like President Ford's last-minute surge to win, describing the scene as "Ford Fever."

Anthony Delano wrote in the *Daily Mirror* that "in a big political battle the taller men always move out at the polls." After voting in Michigan, President Ford returned to the White House. "Here he hung up the bulletproof vest which the Secret Service men urged him to wear after women started pointing guns at him," Delano said. The *Daily Mirror* reporter wrote that the President waited "unworriedly" to see if enough of his "fellow Americans would permit him to stay in the White House for the next four years by actually electing him President." Ford had made history by taking office as Vice-President and, subsequently, as President without having been elected to either office. "If plain Gerry could do it then, truly anyone should be able to," thought Delano. "Ford's amazing comeback against Jimmy Carter," Delano thought, "showed that there was more to this Accidental President than legendary physical and verbal clumsiness." It was doubtful, stated Delano in the *Daily Mirror,* if any President had ever come into office with as much goodwill going for him as Ford. "In the sour-smelling wake of Nixon, the country was delighted with Ford—the bluff, pipe-smoking, kindly, comfortable, paternal figure who got his own breakfast and mispronounced big words."

The *Daily Mirror* contended that President Ford never questioned the axiom that what was right for General Motors was right for the country. He had been too softhearted for the stern right wing of the party and nearly suffered the unprecedented indignity of a serving President being run out of his candidacy by Ronald Reagan. The President, Delano wrote in the *Daily Mirror,* had been too easygoing to fire assistants who proved inefficient and he was surrounded by old cronies from Grand Rapids who used the White House like a social club.

John Pilger published in the same paper—the *Daily Mirror*—on the same day, November 2, a sketch of the Democratic challenger. When asked why many people were unsure who he was, Carter answered forthrightly: "I guess in a campaign as long as this one you lose a little of yourself along the way. I would have preferred to have time to be more natural with people, as I used to be, but a candidate has to meet the demands of the media and I've learned to watch everything I say or do."

Pilger believed that if Carter were defeated a major reason would be the "uncertainty of how Americans feel about his identity and what he really stands for." Furthermore, the fault for this situation was partly Carter's. It lay with a farcical marathon of campaigning, which, at a cost of millions of dollars, converted an interesting politician into a zombie and made the voters' knowledge of his real worth almost impossible, Pilger said.

"While Ford is clearly a simple soul, Carter is a complex politician," Pilger thought. Indeed, Carter was something of a phenomenon, which was one reason why he was projected as "vague." Carter could not be labeled, and yet, paradoxically, his policies apparently were laid out in detail. What his message lacked was a simple rallying slogan like "The New Frontier," "The Great Society," or "The New Day"—a media "image," easily compressible into a thirty-second television commercial, which, declared the *Daily Mirror,* was how most Americans were sold their Presidential candidates. "The most interesting side of Carter represents a genuine alternative to Ford, who is little more than an obedient butler to the 2,000 corporations which control the economy and the military establishment, which accounts for almost half of every dollar spent," the *Daily Mirror* said. It was extremely doubtful that Carter could change this structure, but he might be able to make it work for more people, the *Daily Mirror* added.

Pilger published a Carter program, which Pilger assured others that Carter, if elected, would carry out. Pilger said that Carter would create jobs for the unemployed by rebuilding the railroads, as well as establishing centers for drug victims, alcoholics, the mentally ill, and others who had been swept aside by the American dream. Carter saw himself as a healer, Pilger wrote. Carter would bring new pride to the South. Southerners who retained their accents had been looked down upon and excluded, but no more, thanks largely to Carter, Pilger wrote. The reporter quoted the candidate's mother, Miss Lillian: "To my mind that boy's got two strengths: (1) He can explain to deeply conservative people why they should support his liberal policies. (2) He has a definite sense of mission."

The *Daily Mirror*'s commentary revealed an English trait, not shared by all Americans. "Carter's mission may be good for America," Pilger said, "but when applied abroad it is worrying." The Democratic nominee believed that all of the world's problems had American solutions. The role of the United States as the world's Godfather, indiscriminately doling out weapons to military dictators was "hardly in the best interest of mankind." Pilger added that "in their hearts most Americans want a king"—a statement many Americans would challenge.

The *Daily Mail* in huge black letters on two lines announced, "Now It's Ford in the Lead," but William Lowther stated that the American election was too close to call and that the results would be influenced somewhat by the weather. The meteorologists predicted fine weather throughout the country, which generally meant a big vote favoring the Democrats. Noting President Ford's and Carter's frantically scrambling the night before the election to persuade the last handful of voters, the *Daily Mail*'s leading editorial, "Democracy's Endurance Test," began by saying that "demoralized by military defeat and jaded by political chicanery the greatest democracy on earth shakes itself out of its torpor to pick its next leader." The *Daily Mail* was surprised that the American Constitutional show devised two centuries earlier was still actively used. The newspaper said, "The clanking machinery for choosing the President of the United States favors mediocrity. Only the candidate who is all things to all interests in America can survive the grueling months of the campaign. It is a celebration of platitude over principle. Certainly it's one hell of an endurance test." The *Daily Mail* added that the voting was neck and neck as the polls opened in the United States, "which goes to show, despite the traumas of recent years, how infuriatingly imperturbable and reassuringly balanced the American electorate remains."

The *Daily Telegraph*'s leading editorial, "Neck and Neck," discussed the American electoral system, as the *Daily Mail* had done. The *Daily Telegraph* said that England did not like the peculiar American system of the winner take all in an Electoral College. The *Daily Telegraph* found little to choose between the two contenders, with the enduring campaign mainly confusing for foreigners to follow. Neither the President nor Carter, the London daily paper contended, would revolutionize world relations. Each man could be counted on to maintain the Western alliance. American leadership would be wanted by the free world as never before. The *Daily Telegraph* editorially wished America well and hoped that she would receive and give that leadership.

The *Daily Express* summarized the campaign succinctly when it said, "Carter has grinned and goofed and gospelled [while] Ford has fumbled, bumbled and stumbled." *Daily Express* reporter Ross Mark was fortunate to obtain from both candidates a brief statement on the campaign just hours before it ended. Carter said, "I have enjoyed this campaign and I believe we have won it. I learned a lot about this country. I think I've got a good, natural and accurate sense of the hopes and aspirations of the American people." President Ford declared, Mark wrote, that "we are going to win this election because you just cannot tell where the man [Carter] stands. I'm not all things to all people. I stand for the same thing to all people."

The *Evening News* announced briefly that "the American election is a photo finish for Ford," but most British newspapers declined to predict the winner in the Presidential election, for it was expected to be the closest in modern history.

President Ford, reported the *Evening Standard,* made his final pitch to the American voters with a nearly $500,000 television extravaganza that threw in everything, including Pearl Bailey, Susan Ford's birthday cake, and World War II, ending with a shot of Air Force One landing over a magnificent panorama of New York City, as an angelic choir sang, "I'm feeling good about America, I'm feeling good about me." The *Evening Standard* said that the President's commercial, blanketing all three major networks for most of the evening, alternated with a sober thirty-minute lecture on the political issues by Carter sitting in his study at Plains, dwarfed by an enormous shelf of books and toying with a pair of reading glasses. The battle of the tube, the *Evening Standard* said, cost more than $1.5 million.

The *Evening Standard* reported that President Ford's television spectacular began with sports broadcaster Joe Garagiola euphoric in the cabin of Air Force One, then cut to Pearl Bailey sitting in a posture of almost religious beseeching on a white sofa and saying, "He's made some mistakes, honey, you better believe it, but the man is trying and has more than brains, something like get up and go." The TV pitch then plunged into scenes of merrymaking filmed on the Fourth of July. The program continued with baby snapshots of Ford, Eagle Scout memorabilia, football team photos and select sepia pictures of the war hero Ford shooting down two Japanese torpedo bombers from the gun deck of the carrier *Monterey.*

The *Evening Standard* said that the commercial, to show President Ford as the restorer of peace to a troubled nation, included shots of street riots followed by fountains playing tranquilly in the garden of the White House. President Ford, the statesman, was glimpsed with furrowed brow and pipe in the Oval Office as the foe battled in Red Square. The role of the President as the author of prosperity was highlighted by shots of workers streaming into factories against a soundtrack of roaring tractors and pneumatic drills. President Ford the family man was profiled by an announcer reverently intoning "Gerald and Betty as a love story."

As a finish, the *Evening Standard* reported, President Ford sat shirt-sleeved in the cabin of Air Force One, looking briefly at a book in front of him, promising a tax cut as soon as Christmas was over and aligning his metaphors for a last summation of his accomplishments: "I put the Ship of State on an even keel. I put a firm hand on the tiller." Never, in all the annals of American national elections, wrote the *Evening Standard,* had there been such a well-planned, excellently executed extravaganza as the Ford Election Committee aired on the Monday night before the election.

The President's unashamed appeal to America's middle class, said the *Evening Standard,* was in sharp contrast to Carter's "unvarnished and unrehearsed" session of answers to questions of ordinary Americans in the street. This placed heavy emphasis on Carter's direct personal concern for people who, he thought, were disturbed by crowds and news coverage of the election campaign. In fact, Carter stated that he could "understand how many Americans have been deeply hurt and are embarrassed, even ashamed of their own government."

Other members of the city press expressed opinions on the closeness of the Presidential race in America. The *Times,* for example, cited the latest Gallup Poll to emphasize the extreme closeness of the election, with both candidates active in their campaign until the last minute. The Carter strategists, according to the *Times,* said "Carter would try to relax and enjoy the position of being Dr. Gallup's underdog for twenty-four hours." The President's campaign, noted the London daily, "husbanded its funds for a nationwide blizzard of political advertising on television and in the press—forty metro-dailies carried full page advertisements today [November 2] paid for by the Ford Election Committee." The closeness of the race could ensure a last-minute increase of interest, which, in turn, would probably cause a greater vote total than previously expected, the *Times* predicted.

The *Times* also reported Carter's disgust with the Reverend Clemon King incident. Patrick Brogan reported in the *Times* that King, leader of the Diane Mission Church, had been a candidate for President, on an Afro-American ticket, in 1960. In 1962, King in vain sought asylum in Jamaica on the grounds that he had been persecuted in the United States, Brogan noted.

Meanwhile, the *Sun* declared that the United States was "Fording Ahead." The *Times* revealed that the gamblers had bet more than $150,000 on President Ford in the closing hours of the campaign. Eighty million Americans would decide the greatest cliff-hanger election since 1960, the *Times* concluded.

Ian Brodie reported in the *Daily Telegraph* that Carter, preceded by Rosalynn, spoke effectively in Spanish to a huge crowd of 30,000 to 50,000 mostly Mexican-Americans, in California on the eve of the election. These binational Americans roared their approval as the Georgian begged for their support, Brodie wrote and quoted Carter: "You help me tomorrow, and I'll help you for the next four years to have a great country again. I need you."

The provincial British press expressed as much interest in the election as the metropolitan newspapers did. Hella Pick in the *Guardian* reported that in America all liquor stores were closed on Election Day to "ensure that the electorate would be sober" when it went to the polls to vote for the President and the Vice-President and one-third of the United States Senators. Pick noted that the national election involved all members of the House of Representatives and many officials of the respective states, including their governors, and that several states had propositions, including proposed amendments to their constitutions, with Georgia leading the fifty states with a total of a hundred separate propositions on its ballot. Although the state electoral delegates were not legally bound to support the majority vote, Pick noted that, with only one or two exceptions in recent history, the electors in each state had always cast their ballots according to popular mandate. In America, Pick emphasized, a candidate receiving only a minority vote could become President. In fact, this happened on four occasions, in 1824, 1860, 1888, and 1912. Nevertheless, voting in the United States, reported the *Guardian,* had been steadily declining. Within the United States there were about a hundred and forty million people of voting age, the *Guardian* said, but only a hundred million were registered to vote— "particularly disturbing because the highest percentage of nonregistered eligible voters was among the young people."

Simon Winchester related, again, in the *Guardian,* the story of the black preacher trying to worship in the Plains Baptist Church, only to be turned away by the Reverend Bruce Edwards. The incident threw some confusion into the Carter campaign, the *Guardian* said, but the Ford headquarters forbade the President's staff to comment on the incident. Several black leaders in Georgia and throughout the country explained to large black audiences that the Plains Baptist Church incident was "an outrageous example of Watergate influence and dirty tricks" and had no place in the closing hours of the campaign, the *Guardian* reported. The Reverend Andrew Young, a Georgia Congressman, contended that it was an overall strategy of the Republicans to capture the black vote. The result, the *Guardian* said, was to make the people angry, leading to an even bigger black turnout. All citizens of Plains knew that Pastor Edwards and the Carters had for years opposed the church's policy of refusing membership to blacks.

A vote for Carter, said the *Guardian,* was a vote for women's rights. Although women composed 51.3 percent of the American population, they held only three percent of the "super-roles" in the federal government. Carter promised to reduce this differential. *Guardian* reporter Pick asked which hostess—Betty Ford or Rosalynn Carter—had the edge. Pick knew how "passionately and ardently" Mrs. Carter desired for her husband to become President of the United States. For months she had been out on the political trail—mostly by herself rather than by his side. If Carter "wins today it will be their joint victory not just his," Pick said. In Mrs. Carter's campaign speeches, she had habitually declared, "We will win." Many Americans, said the *Guardian,* might think that they liked Carter better and trusted him more "because he had sense to have chosen Rosalynn as his wife." On the political stump she had succeeded better than her husband in getting a positive response out of her audiences. "Youthful and pretty, blue-eyed, dark-haired, simply dressed, she comes across even on the television screen as a real person, not a media product," Pick wrote. At her speaking engagements she rarely ever used previously prepared texts. She spoke without affectation. "She neither pretends to be shy nor seems pushing and aggressive," Pick added. "Relentlessly, she has been zooming from state to state, city to farm, supermarket to crossroads country store making people feel that she is interested in them as well as their problems."

The Presidential campaign, summarized Pick, was "littered with happy families, all of whose members were politically active." The Fords had all spoken, handed out literature, and solicited votes for the President. Nor were the families of the Vice-Presidential candidates inactive— especially the Mondales. There were endless scenes with rapturous wives embracing their husbands before and after campaign speeches. Pick noted that Mrs. Ford did some traveling and speechmaking on her own, but, in contrast to Mrs. Carter, Mrs. Ford "preferred to fall back on dancing a few remembered steps in public and leaving the speeches to the men." Usually, she was just present as a decorative adjunct to her husband, the President, Pick wrote.

Emphasizing the contrast between the candidates' wives, Rosalynn Carter from the outset had an independent role and established an identity of her own, "even if she has no other career ambition beyond being an active First Lady." "No," wrote the *Guardian,* "she does not want to be President, only Jimmy to be the President." She was not worried about living in a fish bowl—the White House; she had always lived in a fish bowl, for Plains was so small that everybody knew what everyone did.

Pick revealed that Rosalynn and Jimmy had always known each other. He proposed to her when she was seventeen, but she refused. Then, one month before she was nineteen, they were married with a "mutual love that had grown and strengthened for thirty years." Pick wrote that, with Jimmy describing Rosalynn as his "best friend and chief adviser, they built up the peanut business and they will, if elected, build up the White House business." Mrs. Carter was especially interested in the mentally handicapped and the elderly, Pick reported. Mrs. Carter spoke with feeling about the unemployed. She fought for the Equal Rights Amendment. She advised her husband on some appointments, for Jimmy knew the value of having qualified women to aid him, without any prodding from her. "She means to see he practices what he preaches," concluded Pick.

The *Yorkshire Post,* supporting President Ford, noted the closeness of the election by publishing the straw vote at Harry's American Bar in Paris: President Ford 238; Carter 236. The *Yorkshire Post* quoted proprietor Andy MacElkone, behind the bar, as saying, "Harry's Bar has never been mistaken on an American Presidential election since we opened in 1923." At Harry's Bar in Munich, West Germany, a similar straw ballot resulted in President Ford receiving eighty-three votes, while Carter got only eighty-one votes, the *Yorkshire Post* reported.

From its reporter with Carter in California, the *Yorkshire Post* published a report saying that Carter was "looking grim and tired" as he discussed the attempt of a black preacher to join his church in Plains. Carter was saddened by the controversy that had resulted over the deacons' decision to cancel the church services rather than allow the black Reverend Clemon King to join the church. He disagreed with the decision but would not resign from the church, the *Yorkshire Post* said, quoting Carter: "I can't resign from the human race because there is discrimination. I don't intend to resign from my church. It's God's church." Meanwhile, the *Scotsman* quoted the Reverend King as saying, "I don't know why God timed it [his seeking membership in Carter's church on Sunday before the election on Tuesday] this way." The *Scotsman* noted that King was the leader of a Divine Mission Church and not a Baptist.

Backing the President, the *Yorkshire Post* described Ford standing with perspiration trickling down the side of his face as he spoke in California, "proclaiming that he restored dignity to the White House, turned the economy from recess to recovery, cut inflation to more than half, secured our return to peace and deserves four years in the White House." The President was most euphoric at shedding his image as an underdog, the *Yorkshire Post* said, after erasing a thirty-three-point lead Carter held in August to make the most striking comeback in the history of United States Presidential politics.

The *Scotsman* emphasized the psychological boost that the most recent public opinions polls gave to the President and the depressive blow they gave to Carter. In an effort to belittle the reports of the polls, the *Scotsman* said, Carter declared that the polls were not a "popular vote election across the United States; they were only a mini-election in each of the fifty states plus the District of Columbia."

Mark Frankland wrote in the Edinburgh newspaper that America was campaign-weary. Many people were relieved that the whole disappointing campaign was over. Some journalists, Frankland thought, including British reporters, blamed their profession for the public's lack of interest. In fact, neither President Ford nor Carter had fully recovered from the trials and the exhaustion of the tough primary campaigns, Frankland explained. Carter's triumphal coronation at the Democratic convention did not translate into popular enthusiasm among the kind of people whose volunteer work makes a campaign roar. The Edinburgh reporter added that the wounds of the primary campaign had never entirely healed—especially among the Republicans.

Both President Ford and Carter suffered from a lack of enthusiasm in California; Ford from the followers of Ronald Reagan, and Carter from the supporters of Jerry Brown. The *Scotsman* believed it was easy enough to see why the two candidates proved disappointing. President Ford thought Americans perfectly happy, Frankland said, and he was able to ignore the inevitability of change in the modern world. Carter, by contrast, stated repeatedly that he was convinced that many things were wrong with the nation and that he wanted to change them, but Frankland quoted Carter as saying he "was not able to shrug off the accusations made first by the Democrat rivals in the primaries that he was a double-talker."

Realistically, wrote Frankland, Carter was a mixture of a liberal and a conservative—a "liberal in his sympathies to the suffering and less-well-off, but conservative when it comes to questions of the size of government and its spending." The strange economic situation in which the United States found itself, a combination of inflation and unemployment, made it difficult for Carter to stick to traditional Democratic economic concerns and remedies, Frankland said. Carter could not, for example, urge an all-out attack on unemployment without opening himself to the charges of rising inflation.

Frankland contended that America was much more staid than most foreigners thought. How could a man like Carter be so obsessed with personal morality and yet have such a huge passion to be the next President of the United States? Frankland asked. The televised Presidential debates did not provoke the public interest that many had hoped they would. Indeed, the debates were definitely a disappointment. Frankland lamented, as other British journalists did, that the American political system had changed little in two centuries and it was astonishing to him, and to many other Britishers, that the President was not chosen by the people directly but by a college of electors, despite the belief that American society generally was in the process of rapid and disconcerting changes.

The *Herald* proclaimed, in an article under large black letters, "Apathetic America," that the Presidential campaign had been a flop. Although America was equally divided between Carter and President Ford, the people were nearly unanimous in voting that the 1976 national election was a dismal flop. Apathy and cynicism, so seldom seen in American Presidential elections, were particularly obvious in this campaign. The long months of the campaign bred boredom and reluctance to change—all of which favored the Administration. Had America, the *Herald* asked, ever produced such an exceptional *fin de siècle* weariness? The ordinariness of the election accounted for the lack of enthusiasm. This had been a normal election, the *Herald* reported; there were no charismatic candidates, no extremists, no searing issues like Vietnam or civil rights—only a moderate conservative versus a moderate liberal. The only extraordinary feature of the campaign, declared the *Herald,* was the role of the South, which reflected the demographic and ideological changes and the "new waywardness of public opinion."

The American political climate, like the British weather, seemed increasingly subject to sudden and unpredictable swings, the *Herald* wrote. The Glasgow paper contended that the American conservatives had a growing distrust of Carter's "politics of trust me" and others possessed a growing awareness of the President's insensitivity, his limited imagination, and a lack of compassion. These conditions gave the rejected South a chance for power. This campaign, concluded the *Herald,* was the least corrupt of modern times.

Editorially, the *Herald* stated, Americans were voting for freedom, and the paper explained that the United States had just completed an exceptionally negative Presidential campaign—so negative in mood that many people seemed indifferent to the outcome. Yet the White House remained the focal point of all Western democracies, and its occupant was a man of great significance for all who cherished the ideals and priorities of freedom. The *Herald* said that, after the traumas of Watergate and Vietnam, the American people needed to be convinced that their system of government was worth supporting. The Americans had always prided themselves on the fact that power springs from the people, the *Herald* added; thus the election would be a major test of America's resilience. The voters had a chance to accept past disappointments, to learn from them, and to begin work on building something new.

The Irish interest in the American election was well establi hed by the appearance of five articles about the American election in the *Irish Times* on November 2. Sean Cronin stated that the United States election had changed from "a dead cut to a dead beat." He predicted that the popular vote would be a photo finish because several public opinion polls showed an unusually large number of undecided voters. Moreover, candidate Eugene McCarthy, a former Democrat, now an independent, had been kept off of the official ballot in California and in New York, but won the ballot in six of the eight states that were rated too close to call. If he received two percent of the vote cast, Cronin predicted, McCarthy would throw the election to President Ford, because his supporters were non-farm voters. The last day's transformation of the election from a "dead cut to a dead beat," Cronin wrote, had ensured a last-minute surge of interest and a higher turnout than had previously been expected.

Dennis Kennedy asked in the *Irish Times,* "Just what are Americans voting for today?" The need to get a majority in the Electoral College, Kennedy thought, dominated the pattern of campaigning and accounted for the emphasis given to particular issues and especially to the selection of the Vice-Presidential running mate. Clair Cockburn, another *Irish Times* reporter, wanted to know what difference it made who won the American election. Carter's battle for the Democratic nomination for President was considered by many political observers to be one of the most extraordinary phenomena of the post-Nixon era in the United States, Cockburn wrote. His surprising defeat of George Wallace in the Florida primary and of Senator "Scoop" Jackson in Pennsylvania was phenomenal. Carter was a Baptist, steeped in the fundamental traditions of the American Deep South, but he had promulgated forthrightly a tolerance for all creeds. Definitely he was a shy person who found public speaking trying, Cockburn reported, but with a Bible in one hand and a computer in the other he was a direct contrast to the Republican nominee.

The Republicans pictured Carter, the *Irish Times* reporter said, "as a bogeyman, a dangerous populist, a menace to the business community, a man with delusions of grandeur and little versed in foreign affairs." Cockburn saw that the chief difference between Carter and President Ford was the nature of the gaffes they made. Carter ill-advisedly spoke to *Playboy* about lust and seemed to look indulgently on adultery, but then President Ford's crony and Secretary of Agriculture, Earl Butz, canceled that out by using filthy language about American blacks, and President Ford, in an effort to remember on the television screen just what the clever Henry Kissinger had told him to say about East-West relations, got the formula all knotted up and risked losing the Polish vote in Chicago and the Jewish vote in New York in one sentence, Cockburn said.

In fact, wrote Cockburn in the *Irish Times,* there was no truly deep, divisive issue of fundamental principle and policy at stake in the election. The most obvious difference between Carter and President Ford was that Carter would be dealing with a Democratic Congress and the President would not have a Republican Congress to work with. This fact, said the *Irish Times,* should mean "an easier, more coherent, and more rapid implementation of whatever policy might be agreed upon between the White House and Capitol Hill." It was inevitable in so large and various a country as the United States that each political party was in itself a wide coalition. Furthermore, Cockburn wrote, with increasing frequency a Congressional working coalition between the large conservative wing of the Republican Party and the small conservative wing of the Democratic Party, as opposed to the larger liberal wing of the Democratic Party and the small liberal element in the Republican Party, was obvious in American Congressional voting. Thus there were three groups of abstainers among the American electorate, Cockburn said: those who were too apathetic, those who could not make up their minds, and those who disliked both or all candidates.

Howard Kinlay of the *Irish Times* lunched with Rosalynn Carter and wrote that no one could understand Carter unless he knew Rosalynn. She was probably the most substantial difference between the Democrats and Republicans in the election campaign. The reporter recognized his hostess's campaign ability: "She handles large groups of noisy people crowded into small rooms with impressive ease. . . . She has an easy informality in her speech that borders on the ingenious." In appearance, Kinlay said, she was unusual in that her hair was unstyled, her clothes were lime green, synthetic fibers with dark tan stockings—projecting a modesty that could "more honestly be described as dowdiness." Kinlay added that Rosalynn's eyes were blue and bright and utterly cold. "When they focus on you, suddenly you understand the energy that has driven Jimmy Carter over almost every obstacle in American politics!" Kinlay wrote that, if Carter were defeated, it certainly would not be Rosalynn's fault. "How he could find the courage, if defeated, to face her with the news is difficult to imagine."

The *Daily Post and Mercury* quoted President Ford as saying, "Two years ago on being appointed President I asked you to confirm me with your prayers. Tomorrow I ask you to confirm me with your prayers and with your ballots. I won't let you down." In contrast, the *Daily Post and Mercury* stated that Carter's waning hope was based on the belief that the Democrats, who were the majority party, would rally to his side.

In a discussion of the election, the *Daily Post and Mercury* labeled it one of the most disappointing Presidential campaigns in American history, with less than one half of the hundred and forty million eligible voters expected to cast a ballot. A major wave of apathy was sweeping America, stemming from the major candidates' refusal to adopt clear positions on the issues facing America and her people. The *Daily Post and Mercury* noted that President Nixon, "the most corrupt president in American history, held sway" during six of the eight years the Republicans were in the White House. The *Daily Post and Mercury* stated that his successor, President Ford, had not bolstered his popularity by "permanently pardoning the leader of a band of criminals who themselves have all served or were waiting to serve jail sentences." Noting that Ford was universally acclaimed as a "nice guy," the *Daily Post and Mercury* said that his decency and honesty had never been questioned, but added that he was not considered the intellectual giant needed to govern the most powerful nation in the free world.

On the other hand, the *Daily Post and Mercury* contended that many of the Democratic leaders and most of the American electorate were troubled when an unknown Georgia politician and peanut farmer won the nomination. Although Carter had used his talents and intelligence to build a small farm into a million-dollar-a-year business, the *Daily Post and Mercury* reported that at the beginning Carter unfortunately failed to outline his specific plans for handling the major economic problems that concerned most American voters. Slowly his sixty percent support had diminished, until now pollsters expected the election to be very close.

Like other newspapers, the Belfast *Telegraph* declared that the outcome of the election was in the hands of millions of undecided voters, who were waiting until the very last moment to choose between the incumbent Ford, amiable, safe and trusted by most judgments, and Carter, who was untried in any national office but whose rapid rise to prominence had already written a dramatic new chapter in American political history. The Democratic candidate, the *Telegraph* said, faltered badly in the eyes of the American electorate, conditioned by traditional moral standards, by using *Playboy* for one of the most extensive and outspoken interviews in American Presidential campaign history. The Carter campaign strategists also were frustrated by the President's Rose Garden tactics, which kept President Ford working in the White House.

In the meantime, President Ford was enjoying a last-minute surge toward election. In Ohio he endeared himself to a large and enthusiastic audience by shouting, "This is the most crucial election in our lifetime. I happen to believe that with the momentum we have going we are going to win the election on November 2. Vote for Ford. He won't let you down. Not a single American is fighting or dying on any foreign soil. I will keep it that way for the next four years."

The London *Socialist Standard* claimed the main objective of President Ford and Carter was power. The American Presidency, said the socialist magazine, was a "political cloak for the operation of big business capitalism." The *Socialist Standard* blamed the economic crisis, unemployment, poverty, and wars on the American Presidency or erroneous government policies. "The untruth that capitalism can work effectively without creating social problems," the *Socialist Standard* editorialized, "was kept active by the appearance repeatedly of making a fresh start. A new President, a new Government? For the American people to form judgments on the basis of personality of Ford or Carter is totally futile and irrelevant." Moreover, to think in terms of liberal versus conservative was, thought the *Socialist Standard,* really not to think at all, but to swallow the cut-and-dried concepts of the pundits. However, since the difference between the policies of Ford and those of Carter must be searched for with a large magnifying glass, "personality" necessarily became the only means of telling "t'other from the which."

"Both President Ford and Jimmy Carter were Bible-belters," concluded this socialist magazine. "They placed God in a most difficult position, rather like that of wartime, with both sides praying for victory. In His "infinite wisdom He has the consolation of knowing it will make no difference either way the election goes."

7

The
Election

On Tuesday, November 2, as millions of Americans went to thousands of voting precincts the weather was ideal. The few clouds on the horizon failed to indicate rain, thus increasing the possibility of a Democratic triumph as the turnout increased.

Most British periodicals devoted lengthy columns to the American Presidential election. Several metropolitan newspapers published a "United States Election Special" edition, including the *Daily Telegraph,* the *Evening News,* and the *Evening Standard,* which noted that Carter, voting at Plains, Georgia, had told reporters, "I voted for Senator Mondale and his running mate." President Ford cast his ballot in an elementary school auditorium in his home town of Grand Rapids, Michigan. In an answer to a reporter he stated, "I feel very good and confident." Betty Ford said, "If my husband loses I get him back; if he wins we go to live in the White House four more years. I win either way." They left a feeling of success among their numerous friends as they boarded Air Force One for Washington and the White House.

The *Daily Telegraph* described a drastic last-minute effort by the Ford election committee to capture the black vote. The Ford headquarters sent out a telegram to four hundred black clergymen throughout the United States. It read: "If Jimmy Carter, a lifelong member of the Plains Baptist Church, cannot influence the decisions and opinions of his own church, can we expect him to influence issues and opinions of the United States Congress?" It was signed by Ford's campaign chairman. The Carter campaign headquarters was furious when it saw a copy of the telegram, dated November 1, and, particularly, when the Carter supporters learned that the list of four hundred black clergymen had been compiled weeks before the Reverend King incident occurred at the Plains Baptist Church on the day before the telegram was sent.

After election returns began pouring in, the *Yorkshire Post,* the

Evening News, and other British newspapers defined the Democratic campaign as "Carter's political miracle"—fashioned in twenty-two months of campaigning by traveling 461,000 miles and making 1,500 speeches. The Leicester *Mercury* declared that "in one of the biggest upsets in the United States political history," Carter, the unknown, was going to the White House. The *Mercury* emphasized that the wealthy peanut farmer had become the first President to be elected from the Deep South since 1848; the election had brought about the first defeat of a White House incumbent since 1932; and, for the first time since 1968, a President would be of the same party as the majority members of the Congress.

The *Evening News* was inquisitive as to where Carter would take the world. His triumph showed to all Americans, the *Evening News* said, that, if one were determined enough to get somewhere, even to the White House, one could usually attain the object of his ambition. But the question that most interested the *Evening News* editorially was where Carter, as President, would take America and the world. "The victor had played a Harold Wilson role in keeping his options open," the *Evening News* stated, adding that the style of foreign policy might change with the arrival of Carter in the White House but noting that the policy itself would remain somewhat the same. This London newspaper wrote that the British need not worry about Carter's attitude toward them or toward Ireland. "Having made his successful gesture to his Irish voters, he will forget about the intent as his predecessors have done," the *Evening News* said. The London afternoon paper revealed that the British wanted another loan from the unprecedentedly generous United States, but the newspaper warned that British strength as a debtor was such that her total "economic destruction would cause more havoc than the granting of another loan." This, however, did not bestow on them "a license to be profligate forever" but it would assure them of Carter's continued support.

The *Evening News* said that, although President Ford was not a genius, he was no fool either. He had restored to the "most powerful position in the world judgment, decency and friendliness. For that he deserves our gratitude and our warm wishes for his personal future."

Not only was the *Evening News* interested in the newly elected President's attitude toward the British, but the newspaper reviewed his political background and the contribution of Rosalynn Carter to her husband's success. In 1973 and 1974, Carter, as Governor of Georgia, the *Evening News* pointed out, had used his position to increase his contacts with politicians, businessmen, and journalists. He sought and won in 1974 the chairmanship of the Democratic National Committee's Congressional Committee. As chairman he traveled throughout the country, meeting and cultivating people interested in electing Democrats to Congress. These newly made acquaintances paid rich dividends in 1976, when Carter was contesting in the state primary elections and later in the national election. He carried out his campaign for election with the same steely determination and shrewdness as he had in seeking the Democratic nomination, the paper summarized.

The *Evening News* redescribed Carter's family assisting him in walking the streets of American cities, entering barber shops and beauty salons, visiting the lunch counters and restaurants. They stood in factory shift lines, walked into farmer markets, livestock barns, visited county courthouses and city halls—just learning about the country and letting people get to know them. Carter, said the London daily newspaper, owed much to his blue-eyed, brunette wife for his victory. She was almost constantly at his side, giving advice.

The American people had elected an unknown person to their highest office who was proud of his Southern heritage. The *Evening News* quoted Carter as saying, "The South is where I came from. That's where I live. These poor and black people are my people." The newspaper explained that Carter spoke with a soft Georgia drawl, which masked an astute mind and an erudite language. He listened to constructive advice. An avid reader, he especially liked Reinhold Niebuhr and Dylan Thomas. A fan of rock bands, he frequently spent an evening listening to country singers. He was not given to anything frivolous, and bore up well under tremendous stress; his single-mindedness was unbelievable. His critics spoke of him as "arrogant, self-righteous, unbending, lacking in humor and sensitivity for others." Furthermore, said his enemies, he was a political chameleon. The *Evening News* quoted Carter as saying in a self-analysis, "I am a composite of what my experiences have been"—the preacher, the farmer, the scientist, and the supreme politician.

As many of President Ford's supporters gathered in Grand Rapids and in the White House for victory parties and as Carter's friends and neighbors assembled in Atlanta and Plains to celebrate a Democratic victory, in England both the Democratic and the Republican Party organizations held victory celebration parties on the night of November 2 in the stately rooms of the English-Speaking Union Hall in Mayfair. Organizers of the expatriate American political groups throughout the British Isles were amazed at the large attendance at these parties. More than five hundred showed up at each celebrating party. Amply supplied with drink, they danced the night away waiting for the election results from the United States to appear on the large screens. The Democrats hired a rock band for the occasion. Hours later, when the partying partisans left the Union Hall, some of the guests moved to the American Embassy in Grosvenor Square to await the final election results. The *Evening Standard* quoted Tom Kelly, the Democratic area coordinator for the United Kingdom and Ireland, as saying that he and others had worked for Carter since February. "I never had any doubt right up to the end that he would win," concluded Kelly.

The British learned through their newspapers of the Carter celebration in Atlanta. This whopping victory party was held in the vast and dramatically modern World Congress Center. More than twenty thousand Democrats gathered amid placards of "Peanut Power." A small orchestra played for dancing as the night wore on. It was Atlanta's biggest party since the premiere of *Gone With the Wind* in 1939. This time instead of Vivien Leigh and Clark Gable the crowd came to see a genuine Southern hero. Suddenly in the later hours, long after midnight, screams of frenzied jubilation rent the air when Louisiana went for Carter. The Carter family and his campaign staff of some thirty persons occupied a large suite high up in a nearby hotel. They waited anxiously for an official announcement that Carter had the required 270 votes in the Electoral College. This did not come until about four o'clock in the morning, when the results in Mississippi, which raised Carter's electoral vote count to 272, were flashed on the television screen, followed by the announcement that Carter was the winner. Carter, said the *Evening News,* seated on a couch watching television, suddenly clapped his hands in joy as he leaped to his feet shouting, "All right, all right." Joyous bedlam erupted as the Carter family and staff, "shaking hands excited and exchanging kisses," celebrated the happy occasion.

Minutes later the victor with members of his family and aides left the hotel suite and entered the large convention room of the World Congress Center. There, according to the Belfast *Telegraph,* Carter thanked the huge, elated audience for coming and promised them to do his best in serving the American people. "It is not going to be easy for any of us but I am not afraid to take on the responsibilities of the Presidency of the United States because my strength and my confidence and my counsel and my criticism come from you."

An hour or more later the Carters left the Atlanta celebration, drove to the airport, and boarded a plane for Columbus, Georgia, where they entered cars and drove to Plains, where about a thousand fellow townsmen and friends had waited all night for the arrival of their distinguished citizen. Carter brought home the Presidency, said the *Evening Standard,* "just as the sun was rising over the red clay peanut fields of the normally sleepy hamlet." But that morning the people of Plains were not sleepy. Carter told the crowd, "It's been a long night for all of us, but I guarantee it is going to be worth it for all of us." It indeed had been a long night of anguish and suspense for Carter, because for nearly three hours he lacked only three electoral votes to become the winner.

Miss Lillian Carter showed her delight at her son's victory by unzipping her jacket and displaying a new T-shirt emblazoned with "Jimmy won in '76." She told British reporters, "I think it's just wonderful; it's great to have a son who is the President of the United States. I am a proud mother and I never had any doubts. Victory came as the people came to realize Jimmy is the best man for the job." Two years ago, said the *Evening Standard,* only three percent of the American voters knew who Jimmy Carter was. He had scored one of the most amazing electoral successes in modern history. Editorially, the *Evening Standard* stated that in Britain Carter's success was "less welcome" than a Ford victory would have been. He was a quick learner, however, but much would depend upon his choice of close advisers. He possessed determination in abundance and had a young and interesting team around him. "Let us hope," concluded the London paper, "that he governs the United States as successfully as he ran his own extraordinary election campaign."

The Belfast *Telegraph* used huge block letters across its entire front page, to announce that "JIMMY CARTER DRIVES FORD OUT." The *Telegraph* quoted Carter as saying that "the first task after a close and hard-fought campaign is unification."

The *Evening Standard* told its readers in its "Special American Election Edition" that winning the Mississippi vote was the climax of Carter's phenomenal sweep of his homeland—the American South. Although many opinion polls and predictions gave the Magnolia State to President Ford, a combination of local pride in having the first Southerner of this century to reach the White House under his own steam and a massive turnout of black voters gave Carter Mississippi and the sweetest moment he had known in his political career. According to the London newspaper, Carter's victory was realized by his control of the "classic components of the Democratic Party created by Franklin D. Roosevelt."

Furthermore, in winning the election he turned upside down the usually accepted wisdom of the pundits and pollsters that America is irretrievably conservative and that the voting habit along party lines for a President was dead and gone. Carter was the beneficiary of a Southern regional feeling that its long night of political frustration was over if one of its native sons had become an occupant of the White House. The real heart of Carter's victory, the *Evening Standard* said, was in the poor whites and blacks, the factory workers, the Spanish-Americans—the people trapped in shabby centers of the big cities—and the youthful voters.

Evening Standard reporter Jeremy Campbell noted that months of tension seemed to fall away from Carter's face as the moment of victory came—at 4:00 A.M. in the hotel suite. Shortly afterward, entering the auditorium, where the large crowd awaited his appearance, he told them that he loved every single one of them. In reviewing the campaign from its inception in February to the auditorium appearance, Campbell noted that Carter, a native of "the newly enlightened South and unmarked by the decadence and the vices of Washington," believed he could capture the imagination of the country, which "was hovering between high idealism and hopeless cynicism." Carter contended that the American people had grown deaf to the unkept promises of politicians who sat in Congress for many years doing nothing but making the government larger. Although Carter's aides conveyed to British reporters, including Campbell, that Carter was a straightforward and sophisticated political administrator, the general public did not believe he conformed to that description.

Campbell wrote in the *Evening Standard* that the national campaign was famished for information on what Carter intended to do about jobs, inflation, and the cities. In the final day of the campaign the opinion polls showed that Carter was believed to be too much a mystery and too much of a risk—that the voters were reluctantly drifting to President Ford, who could be trusted to provide America with four more years of quietness and consolidation, Campbell said. But the election was made by the bread-and-butter elements of the great Democratic Party coalition. The Carter victory destroyed the frightened, conservative election the pundits led the world to expect. The triumph was extremely significant, Campbell wrote, for Carter began his campaign as an immaculate outsider disgusted with the antics of the regular Democratic politicians and completely beyond the control of the party bosses.

When the campaign got tough, Campbell explained, Carter began to take shelter under the "embrace of the party bosses and wheelhorses who could get out the vote for him." In the end, Carter returned to the political rather than the personal roots of his campaign. In short, he needed the Democratic Party and it needed him, Campbell stated. Now Carter must deal with the enormous tasks that confronted the United States, which was fundamentally as dynamic and open to change as any country in the world.

The most notorious problem, in reporter Campbell's opinion, was the condition of the cities, which, instead of having masses of happy faces, as in Europe, had become "centers of pathology, clusters of black people, chronically unfit for the normal rigours of American life. They were increasingly forgotten by a generally contented white middle class who lived in suburbs." In the campaign President Ford pretended that the cities did not exist, Campbell wrote, while Carter made an indirect approach to the city problems by suggesting changes in housing, welfare, education, crime prevention, and employment.

The British, concluded the *Evening Standard,* need not worry about Carter's conduction of foreign policy, which generated its own momentum and compiled its own compromises. Carter's victory suggested that the Americans were ready to face their problems as long as they had a President who they were confident could make the government work.

The *Times*'s leading editorial, "A Great But Dull Race," just before the election, stated that the change in the prospects of the election was "due to the failures of Carter—not to the brilliance of Ford's campaign." Indeed, the most striking feature of the long campaign was its quiet, extraordinary dullness, the *Times* said. "It produced no memorable phrases, no new ideas of consequence to capture the heart and win the head of the American voters." Although Carter spoke a great deal about trust, the editorial said, he was not able to command it— partly because his style as a Southern politician did not sit comfortably on a majority of the American electorate. Perhaps the intensity of his religious convictions made others weary. At least, the *Times* concluded, Carter had failed to produce the fondness and vigor that was essential if a challenger were to feel confident of defeating a sitting President. "Moreover," the *Times* said, "Ford represented continuity and safety. He was a decent, friendly man, who inspired trust as a human being and who had shown that he was safe with the awesome powers of the Presidency. If Carter was pronounced the winner a few hours later it would be because of the memory of Watergate and of President Ford's pardon of Nixon."

The *Daily Express,* in its leading editorial, "America and Us," declared that Carter had the "congratulations and good wishes of the people of this country [United Kingdom]." Come January he would have the most demanding and the most thankless job in the Western world. "To us America is and will always be what Churchill called 'The Great Republic.' For us it has been the arsenal of democracy. . . . It is an outstanding success story." America, continued the *Daily Express,* was an egalitarian country in the best sense of the word. It was the first country that gave to the common man the right to make his life what he would without having to say "sir" to anybody. Founded and developed largely by people who rejected Europe, the United States was the power that guaranteed freedom to half of the old continent. However, the *Daily Express* added, "we cannot expect America to go on defending Europe forever unless we make a greater contribution to our own defense. Nothing that anybody can say or do will in any way diminish the vigor, the vitality and the moral energy of the American people. We will always do our best to help."

Jonathan Steele told a provincial audience through the *Guardian* that Carter, upon emerging from the voting precinct in Plains and standing by black laborer Jimmy Wallace, said, "Jimmy and I used to plough a mule together" and the black nodded in assent. The candidate added that he won in the primaries because of his close personal relationship with the people. As Carter prepared to leave for Atlanta, Steele quoted him as saying, "When I am back later tonight to address you all again, I will come back as the President-Elect of the United States."

Another provincial paper, the *South Wales Evening Post,* described the election as a bitter defeat for President Ford, who had pleaded for a full term of his own based on his success in restoring trust and confidence in the White House after the Watergate scandal, while maintaining peace and leading the country out of the recession. The American voters rejected Ford because they regarded him as still tainted by his association with Nixon, the *South Wales Evening Post* said. The voters objected to the President's pardon of Nixon and believed that he lacked the positive qualities needed to meet the challenges of change.

The Birmingham *Evening Mail,* which boasted of the largest circulation in the Midlands, stated that "one could see eyeballs tilt sharply upwards when the news arrived from the new world that Jimmy Carter was elected President." Definitely, Carter's rise from general obscurity twenty-two months earlier to election as President of the United States was the Horatio Alger story of the twentieth century. But, the *Evening Mail* said, one of Carter's greatest drawbacks, ironically, was that he had come so far so fast. Whitehall—the British government—had hoped for a Ford victory. And, the *Evening Mail* contended, Carter would have to do some penance over Ulster before he could hope to come to an easy working relationship with Britain.

"The Winner" was the caption of the *Irish Times*'s leading editorial on the American election. Carter's greatest asset was the hope placed in him by the American people, the *Irish Times* said. It was most important, not only for the United States but for the world, that his ability and judgment measure up to his ambition. The editorial concluded that Carter was now the high priest of the nation, "the center of the establishment for which he had so often expressed suspicion and a measure of contempt."

Meanwhile, the *Guardian* said Carter's success stemmed largely from his exploitation of two cardinal issues: (1) the belief of most Americans, that the Republicans were inherently less concerned with the "ordinary people" than the Democrats, and (2) the increasing tensions between the overwhelmingly Democratic Congress and a stagnation in the White House which had resulted in little domestic legislation being enacted during the last eight years of Republican rule.

The *Guardian* continued that many English probably understood Carter better than the Americans. He was of the gentry, the squire of Plains. He owned the grocery store, the warehouse, the seed establishment, and most of the land. The gentry, as a class, were always nice to the poor—whether black or white. Carter's attitude toward labor was very much that of the rural capitalist. "The Republicans give big business 100 percent cooperation; the Democrats 95 percent and they [the Democrats] get damned for the 5 percent difference," concluded the *Guardian.*

Jonathan Steele and Simon Winchester, reporters for the *Guardian* stationed in Washington, wrote that the President-Elect in two years had turned American politics upside down with a constituency consisting of the blacks, the minorities, the young, the small businessmen, the unions, the factory men, and the blue collars. "Ruthless ambition may have been one factor in the political miracle," Steele and Winchester wrote, "but great strength of character was also required. The determination, the intelligence and the self-discipline which went into the making of this President could make him a good President, even a great one."

According to these journalists, many British were confident that Carter would immediately select his Cabinet members. However, the President-Elect did not name all of his Cabinet for some time. When the Cabinet was completed, the President-Elect asked all of them to remain in their respective positions for four years—yet he would find it necessary within two years to shuffle some members to other positions and to dismiss others.

In a lengthy editorial the *Guardian* declared that "America, after much earnest self-searching, has chosen a fresh start, calmly and deliberately." President-Elect Carter, continued the *Guardian,* was a remarkable man and living testimony of a remarkable political system. "In his two years of battle he brought the South into the broad span of mainstream America," the provincial newspaper said, and killed the George Wallace dragon forever, worsted the old pros, and moved on to unseat an incumbent President. "In two short years one man had turned American politics upside down." Whether liberal or conservative, Carter was an instrument of change, the *Guardian* said. In fact, a good Democratic President always runs America by caring, by innovating, and by reforming. As President Ford, disappointed and disspirited, packed to leave the White House, the *Guardian* said he could depart "knowing that he did a brave job for his country, when, by happenstance, it needed him. Gerald Ford could not rewrite history, but he kept a sturdy head when most around him were in despair. America had swapped a caretaker for a risktaker."

Peter Jenkins, reporting in the *Guardian,* was interested in the powers of the American Presidency. He did not believe that the powers of the President were influenced to any appreciable degree by regional socioeconomic or religious composition of the winning alliance, but it was sometimes affected by more personal debts incurred while obtaining the nomination and getting elected. Carter, wrote Jenkins, could not have been elected without the labor union vote consummated at the national party convention, but the agreement was a marriage of convenience. Despite Carter's promises, he was unlikely to balance the budget in 1980, or to bring American foreign policy into line with any moral precept, Jenkins said. If, however, Carter could build a strong economy and conduct a successful foreign policy he would do well. His ability to do these things, Jenkins explained, depended very largely on his choice of persons and his use of them.

Other members of the *Guardian*'s extensive reportorial staff discussed other phases of the American national election and predicted what the incoming Administration would endeavor to accomplish. Carter's goals, as listed by Jane Rose, included full employment, four percent inflation, a balanced budget, a comprehensive health insurance program, a reformed welfare program, federal aid to halt the decay of American cities, an energy program of research in solar energy, substitution of coal for oil, more federal aid to education, and greatly increased federal aid in mass transportation. Steele wrote that the President-Elect had expressed deep concern about the improper use of multinational corporate funds abroad, repeatedly emphasizing human rights and denouncing the role of the United States as the arsenal for the world, especially for military dictators. He opposed meddling in the domestic affairs of other countries, regardless of the conditions in the foreign country, Steele said.

Steele quoted Carter as saying, "The world is tired of American bluff and bluster." The *Guardian* explained that the chief difference between Carter's proposed intentions in foreign policy and Ford's foreign policy was largely one of style. Carter was preparing a definite South African policy —an aggressive policy for peace. He would work through the whole army of his peace-keeping arsenal—particularly technological assistance in the developing of South African resources.

John Palmer, European editor of the *Guardian,* expressed the hope that Carter would act quickly to prevent an independent business recession in the United States and in the world economy. The Common Market and NATO countries were withholding assessment of what Carter's European relations would be until they could learn the nature of his program. Palmer contended that English bankers and financiers were skeptical about Carter's victory because they thought that he probably would risk more inflation in his efforts to reduce unemployment.

The *Yorkshire Post* declared that Carter had fashioned a political miracle because "his intellectual development showed a breadth that was frequently lacking in other Presidential candidates," as exemplified by his reading voraciously—usually three or four books a week.

In its leading editorial, "America's Choice," the provincial *Yorkshire Post* predicted only time would tell what sort of President Carter was going to be, depending on the "kind of advisers he chooses or has thrust upon him." It was alarming to think, the *Yorkshire Post* added, that in a little more than a year the President-Elect had emerged out of almost total obscurity to become the leader of the free world. The American people, continued the *Yorkshire Post,* "voted primarily on domestic issues without giving more than marginal thought to international affairs."

The British would know whether to be reassured or desperately worried, the *Yorkshire Post* said, only when they saw Carter's list of appointees for the State Department, the Pentagon, and the other departments and agencies that influence the President's thinking on foreign affairs. However, Carter's talk of "morality in foreign policy," thought the *Yorkshire Post,* "together with his holier than thou image which he projected, . . . could become an albatross around his neck when he comes face to face with the real world at home and abroad." The powers of the Presidency and its agencies, as everyone knew, were enormous, and effective leadership could come only from the White House, the provincial paper explained.

Edmund Ions, a political expert at the University of York, predicted in the *Yorkshire Post* that Carter's foreign policy in style and content would change from the Kissinger one-man type of diplomacy to something much more in line with traditional methods. The new Secretary of State, continued Ions, would be much less a prima donna than Kissinger, which would be welcomed by most of America's allies. Carter would be less likely to form alliances with military dictators, the type Kissinger supported in Chile, Iran, and Greece. Ions predicted that Carter's foreign policy would include no sudden or sharp reversals. On the other hand, the *Yorkshire Post* thought that Carter's first preoccupation would be domestic plans for dealing with unemployment, inflation, reform of the tax system, a compulsory national health insurance, changes in the Social Security system, decreasing the Washington bureaucracy, reduction of the power of "big government," cutting waste, and ending profligate spending. "Everyone in Britain and in the United States has a lively interest," the *Yorkshire Post* contended, "in the sort of animal Carter will introduce to the Washington jungle, where he will find his team— whether he will avoid the big names in the world of public affairs and rely on the universities."

The *Yorkshire Post,* like other British papers, anticipated that Carter would have smoother relations with Congress. He was likely to be tough-minded, which would cause his popularity to take knocks and decline sharply. The real tests of his character, his program, and his political leadership would occur during the second year of his Administration and thereafter, the *Yorkshire Post* predicted.

The *Scotsman*'s leading editorial, "Narrow Victory," began by stating that Ford was directly elevated to high office by President Nixon and was indirectly cast out of it by Nixon. Carter rose from gubernatorial obscurity to an impregnable position, although "bad weather on election day could have destroyed his chances. Providence definitely was kind to this Baptist servant," the *Scotsman* said. Senator McCarthy was instru-mental in giving Nixon a narrow victory in 1968 and would have assured a Ford triumph in 1976 had he been able to have his name placed on the ballot in New York, the editorial continued. When McCarthy failed in this endeavor he assured Carter of capturing New York and the Presidency. The *Scotsman* added, "It remains to be seen whether Carter's promises are as empty as much of his rhetoric was as he energetically preached his way to power. More broadly based than the Republicans, the Democratic long-standing control of Congress should provide a new era of constructive cooperation between the White House and Capitol Hill to begin with Carter's inauguration."

Frank Vogt wrote in the *Scotsman* that Carter had everything going for him in this election—ideal voting weather throughout the country, a united party, the receding and unstable economy, Watergate, Ford's blunders, including the pardon of Nixon, and much more. The wonder was that he nearly lost the election. He benefited from the great national desire for a change. Ford, who nearly pulled off the political upset of American history, lost with honor.

The leading editorial in the *Herald,* "Put to the Test," stated that the United States had made the more adventurous choice. "The trusty and genial Ford who entered the White House on Nixon's resignation at the end of a long national nightmare" was not given a popular mandate, the *Herald* said. The American voters opted for the potential "of the undoubtedly abler and interested Jimmy Carter—a remarkable outsider from the long rejected South." To this Glasgow paper the greatest question about Carter concerned foreign affairs, "not so much because of any doubts about his policies but because of doubts about his competence." In conclusion, the *Herald* was convinced that America had elected "the abler, less limited, and more imaginative one—the one with, it seems, the greatest capacity for growing with the job."

Conor Brady emphasized, in the *Irish Times,* the important role that Mondale had played in Carter's election. He certainly contributed much more toward Carter's election than Dole did for President Ford, Brady wrote. "In style, in background, in appeal—some even argue in appearance—Mondale and Carter bear many resemblances. The Vice-Presidential candidate's main interest in his twelve years in the United States Senate was his concern for the underprivileged. As a steady, cautious legislator he became one of the foremost civil rights advocates. His influence resulted in the passage of the Open Housing legislation which improved the living conditions of hundreds of thousands of Americans almost immediately." It would be extremely difficult, said Brady, to find a person in American politics whose appeal covered such a broad span of political, ethnic, and geographical differences as that of Senator Mondale. "The places at the Table of American power have changed," Brady wrote. "Carter and Mondale would soon sit where Nixon and Agnew previously sat. The world would soon see whether Americans in desperate need of a restoration of faith in their leaders would have their trust justified."

The *Daily Post and Mercury* asked editorially, "What's Behind the

Smile?" After Carter's Administration, which would begin in January, he "will have to come to terms with the bureaucratic machine before he can feed them his policies." The American voters would have to wait to see how well he could match up to his smile and his pledge to represent the highest ideals of the American people. He had shown that he possesses courage and determination. "Provided Carter has nerve, sound judgment, necessary strength of character, dedication, practicality, diplomacy, an iron constitution, and forbearance and impatience at the appropriate times, the trust of the American people will not have been in vain," the *Daily Post and Mercury* concluded.

Edna Robertson wrote in the *Herald* that Deep South strength gave Carter the victory. It was illustrative of the New South's return to the mainstream of the United States political leadership that Mississippi's election returns first made it clear that Carter had won. Despite widely heard rumors near the end of the campaign that the lower South was shifting from Carter to Ford, the South proved more solidly in support of Carter than expected. There was no erosion of support from the first Deep South Presidential candidate since before the Civil War. Robertson hailed Carter's victory as "the end of the Civil War and of the Watergate Era." In addition to the South's loyal support of its native son, Robertson said, Carter's election could be attributed to Providence's favoring him with fine weather, adverse economic conditions, the rise of unemployment with more than two million under the poverty line, and the fear that Senator Dole would be only a heartbeat away from the Presidency.

Others agreed with the *Herald*. The *Western Mail* declared editorially that the "Mystery Man would soon be in the White House," noting that Carter was not only the first Southerner to be elected to the White House in more than a century but more significantly the first man to walk into the White House from a "thick political and social obscurity. The American people and the rest of us know very little about the new leader of the free world," the *Western Mail* said. The call for a change in the White House had proved to be irresistible. The American voters would have toppled a Republican Administration regardless of who was President. But the Cardiff provincial paper was convinced there were good reasons to regret Ford's defeat. No intellectual giant, President Ford offered stability when most needed. "He was a realist and his pragmatic philosophies . . . at home and overseas, were more timely than the evangelistic idealism . . . displayed by Carter," the *Western Mail* wrote, explaining that, as a Nixon appointee, President Ford had proved reluctant to dismiss Nixon White House appointees. He became the last and the least deserving victim of Watergate. "His pardoning of Nixon and his choice of a running mate were both serious and telling mistakes," the *Western Mail* concluded.

Correspondent Jon Campbell, with another western provincial newspaper, the *Daily Post and Mercury,* interviewed the President-Elect, then published "From Peanuts to Presidency." With Campbell recording in shorthand, Carter gave the British journalist an autobiographical sketch of himself. During Carter's very young boyhood, his father's farm near Plains, Georgia, shifted from cotton to peanuts as the primary money crop. "Boiled peanuts is one of the great gifts of God to mankind," Carter told Campbell. "From five years of age, I sold boiled peanuts on the streets of Plains. I would walk [from the farm] two or three miles down the railroad to Plains to sell my boiled peanuts. I got to be a businessman in those days, on a small scale, even if it seemed on a big scale to me. My closest friend was a colored boy, A. D. Davis. In fact, for quite a time, all my playmates were blacks. We hunted, fished, explored and worked together. But we never attended the same school or church. Our social life and school life was segregated. . . . I was a farmer's son but I didn't want to stay on the farm near the tiny town of Plains."

As a boy, Jimmy became ambitious to become an officer in the United States Navy. Admitted to Annapolis in 1942, he graduated in 1946, and married his early sweetheart, Rosalynn Smith, an auto mechanic's daughter, a month later. In 1948 he joined the submarine U.S.S. *Panfret*'s crew at Hawaii and left for the Far East. The submarine encountered a severe storm in which he almost lost his life.

"I was seasick for five straight days," Carter told Campbell. "Several ships were lost and once I almost lost my own life. During a deck watch, an enormous wave rose around us to a level of about six feet or so above my head. I lost my grip as the force of the wave tore my hands from the handrail, and I found myself swimming literally within the huge wave, completely separated from the sub itself. After I swam for a good while the wave receded and I landed on top of the five-inch gun about thirty feet aft of where I had been standing. I clung desperately to the barrel and finally was able to lower myself to the deck and return to my watch station."

After his father's death in 1953, Carter, despite the stubborn opposition of his wife, left the Navy, returned to Plains, and began a modest business partnership with his mother, Miss Lillian. They made little profit at first, but, by hard work, efficient management, and staunch economy, he soon became a success, Campbell quoted Carter.

One of the ideas that swept the South after the U.S. Supreme Court decision of 1954 abolishing segregated school systems was the White Citizens Councils. Carter was approached twice—once by the chief of police, once by the railroad depot agent. He told the second person, Campbell wrote, that Carter would "see him in hell before he would give him five dollars to join that organization," and, as a result, the Carter family suffered a temporary boycott by the community.

As a deacon in the Plains Baptist Church, Carter was sincere in his religious convictions, Campbell said. When he was absent the eleven other deacons and the pastor passed a resolution prohibiting blacks from attending the church services. When the resolution was presented to the congregation of the church, Carter spoke strongly against the motion, but it was adopted by a vote of fifty to six, with only the Carter family opposing it.

Soon after returning to Plains, Carter became active in Sumpter County politics, Campbell wrote. Carter was appointed to fill a vacancy to the local school board and was named chairman. In a race for a seat in the Georgia State Senate, Carter uncovered vote fraud at Georgetown. A judge, to whom Carter appealed, threw the Georgetown ballot box out, thus permitting Carter's election. He went to the State Senate in 1963 and to the governorship in 1970. In Georgia politics, Campbell said, Carter realized how vulnerable the American political system was to an accumulation of unchallenged power. Carter stated that "honest and courageous people could be silenced when they come to realize that outspoken opposition was fruitless. Those who were insecure could be intimidated. The dishonest could band together to produce and divide the spoils. But I learned a most vital lesson; people intimidated by corrupt public officials don't necessarily like it and that if given some leadership and a chance, they are willing to stand up and be counted on the side of decency and of honest politics and government."

One of the country's most notorious problems, Carter thought, was "our American cities, which instead of being humanizing forces as in Europe were becoming centers of pathology, clusters of black people chronically unfit for the normal rigors of American life. They were increasingly forgotten by a generally contented white class living in a suburb where political activity was in abeyance." Although Carter's victory was no landslide, Campbell said, it did suggest that America was ready to face its own problems, as big as they were, by choosing a man who could make government work. Read by many Britishers, Carter's interview with Campbell gave the British an insightful account of the new American President-Elect.

The metropolitan papers did not follow the example of some of the provincial members of the press in publishing bits of Carter's autobiography, although the *Daily Telegraph* did print an interview with Mrs. Carter. Would the real Mrs. Carter now speak up in the White House? the *Daily Telegraph* asked, attempting an answer. The quietness of her manner gave a hint of the strength of her will beneath it. The week of the election she appeared relaxed and happy after a long and wearing campaign. "We are a very close family," Rosalynn volunteered, "and the thing we want to do more than anything is just to be with the family." For her the campaign was a great experience, the *Daily Telegraph* wrote, and, as the nation's First Lady, she would work with the mental health program as she had done in Georgia, and do what she could for America's elderly.

Mrs. Carter was an articulate spokeswoman, the *Daily Telegraph* informed its readers, devoted to her family and with a strong independent personality of her own, well versed in all issues, relentless in sticking to the stiff schedule she set for herself, and very effective. "Her habit of extreme orderliness and methodology enabled her to achieve much in the national election," the *Daily Telegraph* said. Possessed of a shy smile, and a voice that appeared to be a little sugary, she had a will no less than her husband's. She promised to "introduce square dancing and to eliminate liquor in the White House."

Editorially, the *Daily Telegraph* discussed Carter and the world, noting that hope and uncertainty hovered over the free world as it waited for the foreign policy of the new administration. Although the British were accustomed to America's large and friendly power and influence, "there had never been so crucial a time for world peace, stability and prosperity as now. Russia's global effective military strength in key areas of potential conflict had become much greater in the last four years as Britain had declined," the *Daily Telegraph* said. As a result, Europe was "overwhelmingly dependent on America for its protection at home and almost totally so for the defense and furtherance of its interests abroad." To have won such a remarkable victory, Carter "must not only be almost incredibly tough, determined and intelligent, he must be a realist," the *Daily Telegraph* continued.

The London daily newspaper also discussed both candidates' chief sources of strength. Geographically, Carter was the most popular in the South and in the northern cities, while Ford's strength lay in the Midwest and in the Far West. Among the social classes Carter's chief support was with the blacks, the Jews, Catholics, and minority groups. Ford won the votes of the big city suburbs, the upper-income groups, the college and university groups—in general the affluent classes. Although Carter's greater intellectual capacity was recognized, it was the South regionally that "tipped the scales for Carter," the *Daily Telegraph* wrote.

Several British newspapers, including the *Daily Telegraph,* reported the successes of two academic scholars in their senatorial races. Daniel P. Moynihan, Democrat, defeated Senator James Buckley, the staunch conservative Republican from New York—the state with the largest Congressional representation and Electoral College vote east of the Mississippi River. S. I. Hayakawa, a Republican college president in California, won over Senator James Tunney, a liberal Democrat. California on the West Coast had the largest Congressional group and the greatest number of delegates to the Electoral College west of the "Father of Waters." The composition of the Congress, the newspapers said, was practically unchanged as the Democrats gained a slim majority of one in the Senate and three in the House of Representatives. Carter would face a slightly more liberal and a slightly younger Congress than President Ford had to contend with. Congress would be under new and, quite possibly, more vigorous leadership. This, concluded the *Daily Telegraph,* indicated no drastic contrast in philosophy of government in the newly elected Congress.

The Scottish papers, the *Scotsman* and the *Herald,* described the Carters' arrival in Plains at dawn on the day after the election, the huge crowd of friends and well-wishers who had stayed up all night, awaiting their arrival; of Carter attempting to speak but choking up: "I didn't get choked up until. . . ." He suddenly stopped in midsentence as tears flowed down his cheeks, the newspapers reported. He embraced Rosalynn, who stood beside him shedding tears of joy. The crowd cheered loudly as some wept openly with their newly elected home town hero's success. In referring to President Ford's telegram, received later, Carter stated, "President Ford's characteristically gracious statement will make my job much easier."

Fred Emery reported in the *Scotsman* that the blacks boosted Carter to victory. In Oregon and four other states, Emery noted, Eugene McCarthy received enough votes to give President Ford the states. Only the overwhelming support of the black voters, who made the difference in marginal states like Mississippi, gave Carter the Presidency. In Ohio, Emery said, where some four million votes were cast, Carter won by some six thousand votes. In California, where more than seven million went to the polls, President Ford carried the state by approximately thirty thousand votes.

Under President Ford, Emery wrote, bills originating in Congress and traveling to the White House had been "like directing traffic the wrong way down a one-way street. The ideas, the impulse for ideas, came from the White House to Congress. With overwhelming Democratic majorities in both houses of Congress," the *Scotsman* contended, "Carter should have no difficulty in getting his priority legislation passed."

The *Scotsman*'s correspondent reported that Jack Watson, a lawyer friend, had headed a Carter Presidency transition team in Atlanta, which had been working since early summer on its assignment. "Carter had doggedly stuck with his strategy," Emery said, "coordinated by the tight little band of loyalists who had proved so effective in winning the Democratic Party nomination." During the national campaign Carter had not demonstrably accepted the advice of previously non-Carter Democrats who had national experience, with the single exception of Robert Strauss, the chairman of the Democratic National Committee, Emery said, then asked: Would Carter's new spirit of "Why not the Best?" reach out for the ablest talent in the United States," or would he remain closeted with the "Georgia Mafia" as Nixon did with his "California Mafia"?

Other sources of British printed opinion told their readers about the Carters' homecoming to Plains at sunrise on November 3. "The sun," said the *Daily Mail,* "glanced over the roof of the peanut museum on Main Street, caught the top of the Black Porch Cafe and brought down a drop of dew from the telephone wires. Then the early golden rays of the sun caught Jimmy Carter squarely in the face against an old wooden street on the freight-loading railroad station." Carter didn't come into Plains sitting in the back of a Cadillac blowing kisses to the girls leaning out of high-rise buildings. Jimmy Carter, the next President of the United States, walked home and shared his triumph with all of the 683 people of Plains. John Edwards stood near as Carter glowed with the reddish sun. There was no apparent tiredness about Carter, as he looked straight into the early dawn golden light. "Earl Godwin stared out through the cluttered window of his little shop, looked across the street and said, 'I do believe—I tell you this is sure hard to believe.' "

The *Daily Mail* continued by noting that, as a youthful band struck up "Happy Days Are Here Again," Rosalynn and Jimmy Carter mounted the steps of an unused freight depot. Here, surrounded by their loved ones and close friends, he began to speak. "I told you I didn't intend to lose. I came all the way"—it trailed off—then the sun picked up the tears as they trickled down his cheeks. He turned toward his wife, who stood by, likewise in tears, and embraced her. The Secret Service men jostled some of the people back from Carter, which was resented by the local folk, because the Carters belonged to them. From the platform Jimmy and Rosalynn Carter walked hand in hand, surrounded by Secret Service men, down the drive to their home. "Upon entering his home Jimmy flopped down on a sofa, his hands clasped as if he were in prayer: 'You know—I just think I might take the rest of the day off.' "

The *Yorkshire Post* described Carter's brilliantly planned and executed campaign, which was conceived four years earlier by his closest Georgia friends. "It was fitting that the belt of Southern States provided him with the margin of victory," the *Yorkshire Post* said. "It was Mississippi with its seven electoral votes that put him over the top. The race was very close, so much so, in fact, that a few voters in several states would have given Ford the most remarkable come-from-behind victory since Harry Truman defeated Thomas Dewey in 1948."

The *Western Mail,* among several sources of British public opinion, quoted President Ford's telegram of congratulations to Carter. The President had gone to bed the preceding night at nine o'clock believing he had won the election and learned his fate the next morning. Shortly after noon the entire Ford family emerged into the crowded press room looking crestfallen, the *Western Mail* reported. Too hoarse to speak, Ford handed a telegram to his wife Betty, who read: "It is apparent you have won our long and intense struggle. I congratulate you on your victory. Although there will continue to be disagreement over the best means to use in pursuing our goals I want to assure you that you will have my complete wholehearted support as you take office in January. I also pledge to you that I and all members of my Administration will do all that we can to ensure that you begin your term as smoothly and effectively as possible. May God bless you and your family as you undertake your new responsibilities."

Mrs. Ford's voice cracked with emotion as she read. Her daughter stood by weeping. Upon the completion of the telegram the entire Ford family, said the *Guardian,* went down among the throng of reporters and cameramen to shake hands and to thank them for their help during the past two years. The Presidential family gave and received many hugs and kisses from their friends in the press corps. It was one of the most moving episodes that veteran White House reporters could recall, the *Western Mail* said.

Carter, said the provincial *Western Mail,* won in a "meteoric rise from obscurity to the White House on a platform that promised a host of innovations and strong leadership." His campaign was a masterpiece of planning—"his critics say cynical manipulation"—but it worked. He was a stranger to Washington from the South who performed a political miracle in seeking and gaining the Presidency on a platform of trust, honesty, and openness. To accomplish his objective, the *Western Mail* wrote, he had to bring to defeat the South's major political figure of the last decade, George Wallace, in the Florida primary. The *Western Mail* said, "Wallace, like so many other Southern political figures, was a captive of the race issue. Carter recognized that the South [was] freed from the stigma of race by the civil rights legislation that gave blacks the vote. Carter did for the South what Kennedy did for the Catholics in 1960."

Philip Finn, one of the writers for the "United States Election Special" edition of the *Evening News,* stated that Carter scraped to victory in one of the most dramatic election finishes in American history. His victory was appropriately signaled by his winning the state of Mississippi, which went Democratic for the first time since 1956. Upon learning that he would be the thirty-ninth President of the United States, Finn wrote, Carter flashed the kind of smile that toothpaste makers love and said, "It is time to tap the tremendous strength and vitality, and idealism, and hope, and patriotism, and sense of brother and sisterhood in this country to unify our nation to make it great once again. I pray that I will live up to your confidence and never disappoint you." As Carter spoke to the large audience in the dance hall of Atlanta's World Commerce Center his eyes were puffy and red, his voice strained. The crowd stopped long enough to listen and to cheer Georgia's famous son before returning to their mint juleps and dancing to the bluegrass band strumming out Dixie songs. Amy, the nine-year-old Carter daughter, up well past bedtime, yawned while her mother beside her wept tears of happiness, Finn added.

From Plains, Stephen Barker reported in the *Daily Telegraph* that Carter's campaign workers would be installed in the White House and create a Georgia Mafia just as Bostonians had created Camelot under Kennedy, Texans had staffed Johnson's stay in the White House, and Californians had served as Nixon's Mafia. Jordan, Powell, Watson and Kirbo, Barber stated, would have positions in the White House. As a touch of folksy Georgia affection, the people of Plains baked Carter a cake in the shape of the White House and presented it to him just before the Secret Service men escorted him to the seclusion of his house. Beneath the front portico of the White House cake hung a single peanut. The *Daily Telegraph* concluded that Carter's Administration would be "more moralistic in its approach to foreign affairs and less Machiavellian than Dr. Kissinger's seemed as he flitted around the globe, practicing jet-shuttle diplomacy."

On the other hand, the stock markets in New York and London, fearful that a Democratic Administration would mean wasteful spending, suffered decisive losses upon receiving the news of Carter's victory. The British stock market, however, recovered the next day, November 4, in all stocks except oils, which was the only Carter casualty. The Wall Street stock market opened 16 points down but recovered to 9.56 points down in active trading.

Carter argued that American multiple national corporations should not be building manufacturing plants overseas as long as there was high unemployment at home. The weakness of the oils stock reflected a concern that the combination of Carter in the White House and a Democratic Congress would mean a less favorable political climate for the oil industry. The gold market revealed Carter's shining hours, declared the *Daily Telegraph,* when the price rose $3.25 to a new high of $125.625 per ounce.

William Lowther wrote in the *Daily Mail* about "The Triumphs and the Tears." There were tears in the White House as Betty Ford read the congratulatory telegram; tears in Plains too as the new First Lady was overcome at her husband's successful quest for the Presidency. Carter's victory, wrote Lowther, was sweeter because he knew he owed it to no one but himself. Shunned by the Democratic Party machine, he literally had no debts outstanding. He successfully appealed directly to the young, the ethnic minorities, the blacks, and the laborers. Carter really did more than get elected President; he bypassed the kingmakers and ended an era of Kennedy domination of the Democratic Party. The interregnum to January 20, the *Daily Mail* contended, with a lame duck President and a lame duck Secretary of State, Kissinger, was bound to cause difficulties—

not least for Britain. "President Ford's strongest qualities were supreme in defeat, with a dignity and generosity not frequently found," the *Daily Mail* said.

When Betty Ford in the White House room finished reading the telegram to Carter, she "took a deep and controlled breath and looked distinctly relieved," the *Daily Mail* added. "Afflicted with crippling arthritic pains, her public limelight must have been agonizing. For two years she was not able to relax and sought relief in pain-killing drugs and whiskey—on a few occasions when she endeavored to speak publicly her speech slurred and she stumbled over simple sentences." Mrs. Ford would subsequently go to the Naval Hospital for treatment for her habits of alcoholism and narcotics.

8

Postelection Comments

The British media did not permit the British people to forget the American Presidential election immediately upon its conclusion. With a large number of British news commentators and reporters in the United States, the gates of information opened during the preelection campaign remained open after the election. Practically all British newspapers and periodicals continued their comments on the American Presidential election after the official election returns were known. Some selective examples of continued British interest in the American election follow.

The *Daily Mail*'s leading editorial, "Forward with Carter into the Unknown," for example, lauded the American political system. "The election of Jimmy Carter was living proof," it declared, "of America's genius in devising a political system whereby an ordinary man can emerge from nowhere and go through the democratic process to become his nation's leader." Carter, the editorial predicted, would take America into the third century of its existence at a time when liberty, democracy, and individualism were under attack everywhere, including Britain, the Carter family ancestral home. The election of Carter, the unknown, inexperienced and surrounded by an equally untried team, said something about the American voters. "It shows they were confident enough about the future to entrust it to an exciting newcomer rather than a decent but uninspiring old-style politician." Furthermore, the narrowness of Carter's victory showed that his election was a trust and that he would have to work very hard in the next four years to win a true national endorsement. In short, "he has his chance, what will he do with it?" the editorial concluded.

As for Britain, the *Daily Mail* believed that Carter was a friend who would be difficult to negotiate with financially. Britain would be told to work its way out of its trouble, in which case he would be helpful. When President Ford departed the White House, the last vestiges of the Nixon Administration went with him, the *Daily Mail* said. A new era of American history would open up next January with Carter. The whole free world must wish him well, concluded the London paper.

William Lowther expressed the same idea when he wrote that, with Carter, the Western world would, in a very real sense, move under new and unknown management. With the fall of President Ford went the end of a diplomatic era in which Henry Kissinger and his policies of detente, secrecy, and sometimes deception dominated foreign affairs. The free world, wrote Lowther, was entering "a new period of international diplomacy which promises to be refreshing and exciting." President Carter would emphasize America's economic and political relations with Western Europe. His foreign policy, contended Lowther in the *Daily Mail,* would consist of three themes of major importance: (1) a new moral authority— a dedication to humanitarian principles and opposition to human injustice abroad; (2) an insistence that Washington would not interfere militarily in the internal affairs of other nations unless the security of the United States were threatened; (3) an openness in foreign policy that would ensure that never again would the American people be misled about options, commitments, progress, or failures.

In the preelection campaign Lowther heard both President Ford and Carter speak generously of America's friendship with Great Britain and of the British's admirable spirit and resilience to overcome adversity. However, as President, Carter would demand that Britain make heavy sacrifices to repay her debts to the International Monetary Fund. The new relation with Britain would be both open and decent, Lowther wrote, so Britain need have no fear.

Fred Emery in the *Times* warned Carter that he must learn from the mistakes he made in the campaign that nearly cost him the election. With a Democratic majority in both the Senate and in the House of Representatives, Emery explained, Carter should have no trouble in his priority legislative program being enacted into law. Although Carter did not have the enormous experience of Senator Mondale on Capitol Hill, would Carter use wisely the talented and experienced Vice-President? asked Emery. As President, Carter would have "enormous opportunities to gain the tone and even the inspiration of the country."

In a leading editorial, "Mr. Carter's Qualities," the *Times* described Carter as a safe and reassuring figure. Few Presidents had ever come to the White House less beholden to his party machine and less committed to any group of advisers to run his Administration than had Carter, the *Times* said. There was no reason to believe that Carter would be safer than President Ford's Administration was in dealings with the Soviet Union, or that his position on detente would be significantly different. The *Times* stated, as other British newspapers were saying, that much depended upon whom Carter surrounded himself with in the White House as his close advisers. "What is now clear is that Carter is a man with a capacity for political maneuver and with an inflexible determination that have been characteristic of great Presidents," the *Times* wrote. In wishing the President-Elect the best, the *Times* recalled that to be the first President from the deep South since the Civil War was a remarkable achievement, and, amid all doubts, it was evident that he had the potential to be a remarkable President.

Frank Vogt discussed the economics of Carter and recalled President Ford's approach to reducing government involvement in the economy, predicting that Carter's Administration would produce an active leadership and involvement in all economic areas. Carter would probably expand public spending with increases in appropriations for jobs and welfare programs. These increases would be partly matched by cuts in defense spending. The new President would demand better coordination of fiscal and monetary policies among Congress, the Administration, and the Federal Reserve Board. Furthermore, the *Times* informed its readers, Carter would "simplify the tax code, shift the tax burden toward richer people by closing the loopholes and making the tax rate more progressive, revise corporate tax laws to encourage business equity . . . and end special tax concessions for companies that decide to locate plants abroad." As the new President, Carter would give more aid to local communities, less to states, and combine ten or twelve government agencies involved in energy. There would be immediate action to reduce American dependence on foreign oil.

The *Sun* announced in large headlines: "Peanut President Cracks It!" The millionaire peanut farmer had cracked the toughest nut of his job career—a remarkable achievement. "The Reign begins in Plains." The *Sun* wrote that in the White House President Ford surrendered amid tears:

"In the press room it was a tearful scene as Betty Ford read the telegram of congratulations to Carter on his victory. The President's daughter Susan wept silently, one of the sons wiped his eyes repeatedly, another blew his nose frequently and many of the White House employees cried noticeably." Carter had fulfilled the "wildest dreams of the old South, astonished his old ma and made it to the White House. We at the *Sun* wish him well in the most powerful and toughest job on this planet."

Anthony Shrimsley wrote from Atlanta that, when the New York vote result was flashed over the wires onto the television screen, showing that Carter had won its forty electoral votes, a black supporter yelled, "We've got the Big Apple." Suddenly Carter's grin took over. "It showed his delighted face and seemed to spread and spread to embrace all America." With the Big Apple vote, Carter had 267 of the 270 electoral votes needed for election. Three more cliff-hanging hours passed before the seven electoral votes came from Mississippi. Where would Carter lead America and the free world? Shrimsley asked. "What was known," concluded the *Sun* reporter, "was that Gerald Ford would have led us nowhere."

With the knowledge that the vote of the blacks had given Carter the Deep South and the Presidency, the *Daily Mirror* published an article written in Southern plantation dialect, beginning, "So Mister Carter is de next pressdin of the Yewnigh States an' Prizzdin Fawd leaves the Whatt House." The *Daily Mirror* said it would be "churlish not to wish the man well, and the sight of Mr. Ford stumbling back into obscurity caused no eye dimming."

Daily Mirror correspondent Anthony Delano, in "All the President's People," said the Carters were a closely knit clan, typical of the Deep South. Big decisions, Delano wrote, were decided at family conferences. A family decision brought Amy Carter into the world. A fifteen-year gap lay between her and her youngest of three brothers. Rosalynn Carter, said the *Daily Mirror* reporter, had plenty of placid, soft-centered Southern womanhood about her. At forty-nine years of age she also had plenty of sex appeal. She was, however, very tough. The President-Elect had declared that his wife would have a kind of Assistant President position after his inauguration. She would represent him in the United States and abroad as his personal envoy. Carter told Delano, "I would never hesitate to ask her to go somewhere, let folks know we care about them and bring me back a report."

Editorially, the *Daily Mirror* stated that "America voted for a new beginning after the stench of Vietnam and the shame of Watergate." Democratic Presidents were usually more sympathetic to Britain than were Republican Presidents. Moreover, with the United Kingdom's economy in the condition it was in 1976, Britishers needed all of the American sympathy and help they could get.

John Pilger, another *Daily Mirror* reporter, spent part of the election victory night in the cabin of two Plains blacks who were retired farm tenants and knew Carter from boyhood. Pilger wrote that, as he and Anzze and Ruth Pittman watched the television set as the returns came in, the aging blacks were beside themselves. ANZZE: "Ain't gonna step aside; ain't gonna shed no tears. We've been down too long fer dat kinda actin' now. We gotta praise de Lord; We gotta sing and laugh and all dat. . . . You knows what I means?" Ruth, who sat loosely in a rocking chair, with knitted shawl round her shoulders, interrupted, "Oh, shat ya mouth, Anzze, yer knows sure as de Lord is here today dat you're gonna bawl ya eyes out and babble yo mouth an' so as I." The Pittmans possessed an ancient "snowbound" black-and-white television set, which, as Pilger wrote, "Anzze finally tuned with body blows and appeals to the Lord." In an analysis of Carter's victory, Pilger reported that Anzze stated that a "lot of Northern folks doubted Jimmy and maybe they still do." But Jimmy had won the Presidency with the vote of the poor black people and the poor white people, mainly in the South, "for the simple reason that he's held true to us all his life."

The next day, as John Pilger prepared to leave Plains, he concluded that the small community where the blacks and the whites were utterly at ease with one another was America at its best. And that Carter's election was America at its very best. The election meant simply that a majority of Americans had rejected the crime of Watergate and its apologists. Pilger left Plains with the tune of little Lynn Moon and the Zuma County band singing the "Peanut Pickin' Politicking Man" ringing pleasantly in his ears.

Paul Daese wrote for the *Daily Express* that Plains represented the "American dream in which a peanut farmer can soar from obscurity to the top of the Western world in two years." From Washington, Ross Mark declared that the election "marked the end of an era in American politics." Mark wrote: "The most notable casualty was Dr. Kissinger. President Ford was an honest but uninspiring man, who worked diligently to heal the rifts in American public life after the disgrace of Nixon." According to Mark, Carter promised the American people not only new names in office but a new style of government. He would staff the White House with many of his present campaign team and call on a "brain trust" from the academic circle to fill his cabinet and administrative posts in his government.

Brian Vine, another *Daily Express* journalist who followed the President-Elect's campaign trail, declared that Carter's road to the White House was "littered with people who underestimated his capabilities." Indeed, he soared like an eagle when he was labeled as a moral and a political survivor. The American people reached out for a man with the "presentations of a savior, instead of settling for just another decent, honest All-American politician." Carter's campaign strategy, drawn up by Hamilton Jordan, started out as a long, cool, cunning game plan and was tirelessly executed. He was groomed as a man of truth and honesty and fed to a public starved for integrity, Vine reported.

As Vine saw it, the Georgia nominee was tailored to appeal to the largest part of the electorate. He was conservative to moderate on economics, on foreign policy, on the death penalty, and on abortion. Religion and politics had fashioned Carter's life. Vine noted, however, that Carter's soft Georgia drawl, the plowboy gait, the naked ambition in those pale blue eyes did not endear him to all people.

Peter Bourne advised his fellow Britishers not to worry about Carter. He'll be Britain's best friend, assured Bourne. He was from the heartland of America, represented the best American qualities of honesty, and possessed a charm when the going got tough. He supported strong use of all mechanisms in vogue to strengthen and stabilize the British pound. As President, contended Bourne, Carter would not thrust the United States forward to interfere in any way in British domestic affairs. He would be a traveling President, and so would members of his family and his staff. America's friends in Europe and elsewhere would find in Carter a true friend, concluded Bourne.

Daily Express reporter George Gale wrote that America gritted its teeth in the election and made a brave and witty choice. Gale believed that the more the people saw of Carter the "more apprehension he aroused; the less reassurance he gave. The election was a rejection of the known and an acceptance of the unknown. It was the thought of Dole succeeding to the Presidency that tipped the scales in favor of Carter and Mondale." Personally, Gale thought that America was right in taking the chance it had made and to give Carter the opportunity he had strenuously sought. "In Britain it was impossible for some one to come blazing through from nowhere and seize the strings of power. Everybody had to go through the political machinery," while in the United States a person could make his own political machine, Gale wrote. Carter was like Pierre in Tolstoy's *War and Peace*—a man of incessant quiet yearning.

The *Daily Express* reported the closeness of Carter's victory. A switch of 1,500 votes in Ohio and of 3,000 votes in Hawaii would have given President Ford the 29 Electoral College votes that Carter received in those two states and an Electoral College vote of 270 to 268 for Carter. Only 4,500 switched votes in those two states would have given the Republicans the Presidency, the *Daily Express* said.

Editorially, the London daily newspaper shouted, "Goodbye, Henry!" Kissinger had dominated American foreign policy since Nixon had brought him to Washington. He now joined Dean Acheson and John Foster Dulles as a man who was in a very real sense the author of America's foreign policy while he was Secretary of State, the *Daily Express* contended.

The *East Anglia Daily Times* announced that the Carter win would end eight years of feuding between the executive and the legislative branches in the United States. In all American history, the *Daily Express* said, few people had burst on the national political scene with such slender political credentials as Carter had.

The *Western Mail* reported on November 5 that Carter held a long conference with Mondale. On the same day the *East Anglia Daily Times* reported Carter having conferences with his advisers about members of his Cabinet and others to be appointed to government positions. Congress appropriateed two million dollars for the transition expenses from the Ford Administration to the incoming Carter Administration, and Jack Watson, who headed Carter's transition team, moved from Atlanta to Washington.

Ian Ball reported in the *Daily Telegraph* that Carter personified the old Dream of Dixie—she would rise again to become a dominant force in national politics. The staff who made the Dream of Dixie an impressive reality met with the Carters as they accelerated their plans for an activist and innovative Presidency. As a crucial item in the transition, Ball reported that Watson had a "heavily indexed blue folder, almost three inches thick, which contains the names of seven thousand men and women who have already been screened in a computerized talent hunt as candidates for jobs in a Carter Administration." It was the most nearly complete and confidential assessment of the abilities of people, stated Ball, that any victor in a Presidential race had ever received. Watson and his staff, Ball said, had done an excellent job in providing the "nuts and bolts" of the Carter Administration.

Simon Winchester reported in the *Guardian* that with all the efficiency and deliberate speed that had characterized Carter's election he began preparing for the takeover of the government. He planned to go to Washington three or four days each week during the next two months to visit the transition office. The transition team, one hundred strong, was very busy with the problems involved. Carter would select Cabinet members in December, give the men and women selected administrative power, and make them responsible for their departments to a degree never favored by Nixon, Winchester wrote. A short time later, Watson recommended, and Carter accepted, that the transition work move to Washington. William Simon, Secretary of the Treasury, offered the victorious Democrats room in the Treasury building to set up offices for the transition of Administrations.

Times reporter Patrick Brogan stated that Carter, after conferring with Mondale, promised him that he would play a greater role in government than any previous Vice-President. In America's foreign policy, Brogan reported, Carter announced there would be continuity. "My Administration is for peace," the President-Elect stated. "We will revive the American traditional alliances."

Most of the British reporters stationed in the United States were interested in the political results of the election. A few reporters, however, ignored the political takeover and wrote of the economic effects of the Presidential transition in America. A *Times* reporter informed his paper that the New York stock market had quickly recovered from its original slump. The *Times* said that few Wall Street professionals accepted the grim prediction of excessive and inflationary spending by the Carter Administration. According to the *Times,* the market on November 4 rose 3.91 points, to 910.44, on the trading of 21.7 million shares.

The *Daily Mirror* declared in an article, "Peanut Power Packs Progressive Pugnacious Punch," that Carter's success could be attributed to George Washington Carver, who was born a slave. Carver's research at Tuskegee Institute, a predominantly black college in Alabama, found nearly three hundred products that could be made from peanuts, the *Daily Mirror* said. These products, reported the London newspaper, included flour, dyes, ink, paint, cheese, milk, and insulating board. Harold

Wilson once appeared in the House of Commons dressed in a suit made from peanuts. Pound for pound, peanuts contained more proteins, minerals, and vitamins than beef liver, more fat than heavy cream, more food value than sugar. The British prefer more frequently salted peanuts, but the Americans like peanut butter best, the *Daily Mirror* said.

Jonathan Steele, in the *Guardian,* announced that Carter planned fortnightly press conferences once he was inaugurated. Acknowledging the President-Elect's concern for the media, Steele contended that Carter's language on foreign affairs seemed vague and unimpressive. Domestically, Carter promised a thorough spring cleaning and a radical reorganization of the executive department, Steele reported. Reflecting on those proposed changes, the professional lobbyists, the media, and other organizations were also changing personnel. "It was a time for head hunting and job hunting," Steele wrote, noting that in America the President had great appointive power but in Britain more of the positions were under the Civil Service.

For days after the result of the American election was widely known, articles and editorials continued to appear in British periodicals and newspapers. Among the latter was a *Times* editorial, "The World and Mr. Carter," in which the importance of the Presidential election in the United States was emphasized. America was a world power whose policies were of decisive importance in many parts of the world, it read. A change of the President of the United States was of intense interest to many millions of people who do not have a vote in American elections. To them and to their governments an American election might be an intensely frustrating and worrying affair. Carter's public record, however, gave the British and the people of Western Europe nothing to go on, since his career in Georgia state politics did not involve him in foreign policy issues at all, the *Times* said.

Peter Greg in the *Daily Mail* and Lillian Hellman in the *Observer* published extensive articles on the place Rosalynn Carter would play in the new Administration. A leader of the Democratic Party told Greg, "That lady is going to be the power behind the throne in Washington today and forty-eight hours after the inauguration Rosalynn Carter is going to be the power beside the throne. Jimmy Carter will not press any button without asking his wife first. When it comes to icy, determined ruthlessness, she is not the kind of lady who is frightened by pressing buttons. There is nothing Carter does—or will continue to do—without consultation with his wife."

A President needed someone like that, Greg wrote in the *Daily Mail.* During the campaign when she was at strategy meetings she spoke up in her soft, gentle Southern drawl. What she said, continued Greg, did not always please the professional organizers around Carter but they listened and so did he. "Neither he nor she see any reason to change their way once the family moves into the White House. Southern men-first ladies were usually a force to be reckoned with," Greg said. Not even Eleanor Roosevelt, as the President's wife, exercised as much influence and power as Rosalynn Carter would enjoy. In opening a role as an activist, the new First Lady had views in her own right, not merely as the President's wife. "Mrs. Carter will dramatically demonstrate one of the new President's deepest beliefs, that it's time for women to play a greater part in running this country," Greg believed. Greg quoted Rosalynn, explaining how she would operate: "I believe it would be a shame . . . not to take advantage of the power that the job offers. I intend to be a First Lady who has something to say and I will not hesitate to say it often." Calling Rosalynn "the steel magnolia," Greg said that she and Margaret Thatcher were not unalike.

In explaining her relations with her husband, Rosalynn told Greg, "Jimmy and I have always been partners. That's how we've got to where we are, working together." The English journalist agreed: "In everything they've done from business to politics it has been a real partnership—and a very good marriage indeed. Carter has been a one-woman man and Rosalynn a one-man woman." Their fierce religion had been a foundation for their marital fidelity, Greg contended. Both husband and wife acknowledged that sometimes they held different, even contrary, views. Rosalynn explained: "Sometimes we argue about a viewpoint. I don't always win. But I sure argue hard with Jimmy; I get mad and I scream and scream. He gets mad, too—and he just listens."

In Greg's opinion, when the Carters entered the White House, Rosalynn Carter would involve herself in several projects in which she was recognized as an expert, such as health and welfare projects: setting up committees to improve mental health services in American hospitals; starting a national campaign on behalf of the elderly to give them special care programs; increasing the number of day-care centers in America for the children of working women; learning Spanish.

After several interviews with Mrs. Carter, *Observer* reporter Lillian Hellman wrote that Rosalynn Carter was a pretty woman, prettier to look at straight than on television. Her eyes, finely spaced, underlay an extraordinary intellect. Although she was not as well educated as her husband, she reads everything she can put her hands on. Hellman said Rosalynn spoke with warmth about the struggles of her mother and her help after her father died. She was proud to be of the working class and was deeply interested in their welfare. She was an active member of the lower middle class and had worked all of her life. The Carters were part of the New South. Their reach for power did not exclude their sincere pride in what they came from. A dedication to work and an abiding pride in their family background might be, thought Hellman, the Carters' greatest gift to their fellow Americans.

In regard to the Vietnam War, Rosalynn stated it approached a national disgrace. She did not blame the students for not caring about the government after Watergate, Vietnam, and Cambodia. She thought that the students turned to religion and that the United States was experiencing a religious reawakening. Hellman reported in the *Observer* that Rosalynn believed the students had a right to be alienated and disgusted but, with decent government and proper leadership, they would turn away from that feeling toward their country. When asked about who controlled her husband, Mrs. Carter was emphatic: "Nobody controls Jimmy and nobody ever will."

Hellman's final impression was quite favorable: "When I left Mrs. Carter, I was impressed with the cool, the calm, the ability to handle whatever comes up, or to turn it 'aside.' " This *Observer* journalist confessed that she did not know exactly what the Americans wanted in the new Mrs. President but they would have an intelligent and a remarkable First Lady.

Nora Beloff, another member of the *Observer*'s reportorial staff stationed in the United States, wrote a series of articles on Carter's program for bolstering the economy and lowering the unemployment. From Washington, the reporter described the creation of a joint economic effort by Britain and the United States to solve their common problems. The Ford Administration, Beloff said, actually embarrassed Britain by its somewhat dictatorial approach rather than a cooperative approach to help Britain meet its immediate debts.

Beloff predicted that the raising of oil prices by OPEC countries would force the Carter Administration to speed up the United States' development of nuclear power. Carter must choose between an increasing dependence upon Middle Eastern oil and faster construction of nuclear power plants. In recent years nuclear development was hobbled by the economic uncertainty and environmental opposition in the United States. A new energy policy, Beloff reported, was worked out by Watson's transition team, which included seven areas: creation of a new Cabinet-level Department of Energy with one person in charge; correcting a mistake previously made, which resulted in maintaining the price of energy on the American domestic market at a level far below the international price; increasing the production of offshore and Alaskan wells; agreeing to allow natural gas prices to go up to encourage further drilling of both oil and gas; arguing for the better use of American coal, of which the U.S. had an almost limitless supply, which could eliminate American dependence on foreign energy; exploring the use of solar, geothermal, and synthetic fuels.

Editorially, the *Observer* played down the American electoral process. In electing Carter by a narrow majority, the American people had chosen for the world's most important job a man of sharp intelligence and obvious energy, but with little experience in either national government or international affairs. The *Observer* said that Carter should enjoy a security of tenure at home greater than that of either of his predecessors. He would be dealing with a Congress controlled by his own party. Congress could be expected to try to maintain greater influence over foreign policy than it successfully asserted under President Ford, predicted the *Observer,* but cooperation between the White House and Capitol Hill was likely to run more smoothly. The influence of the United States on the rest of the world depended on the political, economic, and racial health of the American society as well as its stated foreign policy. The metropolitan newspaper contended that, during the later years of Republican rule, several events combined to shake not only the confidence of America's allies, but also the self-confidence of Americans themselves in their political system. The painful blow of Watergate was partially restored by relentless exposure, culminating in the resignation of President Nixon.

President Ford's personal image as an honest, plain man helped to heal the wounds, the *Observer* contended. Certainly Watergate contributed to a feeling among the American people that a change was needed in Washington. During the Ford Administration, continued the *Observer,* unemployment continued high, which hit the blacks hardest and represented a setback for social equality in America. The rest of the world expected a mild inflation during the Carter Administration. A substantial inflation, argued the metropolitan paper, would raise world prices and upset efforts that were being made in Britain and elsewhere to reduce inflation. The world economy required more international management. "America's ability to combine economic well-being with greater social justice and to end racial discrimination was its strongest argument in the worldwide ideological competition," the *Observer* thought.

America's other great question—Vietnam—resulted in a popular revulsion against the commitment of American military power abroad, especially in a civil war. Indeed, Congress would probably oppose any actions likely to lead to United States military intervention abroad, as in the invasion of Cambodia. Furthermore, the *Observer* said, Congress was almost certain to check any policy, such as the Nixon Doctrine, whereby the United States relied heavily on the armies of its strongest local allies and backed them with sea and air power. Under the Nixon Doctrine, America took the risk, as in the Middle East, that an ally would drag the United States into eventual confrontation with the Soviet Union. Carter's assurance of continuity in foreign policy would surely have changes in style and priority. He would not give anyone a free hand as Dr. Kissinger had under Nixon and Ford. "The scholarly doctor [Kissinger] left Carter with a mixed bag of achievements, mistakes and unfinished tasks. . . . A more determined attempt at a comprehensive Middle East settlement guaranteed by both the United States is one of the most urgent needs facing the Carter Administration," the *Observer* continued.

Connected with the Middle East peace was a complex of problems, thought the *Observer,* which stemmed from the "oil revolution." These problems involved oil supplies and prices, and the Third World and its demand for a new international economic order. "The Kissinger-Ford Administration revealed little understanding of these vital issues. Its policy of seeking self-sufficiency in energy was a total failure. Towards OPEC and the Third World generally, it used the stick rather than the carrot, though some American threats were clearly empty," the *Observer* stated. Only after Angola did Kissinger realize the serious possibilities of international conflict in South Africa if African aspirations were not recognized. Carter was more detached, contended the *Observer,* about letting the Third World settle its evolution problem without Soviet intervention. The newspaper asked pointedly if Carter were going to make a positive commitment on economic aid and trade that developing countries desperately needed from richer states if they were to have a chance of achieving political stability. The way Dr. Kissinger was able to recognize and develop a common interest between the nuclear superpowers in preventing war was his greatest achievement. "It is only a beginning of that embryonic world order which can be dimly discerned as the alternative to nuclear destruction. But it is a foundation upon which Carter and Brezhnev need to build," the *Observer* said.

To Mark Frankland, writing for the *Observer,* Carter was a Southern enigma. Riding in a taxi Frankland listened to the driver: "I don't know anything about Carter. Except the South whose regional pride apparently moved people to vote for a fellow Southerner. . . . Carter's greatest desire was to be a Southerner. Up here [in New York] the South and especially Southern politics are little known. Carter's behavior on race is impeccable." Frankland realized many liberals and conservatives thought Carter untrustworthy—that he was peculiarly double-faced even for a politician. For example, Carter stated he would attack unemployment and at the same time fight inflation; the two were incompatible. Again, he attacked established politicians but at some time sought their support in northern cities. He seemed, to this British reporter, to be constantly under strain and frequently was short-tempered. He gave the impression that he had to win at all costs. Toward the end of the campaign he lost much of his earlier self-assurance, Frankland wrote.

Frankland reported that at twelve years of age Jimmy Carter wrote an intriguing document, "Jimmy Carter's Health Report," which contained several illuminating character projections, including a concern for cleanliness in mouth and body, and the admonition to breathe through the nose, not through the mouth. Among young Jimmy's healthy mental habits were expecting to accomplish what you attempt; deciding quickly what you want to do and doing it; and the habit of sticking to the task once undertaken without looking back and regretting the decision.

Carter's mind, said Frankland, was an extremely effective machine, thorough, retentive, curious. Some people with whom Frankland talked expressed concern about Carter's "born-again" religion. They concluded that he might not be a "dangerous, self-righteous sort of person who would be willing to take on the rest of the world because he believes God is on his side." Carter had an inner directive, unique and constant, as the President-Elect stated: "I have a constant drive to do just the best I can." Frankland predicted that Carter's Administration would be stormy, for he planned to be an aggressive President and he expected Congress to follow him. Apparently, he did not intend to compromise, Frankland wrote, and this would result in confrontation.

The Irish and the Scotch newspapers had some comments to make in the final analyses of the American election and a few prophesies to state. M. Francois Xavier Ortoli, president of the European Economic Community (EEC), stated, for the *Irish Times,* his view of Carter's election. He was expecting the development of close relations at all levels with the new Administration with the "view to ensuring peace and prosperity of the peoples on both sides of the Atlantic." He awaited Carter's views on two very important issues, namely, the American contribution to plans to restore stability to the world economy and the monetary situation and trade relations with the United States on a number of problems, such as America's quotas on the imports of steel.

In the *Irish Times,* David Bell noted that Hamilton Jordan, Carter's campaign manager, and Jody Powell, the press secretary, did their laundry in their motel rooms during the campaign to keep expenses down. Jordan always appeared relaxed and possessed a very nimble mind, whereas Powell, not gifted quite as much as Jordan, was more likely to reveal stress and strain. Carter was a moderate liberal Democrat whose election "may well mark the South's coming of age," concluded Bell.

The *Irish Times* believed that Carter's election meant the lack of a monetary policy. As a result there was a cautious reaction among European financial institutions. The Dublin newspaper was the only public source on the American national election to express the idea that the James "Jack" Watson transition team interfered with the election. Preparations for the transition were under way for months before the election, the *Irish Times* said, and the group of "planners so botched the campaign they almost lost the election," concluded the *Irish Times.*

In analyzing the election, the Irish paper declared that the Republican Party was in deep trouble. "With the defeat of President Ford and the total failure to make Congressional gains, the Republicans were left weak, divided and largely powerless," the *Irish Times* argued, adding "nor were minorities in Congress increased—only 17 blacks won seats in the House of Representatives and there would be 18 congresswomen." Overall, the Senate remained the same: of 33 Senators up for reelection, 14 lost their positions—7 Democrats and 7 Republicans, the newspaper added.

Generously, several newspapers throughout the British Isles accepted the new President-Elect's statement that his foreign policy would operate on the principle of world order instead of power politics. Carter promised to try to dismiss the permanently divisive ideological basis for foreign relations and to "deal with nations on an individual basis as far as what is best for their own people. Instead of trying to force people to choose between us and the Soviet Union, I hope to let them choose our country because our system works best and because their trade with us and their open feeling for us would be in their best interest. I will treat each developing nation individually, not as a bloc," the *Irish Times* quoted Carter. The newspaper noted that Carter strongly favored majority rule in Rhodesia and in South Africa, and he planned to make that decision public policy. Certainly, there was no vagueness in this policy statement, the newspaper said.

Stelle Winston, writing from New York for the Birmingham *Evening Mail*, declared that Carter's success in politics came from work at the local level. The early weeks of the new Administration would show "whether the Carter flame is going out or only flickering or burning brightly," Winston wrote. Helen Pick warned in the *Guardian* that the new Administration faced a stiff uphill battle in putting Americans back to work, in halting inflation, in putting momentum into the American economy, and in seeking to prevent worldwide recession. Pick argued that business and the labor unions both were worried: the unions wanted money appropriated for jobs, while business was fearful of inflation. "The incoming Administration marked the end of an era of benign neglect," Pick said, explaining it was obvious that Carter wanted to do more for the Third World than President Ford ever did.

The Republicans, argued Pick, "were badly debilitated, and had turned sour. There was bitter infighting between the conservatives and the liberals." Many Republicans believed that the party should establish a broader base, Pick wrote. In fact, President Ford received nearly half of the votes cast when the registered Republicans numbered less than one-fifth of the total registered voters, Pick said. The old-style conservative Southern Democrats, continued the *Guardian* reporter, who dominated the Congressional committees, and often allied themselves with Republicans, had been largely eclipsed. In the new Administration the Southern members of Congress became a Grand New Party. The Grand Old Party must change its image or become the party of Big Business, concluded Pick.

Grace Durham wrote for the *Scotsman* a long article under the heading

"The Hand That Rocked the Carter Cradle." It was a biographical sketch of the President-Elect's mother—a registered nurse and a most unusual person. She was known affectionately as "Miss Lillian" by thousands of young and old, black and white. In 1976 she was more than seventy-five years of age, spry and alert and showing lots of stamina. In the last week of her son's campaign she visited twenty-one towns across the United States, traveling in a private Lear jet. She was warm and compassionate, and frequently exuberantly extroverted in her busy life. In contrast, Durham wrote, Jimmy was a cool, collected, introverted person who rarely showed any emotions, yet inwardly the son was very much like his mother —both of them were deeply religious with a high regard for human nature. She preached integration long before it became the law of the land, even though her husband was horrified by the idea of black and white mixing.

At sixty-eight she persuaded the Peace Corps, much to the dismay of her children and the opposition of her doctor, Durham reported, to accept her for a two-year stay in India. She worked in a health clinic among poverty-ridden diseased Indians. When she returned she was painfully thin but exuded a marvelous spirit. She benefited greatly from her work in India and was named a member of the Board of the Department of Human Resources by Jimmy when he became Governor of Georgia. She used her appointment to promote social reform throughout the state.

Jeremy Campbell learned from Carter about his early years on a farm and published the history in the *Daily Post and Mercury*. The Carters lived in a wooden clapboard house alongside the dirt road that led from Savannah to Columbus, Georgia. There was no source of heat in young Jimmy's bedroom, "but hot bricks and an eiderdown helped to ease the initial pain of a cold bed in winter," Campbell quoted Carter as saying. The President-Elect remembered that "for years we used an outdoor privy in the backyard and a hand pump for water supply." During the Depression years when the lad was growing into manhood the "amount of labor expended compared with any sort of cash return was almost unbelievable." In the 1930s peanuts sold for one cent per pound. A farmer's average yield was seven hundred pounds per acre, which gave him a gross return of $7 per acre. As a small boy Carter ran errands for the laborers in the fields, including carrying water from a nearby spring and filling the seed planter and the fertilizer distributor. "Only later did he become a proud lad as he learned to plough by himself," Campbell said. During those years he worked steadily, with brief breaks for breakfast and dinner. At sundown the mules were unhitched from the plows, hitched to the wagon, and back to the barn lot they went. The daily wages were $1 per day for men, 75 cents for women, and 25 cents for children. Carter's father was an extremely competent farmer and business-man who later in his life developed a wide range of interests. He was a natural leader, his son remembered.

The *Daily Post and Mercury* quoted the President-Elect as saying, "I'll be aggressive to keep my promise. I don't feel timid, or reticent about being aggressive." But the *Evening Mail* quoted Carter as saying, in an early postelection press conference, "We can't do everything. A great deal of cooperation between me and you, the American people and the Congress is necessary. We must all work together to succeed." In foreign affairs he was not likely to upset the applecart in diplomacy, but in this sphere even nuances and shades may make a great deal of difference, the *Evening Mail* said. The United States had become the greatest salesman of modern military weapons, and Carter wished to decrease sales of American arms abroad. He wanted more curbs on nuclear weapons and energy. He urged the Third World to undertake to help itself; the time had come to stop poor people in rich countries paying for the benefit of rich people in poor countries, the *Evening Mail* added.

P. T. Bangsberg wrote in the *Evening Mail* that Carter would need to do penance over Ulster before he could hope to come to an easy working relationship with Britain. Indeed, Whitehall had by and large hoped for a Ford victory, Bangsberg contended, because one of Carter's biggest drawbacks, ironically, was that he had come "so far so fast." Carter's victory created a natural reservation about a man so unknown as he, Bangsberg said, and "the paralysis which had already gripped the world for three months would drag on while Carter assembled his team."

Jeremy Campbell reported in the *Evening Standard* that Lawrence Klein, the leader of Carter's brain trust, wanted the United States to set up its own recovery as a first priority and to use it as a springboard for a serious, concerted attack on the deteriorating European economic trends, especially the collapse of the British pound. Campbell reported that in foreign policy Carter would strive for world order instead of world power politics. World order was an avenue to world peace. President Ford and Kissinger divided the world into two major power blocs, Campbell said, pressuring nations to take a stand either for the United States and against the Soviet Union or against America and her allies. Campbell quoted Carter: "I think that a permanently divisive attitude to take into world affairs is wrong. What I'll do is to get away from that position and to deal with nations on an individual basis."

The weekly periodicals and journals published comments and opinions on the American Presidential election, as did the daily newspapers. The London *Sunday Illustrated News* asked this question: What was America electing? It answered that the American Presidency was a peculiar institution, in that it combined the head of state and head of government. The voters had chosen someone who would both govern them and represent their flag, who would fulfill two functions—the mystical and the practical, as Walter Bagehot, a renowned British statesman of an earlier century, called them. The American Presidency was created when a republican constitution existed only in utopian blueprints and there were no guidelines, no balance of powers but three branches of government, not static but dynamic, the *Illustrated News* said. "In Britain the voters elected a party to power, in the United States the people elected an individual."

The *Economist* produced a full-page portrait of Carter's face with the caption "By the skin of these teeth." In discussing the election, the widely read periodical stated that Carter won in New York, Pennsylvania, and Ohio only by "desperate efforts" of the Democratic Party organization—the labor unions and the local Democratic chieftains—to get out the vote. Through the Democratic Party bosses' exertions, Carter got narrow, grudging majorities in states and in districts that returned Democratic Senators and Congressmen by generous margins. "The challenger to the political establishment was reached on the coattails of the regular Democratic Party and decidedly not the other way around," the *Economist* said. The American voters easily decided that they would rather be led by Carter than by President Ford.

The public mood of doubt, the *Economist* explained, about the established leaders aided Carter. Americans wanted something new and different, but "now they were nervous about what they received," the *Economist* said, explaining that Carter was a Southerner, an odd person who talked about prayer and love and truth and kept trying to bare his soul. This type of politician was not what the common voters were used to. "President Ford was a well-organized limited man whose campaign decreased nine-tenths of Carter's lead and came astonishingly close to gobbling up the last morsel of it." The *Economist* added that the American people felt comfortable with President Ford, while Carter had a "glint of steel and an appetite for power" that the people were not accustomed to.

Most countries believed that Carter would be temperate in using his power, the *Economist* said. Character and habit made him want to be a strong President. Not all Presidential powers were built in the office or were automatic, the *Economist* stated, noting that President Ford found them limited. Presidents Johnson and Nixon stretched the office and discovered it to be fragile. "Their experiences produced a shift from Presidential supremacy toward Congressional government," the *Economist* explained; thus the "country gave President Ford the problem of cleaning and calming the stables of government."

Hamilton Jordan told the *Economist* that there would be new faces in government. It was "going to be run by the people you have never heard of. Carter is going to appoint more blacks, women and minority groups to office than earlier Presidents." The President-Elect was taking advice from a large circle of Democrats who were experts in diplomacy and defense, but there would be no "palace guard" in the White House during Carter's Administration, Jordan affirmed.

Editorially, the *Economist* declared, "Thank God It's Over." The American Presidential campaign was too long. The United States Constitution prescribed a year for its fulfillment, a year of procrastination with the incumbent Administration, of decisions deferréd and of policies diffused. Fewer registered voters participated in American elections than in any other Western democracy. The cost of the whole procedure was unseemly and preposterous. The British, admitted the *Economist,* were dependent upon the United States. Everything that America did or left undone was relevant to the hopes and the fears of her allies. The American system of politics, contended the *Economist,* left much to be desired from the point of view of efficient conduct of the nation's business. In America there was a basic consensus of opinion about the nature of a free society, which was absent in Britain; the Americans should be grateful for that, the *Economist* concluded.

Alexander Cockburn wrote in the *New Statesman* that President Ford defied the disadvantages of Watergate, of Nixon's pardon, of a business recession, or renewed weakness in the economy, of often visibly fumbling in office to come within a hair of beating a man given a thirty-point lead in midsummer. "He did it because he has an honest face and because the issue of the campaign became the character of Jimmy Carter rather than the record of Gerald Ford," Cockburn said. "Many voters felt that they didn't actually know what Carter stood for." His accent and his religion bothered many voters outside of the South. Carter's *Playboy* interview appeared, to Cockburn, to have had little effect on the election, nor did President Ford's gaffe on the political status of Eastern Europe have any enduring resonance. The *New Statesman* thought that Carter's running mate, Mondale, assured him at least three percent ballot edge over Ford's Dole.

Godfrey Hodgson reported in the same weekly journal that, of the last four American Presidents, one was assassinated, two were driven from office, and one was defeated in seeking reelection. A majority of American informed opinion held that the power of the President had increased and that it ought to be diminished. Congress, Hodgson stated, was mounting a determined and partially successful counteroffensive, aimed at recapturing the power lost to the Presidency since 1933. Watergate proved the worth of the United States Constitution and its eighteenth-century system of checks and balances. "The safeguard against any future Vietnams and Watergates," Hodgson thought, "lies not in weakening the President in his relations to Congress but in strengthening both the Presidency and the Congress."

In 1974 Congress began to put its own house in order, Hodgson wrote. In 1976 Congress was a far more plausible competitor to the White House, a representative of the popular will and the protector of the national interest than it was earlier. "Even without the assistance of Fannie Fox and Elizabeth Ray, Congress had freed itself from the Wilbur Mills and the Wayne Hays," Hodgson said. "The seniority system under which legislation was voted on the whim and interest of autocratic old chairmen was abolished; Congressional staffs in 1976 numbered 1,800 for the 535 members; they had swollen faster than the White House staff."

The *New Statesman* noted that the U.S. Supreme Court gave Congress the power to name a Committee on the Budget to draw up a Congressional budget. "Definitely, Congress has a new consciousness of its strength, and most of its members were well aware that they are far more politically popular in their respective states and districts than is Carter," Hodgson wrote. The *New Statesman* reporter quoted Jack Watson, in charge of the new President's transition team, as saying that Carter saw his role as a moral leader—"not piously, not religiously, but as the center of the nation's moral standards." Hodgson concluded that "the American President is monarch even more than he is manager."

In mid-December the *New Statesman* commented that Carter's first appointments seemed "somewhat bizarre." It had been widely assumed since last February, the *New Statesman* said, that Cyrus Vance would be Secretary of State in any Democratic Administration. Nevertheless, Carter selected Vance only after consultation with virtually every vested interest in the country and with the strong recommendation of former Secretary of State Dean Rusk, who, with Vance, participated in the expansion of the Vietnam War during the Johnson Administration. With Vance at the State Department and James Schlesinger in some superior advisory post, the Carter Administration maintained continuity with the Johnson and Nixon Administrations, the *New Statesman* revealed. "This would be truly overwhelming."

Carter reassured the business community, the weekly argued, with the naming of Bert Lance, a millionaire Atlanta banker who had made loans repeatedly to Carter for his peanut business. The President-Elect's demonstration of fiscal sobriety had not discomfited those who had likened his elevation to power to that of Franklin D. Roosevelt in 1932, the *New Statesman* said. "In his early appointment he had resembled Herbert Hoover much more. There was no disruptive populist striding towards inauguration, January 20, 1977. That was obvious," the weekly concluded.

British popular opinion on the American Presidential campaign of 1976, as published in newspapers and magazines, was prolific and varied, as in *Punch,* which in a postelection comment stated, "Americans are addicted to change, often for its own sake." American voters were bombarded every day with the message that new inevitably meant better, *Punch* said, asking whether the new Administration would be better for the American people than the previous one. In 1980 the voters would have an opportunity to decide, and the British media would be most interested in the formation and result of this decision, *Punch* concluded.

This review of the role of British public opinion in the American Presidential election of 1976 revealed a wide interest among the published sources in the American national election. In the Presidential election of 1976, print media of British opinion told of several innovations in covering the campaign and the election. For example, the British Broadcast Corporation covered the total procedures of both of the American parties' national conventions. Moreover, the number of reporters representing the British newspapers and periodicals sent to America to report on the issues and personalities of the marathon campaign was greatly increased over any previous American national election. Furthermore, the employees of the British press continued to make numerous post-election reports on the issues and personalities of the new Administration. For the first time in American history, expatriate Americans could vote in American national elections. Both major American political parties promoted organizations in the British Isles for the party nominees and endeavored to raise money for campaign expenses. All of these innovations are interesting and perhaps will be of more significance in Anglo-American relations in the future.

Bibliography

Belfast *Telegraph*
Birmingham *Evening Mail*
Cardiff *Western Mail*
Dublin *Irish Times*
Edinburgh *Scotsman*
Glasgow *Herald*
Ipswich *East Anglia Daily Times*
Leeds *Yorkshire Post*
Leicester *Mercury*
Liverpool *Daily Post and Mercury*
London *Daily Express*
London *Daily Mail*
London *Daily Mirror*
London *Daily Telegraph*
London *Economist*
London *Evening Mail*
London *Evening News*
London *Evening Standard*
London *Illustrated Daily News*
London *New Statesman*
London *Observer*
London *Punch*
London *Socialist Standard*
London *Spectator*
London *Sun*
London *Times*
Manchester *Guardian*
Swansea *South Wales Evening Post*

Index